MINDSET

Carol Dweck

ROBINSON

ROBINSON

First published in Great Britain in 2012 by Robinson

First published in the US by Random House, an imprint of The Random
House Publishing Group, a division of Random House Inc., New York, 2006

Published in hardcover in the US by Ballantine, an imprint of The Random
House Publishing Group, a division of Random House Inc., New York, 2007

Grateful acknowledgment is made to Jeremy P. Tarcher, an imprint of Penguin
Group (US), for permission to reprint four illustrations of *The New Drawing on the
Right Side of the Brain Workbook* by Betty Edwards 2003 by Betty Edwards. Reprinted
by permission of Jeremy P. Tarcher, an imprint of Penguin Group (US).

A CIP catalogue record for this book
is available from the British Library.

ISBN 978-1-78033-200-0 (paperback)
ISBN 978-1-78033-393-9 (ebook)

Printed and bound in Great Britain by CPI Mackays

Robinson
is an imprint of
Constable & Robinson Ltd
100 Victoria Embankment
London EC4Y 0DY

An Hachette UK Company
www.hachette.co.uk

www.constablerobinson.com

7 9 10 8 6

CONTENTS

INTRODUCTION

One day, my students sat me down and ordered me to write this book. They wanted people to be able to use our work to make their lives better. It was something I'd wanted to do for a long time, but it became my number one priority.

My work is part of a tradition in psychology that shows the power of people's beliefs. These may be beliefs we're aware of or unaware of, but they strongly affect what we want and whether we succeed in getting it. This tradition also shows how changing people's beliefs—even the simplest beliefs—can have profound effects.

In this book, you'll learn how a simple belief about yourself—a belief we discovered in our research—guides a large part of your life. In fact, it permeates *every* part of your life. Much of what you think of as your personality actually grows out of this "mindset." Much of what may be preventing you from fulfilling your potential grows out of it.

No book has ever explained this mindset and shown people how to make use of it in their lives. You'll suddenly understand the greats—in the sciences and arts, in sports, and in business—and the would-have-beens. You'll understand your mate, your boss, your friends, your kids. You'll see how to unleash your potential—and your children's.

It is my privilege to share my findings with you. Besides accounts of people from my research, I've filled each chapter with stories both ripped from the headlines and based on my own life and experience, so you can see the mindsets in action. (In most cases, names and personal information have been changed to preserve anonymity; in some cases, several people have been condensed into one to make a clearer point. A number of the exchanges are re-created from memory, and I have rendered them to the best of my ability.)

At the end of each chapter and throughout the last chapter, I show you ways to apply the lessons—ways to recognize the mindset that is guiding your life, to understand how it works, and to change it if you wish.

A little note about grammar. I know it and I love it, but I haven't always followed it in this book. I start sentences with *and*s and *but*s. I end sentences with prepositions. I use the plural *they* in contexts that require the singular *he or she*. I've done this for informality and immediacy, and I hope that the sticklers will forgive me.

I'd like to take this chance to thank all of the people who made my research and this book possible. My students have made my research career a complete joy. I hope they've learned as much from me as I've learned from them. I'd also like to thank the organizations that supported our research: the William T. Grant Foundation, the National Science Foundation, the Department of Education, the National Institute of Mental Health, the National Institute of Child Health and Human Development, and the Spencer Foundation.

The people at Random House have been the most encouraging team I could wish for: Webster Younce, Daniel Menaker, Tom Perry, and, most of all, Caroline Sutton, my editor. Your excitement about my book and your great suggestions have made all the difference. I thank my superb agent, Giles Anderson, as well as Heidi Grant for putting me in touch with him.

Thanks to all the people who gave me input and feedback, but special thanks to Polly Shulman, Richard Dweck, and Maryann Peshkin for their extensive and insightful comments. Finally, I thank my husband, David, for the love and enthusiasm that give my life an extra dimension. His support throughout this project was extraordinary.

My work has been about growth, and it has helped foster my own growth. It is my wish that it will do the same for you.

MINDSET

Chapter 1

THE MINDSETS

When I was a young researcher, just starting out, something happened that changed my life. I was obsessed with understanding how people cope with failures, and I decided to study it by watching how students grapple with hard problems. So I brought children one at a time to a room in their school, made them comfortable, and then gave them a series of puzzles to solve. The first ones were fairly easy, but the next ones were hard. As the students grunted, perspired, and toiled, I watched their strategies and probed what they were thinking and feeling. I expected differences among children in how they coped with the difficulty, but I saw something I never expected.

Confronted with the hard puzzles, one ten-year-old boy pulled up his chair, rubbed his hands together, smacked his lips, and cried out, "I love a challenge!" Another, sweating away on these puzzles, looked up with a pleased expression and said with authority, "You know, I was *hoping* this would be informative!"

What's wrong with them? I wondered. I always thought you coped with failure or you didn't cope with failure. I never thought anyone *loved* failure. Were these alien children or were they on to something?

Everyone has a role model, someone who pointed the way at a critical moment in their lives. These children were my role models. They obviously knew something I didn't and I was determined to figure it out—to understand the kind of mindset that could turn a failure into a gift.

What did they know? They knew that human qualities, such as intellectual skills, could be cultivated through effort. And that's what they were doing—getting smarter. Not only weren't they discouraged by failure, they didn't even think they were failing. They thought they were learning.

I, on the other hand, thought human qualities were carved in stone. You were smart or you weren't, and failure meant you weren't. It was that simple. If you could arrange successes and avoid failures (at all costs), you could stay smart. Struggles, mistakes, perseverance were just not part of this picture.

Whether human qualities are things that can be cultivated or things that are carved in stone is an old issue. What these beliefs mean for you is a new one: What are the consequences of thinking that your intelligence or personality is something you can develop, as opposed to something that is a fixed, deep-seated trait? Let's first look in on the age-old, fiercely waged debate about human nature and then return to the question of what these beliefs mean for you.

WHY DO PEOPLE DIFFER?

Since the dawn of time, people have thought differently, acted differently, and fared differently from each other. It was guaranteed that someone would ask the question of why people differed—why some people are smarter or more moral—and whether there was something that made them permanently different. Experts lined up on both sides. Some claimed that there was a strong physical basis for these differences, making them unavoidable and unalterable. Through the ages, these alleged physical differences have included bumps on the skull (phrenology), the size and shape of the skull (craniology), and, today, genes.

Others pointed to the strong differences in people's backgrounds, experiences, training, or ways of learning. It may surprise you to know that a big champion of this view was Alfred Binet, the inventor of the IQ test. Wasn't the IQ test meant to summarize children's unchangeable intelligence? In fact, no. Binet, a Frenchman working in Paris in the early twentieth century, designed this test to identify children who were not profiting from the Paris public schools, *so that new educational programs could be designed to get them back on track.* Without denying individual differences in children's intellects, he believed that education and practice could bring about fundamental changes in intelligence. Here is a quote from one of his major books, *Modern Ideas About Children,* in which he summarizes his work with hundreds of children with learning difficulties:

> A few modern philosophers . . . assert that an individual's intelligence is a fixed quantity, a quantity which cannot be increased. We must protest and react against this brutal pessimism. . . . With practice, training, and above all, method, we manage to increase our attention, our memory, our judgment and literally to become more intelligent than we were before.

Who's right? Today most experts agree that it's not either—or. It's not nature *or* nurture, genes *or* environment. From conception on, there's a constant give and take between the two. In fact, as Gilbert Gottlieb, an eminent neuroscientist, put it, not only do genes and environment cooperate as we develop, but genes *require* input from the environment to work properly.

At the same time, scientists are learning that people have more capacity for lifelong learning and brain development than they ever thought. Of course, each person has a unique genetic endowment. People may start with different temperaments and different aptitudes, but it is clear that experience, training, and personal effort take them the rest of the way. Robert Sternberg, the present-day guru of intelligence, writes that the major factor in whether people achieve expertise "is not some fixed prior ability, but purposeful engagement." Or, as his forerunner Binet recognized, it's not always the people who start out the smartest who end up the smartest.

WHAT DOES ALL THIS MEAN FOR YOU? THE TWO MINDSETS

It's one thing to have pundits spouting their opinions about scientific issues. It's another thing to understand how these views apply to you. For twenty years, my research has shown that *the view you adopt for yourself* profoundly affects the way you lead your life. It can determine whether you become the person you want to be and whether you accomplish the things you value. How does this happen? How can a simple belief have the power to transform your psychology and, as a result, your life?

Believing that your qualities are carved in stone—the *fixed mindset*—creates an urgency to prove yourself over and over. If you have only a certain amount of intelligence, a certain personality, and a certain moral character—well, then you'd better prove that you have a healthy dose of them. It simply wouldn't do to look or feel deficient in these most basic characteristics.

Some of us are trained in this mindset from an early age. Even as a child, I was focused on being smart, but the fixed mindset was really stamped in by Mrs. Wilson, my sixth-grade teacher. Unlike Alfred Binet, she believed that people's IQ scores told the whole story of who they were. We were seated around the room in IQ order, and only the highest-IQ students could be trusted to carry the flag, clap the erasers, or take a note to the principal. Aside from the daily stomachaches she provoked with her judgmental stance, she was creating a mindset in which everyone in the class had one consuming goal—look smart, don't look dumb. Who cared about or enjoyed learning when our whole being was at stake every time she gave us a test or called on us in class?

I've seen so many people with this one consuming goal of proving themselves—in the classroom, in their careers, and in their relationships. Every situation calls for a confirmation of their intelligence, personality, or character. Every situation is evaluated: *Will I succeed or fail? Will I look smart or dumb? Will I be accepted or rejected? Will I feel like a winner or a loser?*

But doesn't our society value intelligence, personality, and character? Isn't it normal to want these traits? Yes, but . . .

There's another mindset in which these traits are not simply a hand you're dealt and have to live with, always trying to convince yourself and others that you have a royal flush when you're secretly worried it's a pair of tens. In this mindset, the hand you're dealt is just the starting point for development. This *growth mindset* is based on the belief that your basic qualities are things you can cultivate through your efforts. Although people may differ in every which way—in their initial talents and aptitudes, interests, or temperaments—everyone can change and grow through application and experience.

Do people with this mindset believe that anyone can be anything, that anyone with proper motivation or education can become Einstein or Beethoven? No, but they believe that a person's true potential is unknown (and unknowable); that it's impossible to foresee what can be accomplished with years of passion, toil, and training.

Did you know that Darwin and Tolstoy were considered ordinary children? That Ben Hogan, one of the greatest golfers of all time, was completely uncoordinated and graceless as a child? That the photographer Cindy Sherman, who has been on virtually every list of the most important artists of the twentieth century, *failed* her first photography course? That Geraldine Page, one of our greatest actresses, was advised to give it up for lack of talent?

You can see how the belief that cherished qualities can be developed creates a passion for learning. Why waste time proving over and over how great you are, when you could be getting better? Why hide deficiencies instead of overcoming them? Why look for friends or partners who will just shore up your self-esteem instead of ones who will also challenge you to grow? And why seek out the tried and true, instead of experiences that will stretch you? The passion for stretching yourself and sticking to it, even (or especially) when it's not going well, is the hallmark of the growth mindset. This is the mindset that allows people to thrive during some of the most challenging times in their lives.

A VIEW FROM THE TWO MINDSETS

To give you a better sense of how the two mindsets work, imagine—as vividly as you can—that you are a young adult having a really bad day:

One day, you go to a class that is really important to you and that you like a lot. The professor returns the midterm papers to the class. You got a C+. You're very disappointed. That evening on the way back to your home, you find that you've gotten a parking ticket. Being really frustrated, you call your best friend to share your experience but are sort of brushed off.

What would you think? What would you feel? What would you do?

When I asked people with the fixed mindset, this is what they said: "I'd feel like a reject." "I'm a total failure." "I'm an idiot." "I'm a loser." "I'd feel worthless and dumb—everyone's better than me." "I'm slime." In other words, they'd see what happened as a direct measure of their competence and worth.

This is what they'd think about their lives: "My life is pitiful." "I have no life." "Somebody upstairs doesn't like me." "The world is out to get me." "Someone is out to destroy me." "Nobody loves me, everybody hates me." "Life is unfair and all efforts are useless." "Life stinks. I'm stupid. Nothing good ever happens to me." "I'm the most unlucky person on this earth."

Excuse me, was there death and destruction, or just a grade, a ticket, and a bad phone call?

Are these just people with low self-esteem? Or card-carrying pessimists? No. When they aren't coping with failure, they feel just as worthy and optimistic—and bright and attractive—as people with the growth mindset.

So how would they cope? "I wouldn't bother to put so much time and effort into doing well in anything." (In other words, don't let anyone measure you again.) "Do nothing." "Stay in bed." "Get drunk." "Eat." "Yell at someone if I get a chance to." "Eat chocolate." "Listen to music and pout." "Go into my closet and sit there." "Pick a fight with somebody." "Cry." "Break something." "What is there to do?"

What is there to do! You know, when I wrote the vignette, I intentionally made the grade a C+, not an F. It was a midterm rather than a final. It was a parking ticket, not a car wreck. They were "sort of brushed off," not rejected outright. Nothing catastrophic or irreversible happened. Yet from this raw material the fixed mindset created the feeling of utter failure and paralysis.

When I gave people with the growth mindset the same vignette, here's what they said. They'd think:

"I need to try harder in class, be more careful when parking the car, and wonder if my friend had a bad day."

"The C+ would tell me that I'd have to work a lot harder in the class, but I have the rest of the semester to pull up my grade."

There were many, many more like this, but I think you get the idea. Now, how would they cope? Directly.

"I'd start thinking about studying harder (or studying in a different way) for my next test in that class, I'd pay the ticket, and I'd work things out with my best friend the next time we speak."

"I'd look at what was wrong on my exam, resolve to do better, pay my parking ticket, and call my friend to tell her I was upset the day before."

"Work hard on my next paper, speak to the teacher, be more careful where I park or contest the ticket, and find out what's wrong with my friend."

You don't have to have one mindset or the other to be upset. Who wouldn't be? Things like a poor grade or a rebuff from a friend or loved one—these are not fun events. No one was smacking their lips with relish. Yet those people with the growth mindset were not labeling themselves and throwing up their hands. Even though they felt distressed, they were ready to take the risks, confront the challenges, and keep working at them.

SO, WHAT'S NEW?

Is this such a novel idea? We have lots of sayings that stress the importance of risk and the power of persistence, such as "Nothing ventured, nothing gained" and "If at first you don't succeed, try, try again" or "Rome wasn't built in a day." (By the way, I was delighted to learn that the Italians have the same expression.) What is truly amazing is that people with the fixed mindset would not agree. For them, it's "Nothing ventured, nothing lost." "If at first you don't succeed, you probably don't have the ability." "If Rome wasn't built in a day, maybe it wasn't meant to be." In other words, risk and effort are two things that might reveal your inadequacies and show that you were not up to the task. In fact, it's startling to see the degree to which people with the fixed mindset do not believe in effort.

What's also new is that people's ideas about risk and effort grow out of their more basic mindset. It's not just that some people happen to recognize the value of challenging themselves and the importance of effort. Our research has shown that this *comes directly* from the growth mindset. When we teach people the growth mindset, with its focus on development, these ideas about challenge and effort follow. Similarly, it's not just that some people happen to dislike challenge and effort. When we (temporarily) put people in a fixed mindset, with its focus on permanent traits, they quickly fear challenge and devalue effort.

We often see books with titles like *The Ten Secrets of the World's Most Successful People* crowding the shelves of bookstores, and these books may give many useful tips. But they're usually a list of unconnected pointers, like "Take more risks!" or "Believe in yourself!" While you're left admiring people who can do that, it's never clear how these things fit together or how you could ever become that way. So you're inspired for a few days, but basically the world's most successful people still have their secrets.

Instead, as you begin to understand the fixed and growth mindsets, you will see exactly how one thing leads to another—how a belief that your qualities are carved in stone leads to a host of thoughts and actions, and how a belief that your qualities can be cultivated leads to a host of different thoughts and actions, taking you down an entirely different road. It's what we psychologists call an *Aha!* experience. Not only have I seen this in my research when we teach people a new mindset, but I get letters all the time from people who have read my work.

They recognize themselves: "As I read your article I literally found myself saying over and over again, 'This is me, this is me!'" They see the connections: "Your article completely blew me away. I felt I had discovered the secret of the universe!" They feel their mindsets reorienting: "I can certainly report a kind of personal revolution happening in my own thinking, and this is an exciting feeling." And they can put this new thinking into practice for themselves *and* others: "Your work has allowed me to transform my work with children and see education through a different lens," or "I just wanted to let you know what an impact—on a personal and practical level—your outstanding research has had for hundreds of students."

SELF-INSIGHT: WHO HAS ACCURATE VIEWS
OF THEIR ASSETS AND LIMITATIONS?

Well, maybe the people with the growth mindset don't think they're Einstein or Beethoven, but aren't they more likely to have inflated views of their abilities and try for things they're not capable of? In fact, studies show that people are terrible at estimating their abilities. Recently, we set out to see who is most likely to do this. Sure, we found that people greatly misestimated their performance and their ability. *But it was those with the fixed mindset who accounted for almost all the inaccuracy.* The people with the growth mindset were amazingly accurate.

When you think about it, this makes sense. If, like those with the growth mindset, you believe you can develop yourself, then you're open to accurate information about your current abilities, even if it's unflattering. What's more, if you're oriented toward learning, as they are, you *need* accurate information about your current abilities in order to learn effectively. However, if everything is either good news or bad news about your precious traits—as it is with fixed-mindset people—distortion almost inevitably enters the picture. Some outcomes are magnified, others are explained away, and before you know it you don't know yourself at all.

Howard Gardner, in his book *Extraordinary Minds,* concluded that exceptional individuals have "a special talent for identifying their own strengths and weaknesses." It's interesting that those with the growth mindset seem to have that talent.

WHAT'S IN STORE

The other thing exceptional people seem to have is a special talent for converting life's setbacks into future successes. Creativity researchers concur. In a poll of 143 creativity researchers, there was wide agreement about the number one ingredient in creative achievement. And it was exactly the kind of perseverance and resilience produced by the growth mindset.

You may be asking again, *How can one belief lead to all this—the love of challenge, belief in effort, resilience in the face of setbacks, and greater (more creative!) success?* In the chapters that follow, you'll see exactly how this happens: how the mindsets change what people strive for and what they see as success. How they change the definition, significance, and impact of failure. And how they change the deepest meaning of effort. You'll see how these mindsets play out in school, in sports, in the workplace, and in relationships. You'll see where they come from and how they can be changed.

Grow Your Mindset

Which mindset do you have? Answer these questions about intelligence. Read each statement and decide whether you mostly agree with it or disagree with it.

1. Your intelligence is something very basic about you that you can't change very much.
2. You can learn new things, but you can't really change how intelligent you are.
3. No matter how much intelligence you have, you can always change it quite a bit.
4. You can always substantially change how intelligent you are.

Questions 1 and 2 are the fixed-mindset questions. Questions 3 and 4 reflect the growth mindset. Which mindset did you agree with more? You can be a mixture, but most people lean toward one or the other.

You also have beliefs about other abilities. You could substitute "artistic talent," "sports ability," or "business skill" for "intelligence." Try it.

It's not only your abilities; it's your personal qualities too. Look at these statements about personality and character and decide whether you mostly agree or mostly disagree with each one.

1. You are a certain kind of person, and there is not much that can be done to really change that.
2. No matter what kind of person you are, you can always change substantially.
3. You can do things differently, but the important parts of who you are can't really be changed.
4. You can always change basic things about the kind of person you are.

Here, questions 1 and 3 are the fixed-mindset questions and questions 2 and 4 reflect the growth mindset. Which did you agree with more?

Did it differ from your intelligence mindset? It can. Your "intelligence mindset" comes into play when situations involve mental ability.

Your "personality mindset" comes into play in situations that involve your personal qualities—for example, how dependable, cooperative, caring, or socially skilled you are. The fixed mindset makes you concerned with how you'll be judged; the growth mindset makes you concerned with improving.

Here are some more ways to think about mindsets:

- Think about someone you know who is steeped in the fixed mindset. Think about how they're always trying to prove themselves and how they're supersensitive about being wrong or making mistakes. Did you ever wonder why they were this way? (Are you this way?) Now you can begin to understand why.

- Think about someone you know who is skilled in the growth mindset—someone who understands that important qualities can be cultivated. Think about the ways they confront obstacles. Think about the things they do to stretch themselves. What are some ways you might like to change or stretch yourself?

- Okay, now imagine you've decided to learn a new language and you've signed up for a class. A few sessions into the course, the instructor calls you to the front of the room and starts throwing questions at you one after another.

  Put yourself in a fixed mindset. Your ability is on the line. Can you feel everyone's eyes on you? Can you see the instructor's face evaluating you? Feel the tension, feel your ego bristle and waver. What else are you thinking and feeling?

  Now put yourself in a growth mindset. You're a novice—that's why you're here. You're here to learn. The teacher is a resource for learning. Feel the tension leave you; feel your mind open up.

  The message is: You can change your mindset.

Chapter 2

INSIDE THE MINDSETS

When I was a young woman, I wanted a prince-like mate. Very handsome, very successful. A big cheese. I wanted a glamorous career, but nothing too hard or risky. And I wanted it all to come to me as validation of who I was.

It would be many years before I was satisfied. I got a great guy, but he was a work in progress. I have a great career, but boy, is it a constant challenge. Nothing was easy. So why am I satisfied? I changed my mindset.

I changed it because of my work. One day my doctoral student, Mary Bandura, and I were trying to understand why some students were so caught up in proving their ability, while others could just let go and learn. Suddenly we realized that there were *two* meanings to ability, not one: a fixed ability that needs to be proven, and a changeable ability that can be developed through learning.

That's how the mindsets were born. I knew instantly which one I had. I realized why I'd always been so concerned about mistakes and failures. And I recognized for the first time that I had a choice.

When you enter a mindset, you enter a new world. In one world—the world of fixed traits—success is about proving you're smart or talented. Validating yourself. In the other—the world of changing qualities—it's about stretching yourself to learn something new. Developing yourself.

In one world, failure is about having a setback. Getting a bad grade.

Losing a tournament. Getting fired. Getting rejected. It means you're not smart or talented. In the other world, failure is about not growing. Not reaching for the things you value. It means you're not fulfilling your potential.

In one world, effort is a bad thing. It, like failure, means you're not smart or talented. If you were, you wouldn't need effort. In the other world, effort is what *makes* you smart or talented.

You have a choice. Mindsets are just beliefs. They're powerful beliefs, but they're just something in your mind, and you can change your mind. As you read, think about where you'd like to go and which mindset will take you there.

IS SUCCESS ABOUT LEARNING—OR PROVING YOU'RE SMART?

Benjamin Barber, an eminent sociologist, once said, "I don't divide the world into the weak and the strong, or the successes and the failures. . . . *I divide the world into the learners and nonlearners.*"

What on earth would make someone a nonlearner? Everyone is born with an intense drive to learn. Infants stretch their skills daily. Not just ordinary skills, but the most difficult tasks of a lifetime, like learning to walk and talk. They never decide it's too hard or not worth the effort. Babies don't worry about making mistakes or humiliating themselves. They walk, they fall, they get up. They just barge forward.

What could put an end to this exuberant learning? The fixed mindset. As soon as children become able to evaluate themselves, some of them become afraid of challenges. They become afraid of not being smart. I have studied thousands of people from preschoolers on, and it's breathtaking how many reject an opportunity to learn.

We offered four-year-olds a choice: They could redo an easy jigsaw puzzle or they could try a harder one. Even at this tender age, children with the fixed mindset—the ones who believed in fixed traits—stuck with the safe one. Kids who are born smart "don't do mistakes," they told us.

Children with the growth mindset—the ones who believed you could get smarter—thought it was a strange choice. *Why are you asking me this, lady? Why would anyone want to keep doing the same puzzle over and over?* They chose one hard one after another. "I'm *dying* to figure them out!" exclaimed one little girl.

So children with the fixed mindset want to make sure they succeed. Smart people should always succeed. But for children with the growth mindset, success is about stretching themselves. It's about becoming smarter.

One seventh-grade girl summed it up. "I think intelligence is something you have to work for . . . it isn't just given to you. . . . Most kids, if they're not sure of an answer, will not raise their hand to answer the question. But what I usually do is raise my hand, because if I'm wrong, then my mistake will be corrected. Or I will raise my hand and say, 'How would this be solved?' or 'I don't get this. Can you help me?' Just by doing that I'm increasing my intelligence."

Beyond Puzzles

It's one thing to pass up a puzzle. It's another to pass up an opportunity that's important to your future. To see if this would happen, we took advantage of an unusual situation. At the University of Hong Kong, everything is in English. Classes are in English, textbooks are in English, and exams are in English. But some students who enter the university are not fluent in English, so it would make sense for them to do something about it in a hurry.

As students arrived to register for their freshman year, we knew which ones were not skilled in English. And we asked them a key question: If the faculty offered a course for students who need to improve their English skills, would you take it?

We also measured their mindset. We did this by asking them how much they agreed with statements like this: "You have a certain amount of intelligence, and you can't really do much to change it." People who agree with this kind of statement have a fixed mindset.

Those who have a growth mindset agree that: "You can always substantially change how intelligent you are."

Later, we looked at who said yes to the English course. Students with the growth mindset said an emphatic yes. But those with the fixed mindset were not very interested.

Believing that success is about learning, students with the growth mindset seized the chance. But those with the fixed mindset didn't want to expose their deficiencies. Instead, to feel smart in the short run, they were willing to put their college careers at risk.

This is how the fixed mindset makes people into nonlearners.

Brain Waves Tell the Story

You can even see the difference in people's brain waves. People with both mindsets came into our brain-wave lab at Columbia. As they answered hard questions and got feedback, we were curious about when their brain waves would show them to be interested and attentive.

People with a fixed mindset were only interested when the feedback reflected on their ability. Their brain waves showed them paying close attention when they were told whether their answers were right or wrong.

But when they were presented with information that could help them learn, there was no sign of interest. Even when they'd gotten an answer wrong, they were not interested in learning what the right answer was.

Only people with a growth mindset paid close attention to information that could stretch their knowledge. Only for them was learning a priority.

What's Your Priority?

If you had to choose, which would it be? Loads of success and validation or lots of challenge?

It's not just on intellectual tasks that people have to make these choices. People also have to decide what kinds of relationships they want: ones that bolster their egos or ones that challenge them to grow? Who is your ideal mate? We put this question to young adults, and here's what they told us.

People with the fixed mindset said the ideal mate would:

Put them on a pedestal.

Make them feel perfect.

Worship them.

In other words, the perfect mate would enshrine their fixed qualities. My husband says that he used to feel this way, that he wanted to be the god of a one-person (his partner's) religion. Fortunately, he chucked this idea before he met me.

People with the growth mindset hoped for a different kind of partner. They said their ideal mate was someone who would:

See their faults and help them to work on them.

Challenge them to become a better person.

Encourage them to learn new things.

Certainly, they didn't want people who would pick on them or undermine their self-esteem, but they did want people who would foster their development. They didn't assume they were fully evolved, flawless beings who had nothing more to learn.

Are you already thinking, *Uh-oh, what if two people with different mindsets get together?* A growth-mindset woman tells about her marriage to a fixed-mindset man:

> I had barely gotten all the rice out of my hair when I began to realize I made a big mistake. Every time I said something like "Why don't we try to go out a little more?" or "I'd like it if you consulted me before making decisions," he was devastated. Then instead of talking about the issue I raised, I'd have to spend literally an hour repairing the damage and making him feel good again. Plus he would then run to the phone to call his mother, who always showered him with the constant adoration he seemed to need. We were both young and new at marriage. I just wanted to communicate.

So the husband's idea of a successful relationship—total, uncritical acceptance—was not the wife's. And the wife's idea of a successful relationship—confronting problems—was not the husband's. One person's growth was the other person's nightmare.

CEO Disease

Speaking of reigning from atop a pedestal and wanting to be seen as perfect, you won't be surprised that this is often called "CEO disease." Lee Iacocca had a bad case of it. After his initial success as head of Chrysler Motors, Iacocca looked remarkably like our four-year-olds with the fixed mindset. He kept bringing out the same car models over and over with only superficial changes. Unfortunately, they were models no one wanted anymore.

Meanwhile, Japanese companies were completely rethinking what cars should look like and how they should run. We know how this turned out. The Japanese cars rapidly swept the market.

CEOs face this choice all the time. Should they confront their shortcomings or should they create a world where they have none? Lee Iacocca chose the latter. He surrounded himself with worshipers, exiled the critics—and quickly lost touch with where his field was going. Lee Iacocca had become a nonlearner.

But not everyone catches CEO disease. Many great leaders confront their shortcomings on a regular basis. Darwin Smith, looking back on his extraordinary performance at Kimberly-Clark, declared, "I never stopped trying to be qualified for the job." These men, like the Hong Kong students with the growth mindset, never stopped taking the remedial course.

CEOs face another dilemma. They can choose short-term strategies that boost the company's stock and make themselves look like heroes. Or they can work for long-term improvement—risking Wall Street's disapproval as they lay the foundation for the health and growth of the company over the longer haul.

Albert Dunlap, a self-professed fixed mindsetter, was brought in to turn around Sunbeam. He chose the short-term strategy of looking like a hero to Wall Street. The stock soared but the company fell apart.

Lou Gerstner, an avowed growth mindsetter, was called in to turn around IBM. As he set about the enormous task of overhauling IBM culture and policies, stock prices were stagnant and Wall Street sneered. They called him a failure. A few years later, however, IBM was leading its field again.

Stretching

People in a growth mindset don't just *seek* challenge, they thrive on it. The bigger the challenge, the more they stretch. And nowhere can it be seen more clearly than in the world of sports. You can just watch people stretch and grow.

Mia Hamm, the greatest female soccer star of her time, says it straight out. "All my life I've been playing up, meaning I've challenged myself with players older, bigger, more skillful, more experienced—in short, better than me." First she played with her older brother. Then at ten, she joined the eleven-year-old boys' team. Then she threw herself into the number one college team in the United States. "Each day I attempted to play up to their level . . . and I was improving faster than I ever dreamed possible."

Patricia Miranda was a chubby, unathletic high school kid who wanted to wrestle. After a bad beating on the mat, she was told, "You're a joke." First she cried, then she felt: "That really set my resolve . . . I had to keep going and had to know if effort and focus and belief and training could somehow legitimize me as a wrestler." Where did she get this resolve?

Miranda was raised in a life devoid of challenge. But when her mother died of an aneurysm at age forty, ten-year-old Miranda came up with a principle. "When you're lying on your deathbed, one of the cool things to say is, 'I really explored myself.' This sense of urgency was instilled when my mom died. If you only go through life doing stuff that's easy, shame on you." So when wrestling presented a challenge, she was ready to take it on.

Her effort paid off. At twenty-four, Miranda was having the last laugh. She won the spot for her weight group on the U.S. Olympic team and came home from Athens with a bronze medal. And what was next?

Yale Law School. People urged her to stay where she was already on top, but Miranda felt it was more exciting to start at the bottom again and see what she could grow into this time.

Stretching Beyond the Possible

Sometimes people with the growth mindset stretch themselves so far that they do the impossible. In 1995, Christopher Reeve, the actor, was thrown from a horse. His neck was broken, his spinal cord was severed from his brain, and he was completely paralyzed below the neck. Medical science said, *So sorry. Come to terms with it.*

Reeve, however, started a demanding exercise program that involved moving all parts of his paralyzed body with the help of electrical stimulation. Why *couldn't* he learn to move again? Why couldn't his brain once again give commands that his body would obey? Doctors warned that he was in denial and was setting himself up for disappointment. They had seen this before and it was a bad sign for his adjustment. But, really, what else was Reeve doing with his time? Was there a better project?

Five years later, Reeve started to regain movement. First it happened in his hands, then his arms, then legs, and then torso. He was far from cured, but brain scans showed that his brain was once more sending signals to his body that the body was responding to. Not only did Reeve stretch his abilities, he changed the entire way science thinks about the nervous system and its potential for recovery. In doing so, he opened a whole new vista for research and a whole new avenue of hope for people with spinal cord injuries.

Thriving on the Sure Thing

Clearly, people with the growth mindset thrive when they're stretching themselves. When do people with the fixed mindset thrive? When things are safely within their grasp. If things get too challenging—when they're not feeling smart or talented—they lose interest.

I watched it happen as we followed pre-med students through their first semester of chemistry. For many students, this is what their lives have led up to: becoming a doctor. And this is the course that decides who gets to be one. It's one heck of a hard course, too. The average grade on each exam is C+, for students who've rarely seen anything less than an A.

Most students started out pretty interested in chemistry. Yet over the semester, something happened. Students with the fixed mindset stayed interested *only when they did well right away*. Those who found it difficult showed a big drop in their interest and enjoyment. If it wasn't a testimony to their intelligence, they couldn't enjoy it.

"The harder it gets," reported one student, "the more I have to force myself to read the book and study for the tests. I was excited about chemistry before, but now every time I think about it, I get a bad feeling in my stomach."

In contrast, students with the growth mindset continued to show the same high level of interest even when they found the work very challenging. "It's a lot more difficult for me than I thought it would be, but it's what I want to do, so that only makes me more determined. When they tell me I can't, it really gets me going." Challenge and interest went hand in hand.

We saw the same thing in younger students. We gave fifth graders intriguing puzzles, which they all loved. But when we made them harder, children with the fixed mindset showed a big plunge in enjoyment. They also changed their minds about taking some home to practice. "It's okay, you can keep them. I already have them," fibbed one child. In fact, they couldn't run from them fast enough.

This was just as true for children who were the best puzzle solvers. Having "puzzle talent" did not prevent the decline.

Children with the growth mindset, on the other hand, couldn't tear themselves away from the hard problems. These were their favorites and these were the ones they wanted to take home. "Could you write down the name of these puzzles," one child asked, "so my mom can buy me some more when these ones run out?"

Not long ago I was interested to read about Marina Semyonova, a great Russian dancer and teacher, who devised a novel way of selecting her students. It was a clever test for mindset. As a former student tells it, "Her students first have to survive a trial period while she watches to see how you react to praise and to correction. Those more responsive to the correction are deemed worthy."

In other words, she separates the ones who get their thrill from what's easy—what they've already mastered—from those who get their thrill from what's hard.

I'll never forget the first time I heard myself say, "This is hard. This is fun." That's the moment I knew I was changing mindsets.

When Do You Feel Smart:
When You're Flawless or When You're Learning?

The plot is about to thicken, for in the fixed mindset it's not enough just to succeed. It's not enough just to look smart and talented. You have to be pretty much flawless. And you have to be flawless right away.

We asked people, ranging from grade schoolers to young adults, "When do you feel smart?" The differences were striking. People with the fixed mindset said:

"It's when I don't make any mistakes."

"When I finish something fast and it's perfect."

"When something is easy for me, but other people can't do it."

It's about being perfect right now. But people with the growth mindset said:

"When it's really hard, and I try really hard, and I can do something I couldn't do before."

Or "[When] I work on something a long time and I start to figure it out."

For them it's not about immediate perfection. It's about learning something over time: confronting a challenge and making progress.

If You Have Ability,
Why Should You Need Learning?

Actually, people with the fixed mindset expect ability to show up on its own, before any learning takes place. After all, if you have it you have it, and if you don't you don't. I see this all the time.

Out of all the applicants from all over the world, my department at Columbia admitted six new graduate students a year. They all had amazing test scores, nearly perfect grades, and rave recommendations from eminent scholars. Moreover, they'd been courted by the top grad schools.

It took one day for some of them to feel like complete imposters. Yesterday they were hotshots; today they're failures. Here's what happens. They look at the faculty with our long list of publications. "Oh my God, I can't do that." They look at the advanced students who are submitting articles for publication and writing grant proposals. "Oh my God, I can't do that." They know how to take tests and get A's but they don't know how to do *this*—yet. They forget the *yet*.

Isn't that what school is for, to teach? They're there to learn how to do these things, not because they already know everything.

I wonder if this is what happened to Janet Cooke and Stephen Glass. They were both young reporters who skyrocketed to the top—on fabricated articles. Janet Cooke won a Pulitzer Prize for her *Washington Post* articles about an eight-year-old boy who was a drug addict. The boy did not exist, and she was later stripped of her prize. Stephen Glass was the whiz kid of *The New Republic*, who seemed to have stories and sources reporters only dream of. The sources did not exist and the stories were not true.

Did Janet Cooke and Stephen Glass need to be perfect right away? Did they feel that admitting ignorance would discredit them with their colleagues? Did they feel they should already be like the big-time reporters before they did the hard work of learning how? "We were stars—precocious stars," wrote Stephen Glass, "and that was what mattered." The public understands them as cheats, and cheat they did. But I understand them as talented young people—desperate young people—who succumbed to the pressures of the fixed mindset.

There was a saying in the 1960s that went: "Becoming is better than being." The fixed mindset does not allow people the luxury of becoming. They have to already be.

A Test Score Is Forever

Let's take a closer look at why, in the fixed mindset, it's so crucial to be perfect right now. It's because one test—or one evaluation—can measure you forever.

Twenty years ago, at the age of five, Loretta and her family came to the United States. A few days later, her mother took her to her new school, where they promptly gave her a test. The next thing she knew, she was in her kindergarten class—*but it was not the Eagles*, the elite kindergarten class.

As time passed, however, Loretta was transferred to the Eagles and she remained with that group of students until the end of high school, garnering a bundle of academic prizes along the way. Yet she never felt she belonged.

That first test, she was convinced, diagnosed her fixed ability and said that she was not a true Eagle. Never mind that she had been five years old and had just made a radical change to a new country. Or that maybe there hadn't been room in the Eagles for a while. Or that maybe the school decided she would have an easier transition in a more low-key class. There are so many ways to understand what happened and what it meant. Unfortunately, she chose the wrong one. For in the world of the fixed mindset, there is no way to *become* an Eagle. If you were a true Eagle, you would have aced the test and been hailed as an Eagle at once.

Is Loretta a rare case, or is this kind of thinking more common than we realize?

To find out, we showed fifth graders a closed cardboard box and told them it had a test inside. This test, we said, measured an important school ability. We told them nothing more. Then we asked them questions about the test. First, we wanted to make sure that they'd accepted our description, so we asked them: How much do you think this test measures an important school ability? All of them had taken our word for it.

Next we asked: Do you think this test measures *how smart you are*? And: Do you think this test measures *how smart you'll be when you grow up*?

Students with the growth mindset had taken our word that the test measured an important ability, but they didn't think it measured how *smart* they were. And they certainly didn't think it would tell them how smart they'd be when they grew up. In fact, one of them told us, "No way! Ain't no test can do that."

But the students with the fixed mindset didn't simply believe the test could measure an important ability. They also believed—just as strongly—that it could measure how smart they were. *And* how smart they'd be when they grew up.

They granted one test the power to measure their most basic intelligence now and forever. They gave this test the power to define them. That's why every success is so important.

Another Look at Potential

This leads us back to the idea of "potential" and to the question of whether tests or experts can tell us what our potential is, what we're capable of, what our future will be. The fixed mindset says yes. You can simply measure the fixed ability right now and project it into the future. Just give the test or ask the expert. No crystal ball needed.

So common is the belief that potential can be known right now that Joseph P. Kennedy felt confident in telling Morton Downey Jr. that he would be a failure. What had Downey—later a famous television personality and author—done? Why, he had worn red socks and brown shoes to the Stork Club.

"Morton," Kennedy told him, "I don't know anybody I've ever met in my life wearing red socks and brown shoes who ever succeeded. Young man, let me tell you now, you do stand out, but you don't stand out in a way that people will ever admire you."

Many of the most accomplished people of our era were considered by experts to have no future. Jackson Pollock, Marcel Proust, Elvis Presley, Ray Charles, Lucille Ball, and Charles Darwin were all thought to have little potential for their chosen fields. And in some of these cases, it may well have been true that they did not stand out from the crowd early on.

But isn't potential someone's capacity to *develop* their skills with effort over time? And that's just the point. How can we know where effort and time will take someone? Who knows—maybe the experts were right about Jackson, Marcel, Elvis, Ray, Lucille, and Charles—in terms of their skills at the time. Maybe they were not yet the people they were to become.

I once went to an exhibit in London of Paul Cézanne's early paintings. On my way there, I wondered who Cézanne was and what his paintings were like before he was the painter we know today. I was intensely curious because Cézanne is one of my favorite artists and the man who set the stage for much of modern art. Here's what I found: Some of the paintings were pretty bad. They were overwrought scenes, some violent, with amateurishly painted people. Although there were some paintings that foreshadowed the later Cézanne, many did not. Was the early Cézanne not talented? Or did it just take time for Cézanne to become Cézanne?

People with the growth mindset know that it takes time for potential to flower. Recently, I got an angry letter from a teacher who had taken one of our surveys. The survey portrays a hypothetical student, Jennifer, who had gotten 65 percent on a math exam. It then asks teachers to tell us how they would treat her.

Teachers with the fixed mindset were more than happy to answer our questions. They felt that by knowing Jennifer's score, they had a good sense of who she was and what she was capable of. Their recommendations abounded. Mr. Riordan, by contrast, was fuming. Here's what he wrote.

To Whom It May Concern:

Having completed the educator's portion of your recent survey, I must request that my results be excluded from the study. I feel that the study itself is scientifically unsound. . . .

Unfortunately, the test uses a faulty premise, asking teachers to make assumptions about a given student based on nothing more than a number on a page. . . . Performance cannot be based on one assessment. You cannot determine the slope of a line given only one point, as there is no line to begin with. A single point in time does not show trends, improvement, lack of effort, or mathematical ability. . . .

Sincerely,
Michael D. Riordan

I was delighted with Mr. Riordan's critique and couldn't have agreed with it more. An assessment at one point in time has little value for understanding someone's ability, let alone their potential to succeed in the future.

It was disturbing how many teachers thought otherwise, and that was the point of our study.

The idea that one evaluation can measure you forever is what creates the urgency for those with the fixed mindset. That's why they must succeed perfectly and immediately. Who can afford the luxury of trying to grow when everything is on the line right now?

Is there another way to judge potential? NASA thought so. When they were soliciting applications for astronauts, they rejected people with pure histories of success and instead selected people who had had significant failures and bounced back from them. Jack Welch, the celebrated CEO of General Electric, chose executives on the basis of "runway," their capacity for growth. And remember Marina Semyonova, the famed ballet teacher, who chose the students who were energized by criticism. They were all rejecting the idea of fixed ability and selecting instead for mindset.

Proving You're Special

When people with the fixed mindset opt for success over growth, what are they *really* trying to prove? That they're special. Even superior.

When we asked them, "When do you feel smart?" so many of them talked about times they felt like a special person, someone who was different from and better than other people.

Until I discovered the mindsets and how they work, I, too, thought of myself as more talented than others, maybe even more worthy than others because of my endowments. The scariest thought, which I rarely entertained, was the possibility of being ordinary. This kind of thinking led me to need constant validation. Every comment, every look was meaningful—it registered on my intelligence scorecard, my attractiveness scorecard, my likability scorecard. If a day went well, I could bask in my high numbers.

One bitter cold winter night, I went to the opera. That night, the opera was everything you hope for, and everyone stayed until the very end—not just the end of the opera, but through all the curtain calls. Then we all poured into the street, and we all wanted taxis. I remember it clearly. It was after midnight, it was seven degrees, there was a strong wind, and, as time went on, I became more and more miserable. There I was, part of an undifferentiated crowd. What chance did I have? Suddenly, a taxi pulled up right next to me. The handle of the back door lined up perfectly with my hand, and as I entered, the driver announced, "You were different." I lived for these moments. Not only was I special. It could be detected from a distance.

The self-esteem movement encourages this kind of thinking and has even invented devices to help you confirm your superiority. I recently came across an ad for such a product. Two of my friends send me an illustrated list each year of the top ten things they *didn't* get me for Christmas. From January through November, they clip candidate items from catalogs or download them from the Internet. In December, they select the winners. One of my all-time favorites is the pocket toilet, which you fold up and return to your pocket after using. This year my favorite was the I LOVE ME mirror, a mirror with I LOVE ME in huge capital letters written across the bottom half. By looking into it, you can administer the message to yourself and not wait for the outside world to announce your specialness.

Of course, the mirror is harmless enough. The problem is when *special* begins to mean *better than others*. A more valuable human being. A superior person. An entitled person.

Special, Superior, Entitled

John McEnroe had a fixed mindset: He believed that talent was all. He did not love to learn. He did not thrive on challenges; when the going got rough, he often folded. As a result, by his own admission, he did not fulfill his potential.

But his talent was so great that he was the number one tennis player in the world for four years. Here he tells us what it was like to be number one.

McEnroe used sawdust to absorb the sweat on his hands during a match. This time the sawdust was not to his liking, so he went over to the can of sawdust and knocked it over with his racket. His agent, Gary, came dashing over to find out what was wrong.

"You call that sawdust?" I said. I was actually screaming at him: The sawdust was ground too fine! "This looks like rat poison. Can't you get anything right?" So Gary ran out and, twenty minutes later, came back with a fresh can of coarser sawdust . . . and twenty dollars less in his pocket: He'd had to pay a union employee to grind up a two-by-four. This is what it was like to be number one.

He goes on to tell us about how he once threw up all over a dignified Japanese lady who was hosting him. The next day she bowed, apologized to him, and presented him with a gift. "This," McEnroe proclaims, "is also what it was like to be number one."

"Everything was about *you* . . . 'Did you get everything you need? Is everything okay? We'll pay you this, we'll do that, we'll kiss your behind.' You only have to do what you want; your reaction to anything else is, 'Get the hell out of here.' For a long time I didn't mind it a bit. Would you?"

So let's see. If you're successful, you're better than other people. You get to abuse them and have them grovel. In the fixed mindset, this is what can pass for self-esteem.

As a contrast, let's look at Michael Jordan—growth-minded athlete par excellence—whose greatness is regularly proclaimed by the world: "Superman," "God in person," "Jesus in tennis shoes." If anyone has reason to think of himself as special, it's he. But here's what he said when his return to basketball caused a huge commotion: "I was shocked with the level of intensity my coming back to the game created. . . . People were praising me like I was a religious cult or something. That was very embarrassing. I'm a human being like everyone else."

Jordan knew how hard he had worked to develop his abilities. He was a person who had struggled and grown, not a person who was inherently better than others.

Tom Wolfe, in *The Right Stuff,* describes the elite military pilots who eagerly embrace the fixed mindset. Having passed one rigorous test after another, they think of themselves as special, as people who were born smarter and braver than other people. But Chuck Yeager, the hero of *The Right Stuff,* begged to differ. "There is no such thing as a natural-born pilot. Whatever my aptitude or talents, becoming a proficient pilot was hard work, really a lifetime's learning experience. . . . The best pilots fly more than the others; that's why they're the best." Like Michael Jordan, he was a human being. He just stretched himself farther than most.

In summary, people who believe in fixed traits feel an urgency to succeed, and when they do, they may feel more than pride. They may feel a sense of superiority, since success means that their fixed traits are better than other people's.

However, lurking behind that self-esteem of the fixed mindset is a simple question: If you're *somebody* when you're successful, what are you when you're unsuccessful?

MINDSETS CHANGE THE MEANING OF FAILURE

The Martins worshiped their three-year-old Robert and always bragged about his feats. There had never been a child as bright and creative as theirs. Then Robert did something unforgivable—he didn't get into the number one preschool in New York. After that, the Martins cooled toward him. They didn't talk about him the same way, and they didn't treat him with the same pride and affection. He was no longer their brilliant little Robert. He was someone who had discredited himself and shamed them. At the tender age of three, he was a failure.

As a *New York Times* article points out, failure has been transformed from an action (I failed) to an identity (I am a failure). This is especially true in the fixed mindset.

When I was a child, I, too, worried about meeting Robert's fate. In sixth grade, I was the best speller in my school. The principal wanted me to go to a citywide competition, but I refused. In ninth grade, I excelled in French, and my teacher wanted me to enter a citywide competition. Again, I refused. Why would I risk turning from a success into a failure? From a winner into a loser?

Ernie Els, the great golfer, worried about this too. Els finally won a major tournament after a five-year dry spell, in which match after match slipped away from him. What if he had lost this tournament, too? "I would have been a different person," he tells us. He would have been a loser.

Each April when the skinny envelopes—the rejection letters—arrive from colleges, countless failures are created coast to coast. Thousands of brilliant young scholars become "The Girl Who Didn't Get into Princeton" or the "The Boy Who Didn't Get into Stanford."

Defining Moments

Even in the growth mindset, failure can be a painful experience. But it doesn't define you. It's a problem to be faced, dealt with, and learned from.

Jim Marshall, former defensive player for the Minnesota Vikings, relates what could easily have made him into a failure. In a game against the San Francisco 49ers, Marshall spotted the football on the ground. He scooped it up and ran for a touchdown as the crowd cheered. But he ran the wrong way. He scored for the wrong team and on national television.

It was the most devastating moment of his life. The shame was overpowering. But during halftime, he thought, "If you make a mistake, you got to make it right. I realized I had a choice. I could sit in my misery or I could do something about it." Pulling himself together for the second half, he played some of his best football ever and contributed to his team's victory.

Nor did he stop there. He spoke to groups. He answered letters that poured in from people who finally had the courage to admit their own shameful experiences. He heightened his concentration during games. Instead of letting the experience define him, he took control of it. He *used* it to become a better player and, he believes, a better person.

In the fixed mindset, however, the loss of one's self to failure can be a permanent, haunting trauma. Bernard Loiseau was one of the top chefs in the world. Only a handful of restaurants in all of France receive the supreme rating of three stars from the *Guide Michelin*, the most respected restaurant guide in Europe. His was one of them. Around the publication of the 2003 *Guide Michelin,* however, Mr. Loiseau committed suicide. He had lost two points in another guide, going from a nineteen (out of twenty) to a seventeen in the *GaultMillau.* And there were rampant rumors that he would lose one of his three stars in the new *Guide.* Although he did not, the idea of failure had possessed him.

Loiseau had been a pioneer. He was one of the first to advance the "nouvelle cuisine," trading the traditional butter and cream sauces of French cooking for the brighter flavors of the foods themselves. A man of tremendous energy, he was also an entrepreneur. Besides his three-star restaurant in Burgundy, he had created three eateries in Paris, numerous cookbooks, and a line of frozen foods. "I'm like Yves Saint Laurent," he told people. "I do both haute couture and ready-to-wear."

A man of such talent and originality could easily have planned for a satisfying future, with or without the two points or the third star. In fact, the director of the *GaultMillau* said it was unimaginable that their rating could have taken his life. But in the fixed mindset, it *is* imaginable. Their lower rating gave him a new definition of himself: Failure. Has-been.

It's striking what counts as failure in the fixed mindset. So, on a lighter note . . .

My Success Is Your Failure

Last summer my husband and I went to a dude ranch, something very novel since neither of us had ever made contact with a horse. One day, we signed up for a lesson in fly fishing. It was taught by a wonderful eighty-year-old cowboy-type fisherman who showed us how to cast the fishing line, and then turned us loose.

We soon realized that he had not taught us how to recognize when the trout bit the lure (they don't tug on the line; you have to watch for a bubble in the water), what to do when the trout bit the lure (tug upward), or how to reel the trout in if by some miracle we got that far (pull the fish along the water; do not hoist it into the air). Well, time passed, the mosquitoes bit, but not so the trout. None of the dozen or so of us made the slightest progress. Suddenly, I hit the jackpot. Some careless trout bit hard on my lure and the fisherman, who happened to be right there, talked me through the rest. I had me a rainbow trout.

Reaction #1: My husband, David, came running over beaming with pride and saying, "Life with you is so exciting!"

Reaction #2: That evening when we came into the dining room for dinner, two men came up to my husband and said, "David, how're you coping?" David looked at them blankly; he had no idea what they were talking about. Of course he didn't. He was the one who thought my catching the fish was exciting. But I knew exactly what they meant. They had expected him to feel diminished, and they went on to make it clear that that's exactly what my success had done to them.

Shirk, Cheat, Blame: Not a Recipe for Success

Beyond how traumatic a setback can be in the fixed mindset, this mindset gives you no good recipe for overcoming it. If failure means you lack competence or potential—that you *are* a failure—where do you go from there?

In one study, seventh graders told us how they would respond to an academic failure—a poor test grade in a new course. Those with the growth mindset, no big surprise, said they would study harder for the next test. But those with the fixed mindset said they would study *less* for the next test. If you don't have the ability, why waste your time? And, they said, they would seriously consider cheating! If you don't have the ability, they thought, you just have to look for another way.

What's more, instead of trying to learn from and repair their failures, people with the fixed mindset may simply try to repair their self-esteem. For example, they may go looking for people who are even worse off than they are.

College students, after doing poorly on a test, were given a chance to look at tests of other students. Those in the growth mindset looked at the tests of people who had done far better than they had. As usual, they wanted to correct their deficiency. But students in the fixed mindset chose to look at the tests of people who had done *really* poorly. That was their way of feeling better about themselves.

Jim Collins tells in *Good to Great* of a similar thing in the corporate world. As Procter & Gamble surged into the paper goods business, Scott Paper—which was then the leader—just gave up. Instead of mobilizing themselves and putting up a fight, they said, "Oh, well . . . at least there are people in the business worse off than we are."

Another way people with the fixed mindset try to repair their self-esteem after a failure is by assigning blame or making excuses. Let's return to John McEnroe.

It was never his fault. One time he lost a match because he had a fever. One time he had a backache. One time he fell victim to expectations, another time to the tabloids. One time he lost to a friend because the friend was in love and he wasn't. One time he ate too close to the match. One time he was too chunky, another time too thin. One time it was too cold, another time too hot. One time he was undertrained, another time overtrained.

His most agonizing loss, and the one that still keeps him up nights, was his loss in the 1984 French Open. Why did he lose after leading Ivan Lendl two sets to none? According to McEnroe, it wasn't his fault. An NBC cameraman had taken off his headset and a noise started coming from the side of the court.

Not his fault. So he didn't train to improve his ability to concentrate or his emotional control.

John Wooden, the legendary basketball coach, says you aren't a failure until you start to blame. What he means is that you can still be in the process of learning from your mistakes until you deny them.

When Enron, the energy giant, failed—toppled by a culture of arrogance—whose fault was it? Not mine, insisted Jeffrey Skilling, the CEO and resident genius. It was the world's fault. The world did not appreciate what Enron was trying to do. What about the Justice Department's investigation into massive corporate deception? A "witch hunt."

Jack Welch, the growth-minded CEO, had a completely different reaction to one of General Electric's fiascos. In 1986, General Electric bought Kidder, Peabody, a Wall Street investment banking firm. Soon after the deal closed, Kidder, Peabody was hit with a big insider trading scandal. A few years later, calamity struck again in the form of Joseph Jett, a trader who made a bunch of fictitious trades, to the tune of hundreds of millions, to pump up his bonus. Welch phoned fourteen of his top GE colleagues to tell them the bad news and to apologize personally. "I blamed myself for the disaster," Welch said.

Mindset and Depression

Maybe Bernard Loiseau, the French chef, was just depressed. Were you thinking that?

As a psychologist and an educator, I am vitally interested in depression. It runs wild on college campuses, especially in February and March. The winter is not over, the summer is not in sight, work has piled up, and relationships are often frayed. Yet it's been clear to me for a long time that different students handle depression in dramatically different ways. Some let everything slide. Others, though feeling wretched, hang on. They drag themselves to class, keep up with their work, and take care of themselves—so that when they feel better, their lives are intact.

Not long ago, we decided to see whether mindsets play a role in this difference. To find out, we measured students' mindsets and then had them keep an online "diary" for three weeks in February and March.

Every day they answered questions about their mood, their activities, and how they were coping with problems. Here's what we discovered.

First, the students with the fixed mindset had higher levels of depression. Our analyses showed that this was because they ruminated over their problems and setbacks, essentially tormenting themselves with the idea that the setbacks meant they were incompetent or unworthy: "It just kept circulating in my head: You're a dope." "I just couldn't let go of the thought that this made me less of a man." Again, failures labeled them and left them no route to success.

And the more depressed they felt, the more they let things go; the less they took action to solve their problems. For example, they didn't study what they needed to, they didn't hand in their assignments on time, and they didn't keep up with their chores.

Although students with the fixed mindset showed more depression, there were still plenty of people with the growth mindset who felt pretty miserable, this being peak season for depression. And here we saw something really amazing. The *more* depressed people with the growth mindset felt, the *more* they took action to confront their problems, the *more* they made sure to keep up with their schoolwork, and the *more* they kept up with their lives. The worse they felt, the more determined they became!

In fact, from the way they acted, it might have been hard to know how despondent they were. Here is a story a young man told me.

I was a freshman and it was the first time I had been away from home. Everyone was a stranger, the courses were hard, and as the year wore on I felt more and more depressed. Eventually, it reached a point where I could hardly get out of bed in the morning. But every day I forced myself to get up, shower, shave, and do whatever it was I needed to do. One day I really hit a low point and I decided to ask for help, so I went to the teaching assistant in my psychology course and asked for her advice.

"Are you going to your classes?" she asked.

"Yes," I replied.

"Are you keeping up with your reading?"

"Yes."

"Are you doing okay on your exams?"

"Yes."

"Well," she informed me, "then you're not depressed."

Yes, he was depressed, but he was coping the way people in the growth mindset tend to cope—with determination.

Doesn't temperament have a lot to do with it? Aren't some people sensitive by nature, while others just let things roll off their backs? Temperament certainly plays a role, but mindset is the most important part of the story. When we *taught* people the growth mindset, it completely changed the way they reacted to their depressed mood. The worse they felt, the more motivated they became and the more they confronted the problems that faced them.

In short, when people believe in fixed traits, they are always in danger of being measured by a failure. It can define them in a permanent way. Smart or talented as they may be, this mindset seems to rob them of their coping resources.

When people believe their basic qualities can be developed, failures may still hurt, but failures don't define them. And if abilities can be expanded—if change and growth are possible—then there are still many paths to success.

MINDSETS CHANGE THE MEANING OF EFFORT

As children, we were given a choice between the talented but erratic hare and the plodding but steady tortoise. The lesson was supposed to be that slow and steady wins the race. But, really, did any of us ever want to be the tortoise?

No, we just wanted to be a less foolish hare. We wanted to be swift as the wind and a bit more strategic—say, not taking quite so many snoozes before the finish line. After all, everyone knows you have to show up in order to win.

The story of the tortoise and the hare, in trying to put forward the power of effort, gave effort a bad name. It reinforced the image that effort is for the plodders and suggested that in rare instances, when talented people dropped the ball, the plodder could sneak through.

The little engine that could, the saggy, baggy elephant, and the scruffy tugboat—they were cute, they were often overmatched, and we were happy for them when they succeeded. In fact, to this day I remember how fond I was of those little creatures (or machines), but no way did I identify with them. The message was: If you're unfortunate enough to be the runt of the litter—if you lack endowment—you don't have to be an utter failure. You can be a sweet, adorable little slogger, and maybe (if you really work at it and withstand all the scornful onlookers) even a success.

Thank you very much, I'll take the endowment.

The problem was that these stories made it into an either-or. Either you have ability *or* you expend effort. And this is part of the fixed mindset. Effort is for those who don't have the ability. People with the fixed mindset tell us, "If you have to work at something, you must not be good at it." They add, "Things come easily to people who are true geniuses."

CALVIN AND HOBBES © 1995 WATTERSON.
REPRINTED WITH PERMISSION OF UNIVERSAL PRESS SYNDICATE

I was a young assistant professor in the psychology department at the University of Illinois. Late one night, I was passing the psychology building and noticed that the lights were on in some faculty offices. Some of my colleagues were working late. *They must not be as smart as I am,* I thought to myself.

It never occurred to me that they might be just as smart and more hardworking! For me it was either-or. And it was clear I valued the either over the or.

Malcolm Gladwell, the author and *New Yorker* writer, has suggested that as a society we value natural, effortless accomplishment over achievement through effort. We endow our heroes with superhuman abilities that led them inevitably toward their greatness. It's as if Midori popped out of the womb fiddling, Michael Jordan dribbling, and Picasso doodling. This captures the fixed mindset perfectly. And it's everywhere.

A report from researchers at Duke University sounds an alarm about the anxiety and depression among female undergraduates who aspire to "effortless perfection." They believe they should display perfect beauty, perfect womanhood, and perfect scholarship all without trying (or at least without appearing to try).

Americans aren't the only people who disdain effort. French executive Pierre Chevalier says, "We are not a nation of effort. After all, if you have savoir-faire [a mixture of know-how and cool], you do things effortlessly."

People with the growth mindset, however, believe something very different. For them, even geniuses have to work hard for their achievements. And what's so heroic, they would say, about having a gift? They may appreciate endowment, but they admire effort, for no matter what your ability is, effort is what ignites that ability and turns it into accomplishment.

Seabiscuit

Here was a horse who was so broken, he was supposed to be put to sleep. In fact, here was a whole team of people—the jockey, the owner, the trainer—who were damaged in one way or another. Yet through their dogged determination and against all odds, they transformed themselves into winners. A down-and-out nation saw this horse and rider as a symbol of what could be accomplished through grit and spirit.

Equally moving is the parallel story about *Seabiscuit*'s author, Laura Hillenbrand. Felled in her college years by severe, recurrent chronic fatigue that never went away, she was often unable to function. Yet something in the story of the "horse who could" gripped and inspired her, so that she was able to write a heartfelt, magnificent story about the triumph of will. The book was a testament to Seabiscuit's triumph and her own, equally.

Seen through the lens of the growth mindset, these are stories about the transformative power of effort—the power of effort to change your ability and to change you as a person. But filtered through the fixed mindset, it's a great story about three men and a horse, all with deficiencies, who *had* to try very hard.

High Effort: The Big Risk

From the point of view of the fixed mindset, effort is only for people with deficiencies. And when people already know they're deficient, they have nothing to lose by trying. But if your claim to fame is not having any deficiencies—if you're considered a genius, a talent, or a natural—then you have a lot to lose. Effort can *reduce* you.

Nadja Salerno-Sonnenberg made her violin debut at the age of ten with the Philadelphia Orchestra. Yet when she arrived at Juilliard to study with Dorothy DeLay, the great violin teacher, she had a repertoire of awful habits. Her fingerings and bowings were awkward and she held her violin in the wrong position, but she refused to change. After several years, she saw the other students catching up and even surpassing her, and by her late teens she had a crisis of confidence. "I was used to success, to the prodigy label in newspapers, and now I felt like a failure."

This prodigy was afraid of trying. "Everything I was going through boiled down to fear. Fear of trying and failing. . . . If you go to an audition and don't really try, if you're not really prepared, if you didn't work as hard as you could have and you don't win, you have an excuse. . . . Nothing is harder than saying, 'I gave it my all and it wasn't good enough.' "

The idea of trying and still failing—of leaving yourself without excuses—is the worst fear within the fixed mindset, and it haunted and paralyzed her. She had even stopped bringing her violin to her lesson!

Then, one day, after years of patience and understanding, DeLay told her, "Listen, if you don't bring your violin next week, I'm throwing you out of my class." Salerno-Sonnenberg thought she was joking, but DeLay rose from the couch and calmly informed her, "I'm not kidding. If you are going to waste your talent, I don't want to be a part of it. This has gone on long enough."

Why is effort so terrifying?

There are two reasons. One is that in the fixed mindset, great geniuses are not supposed to need it. So just needing it casts a shadow on your ability. The second is that, as Nadja suggests, it robs you of all your excuses. Without effort, you can always say, "I could have been [fill in the blank]." But once you try, you can't say that anymore. Someone once said to me, "I could have been Yo-Yo Ma." If she had really tried for it, she wouldn't have been able to say that.

Salerno-Sonnenberg was terrified of losing DeLay. She finally decided that trying and failing—an honest failure—was better than the course she had been on, and so she began training with DeLay for an upcoming competition. For the first time she went all out, and, by the way, won. Now she says, "This is something I know for a fact: You have to work hardest for the things you love most. And when it's music you love, you're in for the fight of your life."

Fear of effort can happen in relationships, too, as it did with Amanda, a dynamic and attractive young woman.

I had a lot of crazy boyfriends. A lot. They ranged from unreliable to inconsiderate. "How about a nice guy for once?" my best friend Carla always said. It was like, "You deserve better."

So then Carla fixed me up with Rob, a guy from her office. He was great, and not just on day one. I loved it. It was like, "Oh, my God, a guy who actually shows up on time." Then it became serious and I freaked. I mean, this guy really liked me, but I couldn't stop thinking about how, if he really knew me, he might get turned off. I mean, what if I really, really tried and it didn't work? I guess I couldn't take that risk.

Low Effort: The Big Risk

In the growth mindset, it's almost inconceivable to want something badly, to think you have a chance to achieve it, and then do nothing about it. When it happens, the *I could have been* is heartbreaking, not comforting.

There were few American women in the 1930s through 1950s who were more successful than Clare Boothe Luce. She was a famous author and playwright, she was elected to Congress twice, and she was ambassador to Italy. "I don't really understand the word 'success,' " she has said. "I know people use it about me, but I don't understand it." Her public life and private tragedies kept her from getting back to her greatest love: writing for the theater. She'd had great success with plays like *The Women,* but it just wouldn't do for a political figure to keep penning tart, sexy comedies.

For her, politics did not provide the personal creative effort she valued most, and looking back she couldn't forgive herself for not pursuing her passion for theater. "I often thought," she said, "that if I were to write an autobiography, my title would be *The Autobiography of a Failure.*"

Billie Jean King says it's all about what you want to look back and say. I agree with her. You can look back and say, "I could have been . . . ," polishing your unused endowments like trophies. Or you can look back and say, "I gave my all for the things I valued." Think about what you want to look back and say. Then choose your mindset.

Turning Knowledge into Action

Sure, people with the fixed mindset have read the books that say: Success is about being your best self, not about being better than others; failure is an opportunity, not a condemnation; effort is the key to success. But they can't put this into practice because their basic mindset—their belief in fixed traits—is telling them something entirely different: that success *is* about being more gifted than others, that failure *does* measure you, and that effort is for those who can't make it on talent.

QUESTIONS AND ANSWERS

At this point, you probably have questions. Let me see if I can answer some of them.

> *Question: If people believe their qualities are fixed, and they have shown themselves to be smart or talented, why do they have to keep proving it? After all, when the prince proved his bravery, he and the princess lived happily ever after. He didn't have to go out and slay a dragon every day. Why don't people with the fixed mindset prove themselves and then live happily ever after?*

Because every day new and larger dragons come along and, as things get harder, maybe the ability they proved yesterday is not up to today's task. Maybe they were smart enough for algebra but not calculus. Maybe they were a good enough pitcher for the minor leagues but not the majors. Maybe they were a good enough writer for their school newspaper but not *The New York Times*.

So they're racing to prove themselves over and over, but where are they going? To me they're often running in place, amassing countless affirmations, but not necessarily ending up where they want to be.

You know those movies where the main character wakes up one day and sees that his life has not been worthwhile—he has always been besting people, not growing, learning, or caring. My favorite is *Groundhog Day*, which I didn't see for a long time because I couldn't get past the name. At any rate, in *Groundhog Day*, Bill Murray doesn't just wake up one day and get the message; he has to repeat the same day over and over until he gets the message.

Phil Connors (Murray) is a weatherman for a local station in Pittsburgh who is dispatched to Punxsutawney, Pennsylvania, to cover the Groundhog Day ceremony. On February 2, a groundhog is taken out of his little house; if he is judged to have seen his shadow, there will be another six weeks of winter. If not, there will be an early spring.

Phil, considering himself to be a superior being, has complete contempt for the ceremony, the town, and the people ("hicks" and "morons"), and after making that perfectly clear, he plans to get out of Punxsutawney as quickly as possible. But this is not to be. A blizzard hits the town, he is forced to remain, and when he wakes up the next morning, it's Groundhog Day again. The same Sonny and Cher song, "I Got You Babe," wakes him up on the clock radio and the same groundhog festival is gearing up once again. And again. And again.

At first, he uses the knowledge to further his typical agenda, making fools out of other people. Since he is the only one reliving the day, he can talk to a woman on one day, and then use the information to deceive, impress, and seduce her the next. He is in fixed-mindset heaven. He can prove his superiority over and over.

But after countless such days, he realizes it's all going nowhere and he tries to kill himself. He crashes a car, he electrocutes himself, he jumps from a steeple, he walks in front of a truck. With no way out, it finally dawns on him. He could be using this time to learn. He goes for piano lessons. He reads voraciously. He learns ice sculpting. He finds out about people who need help that day (a boy who falls from a tree, a man who chokes on his steak) and starts to help them, and care about them. Pretty soon the day is not long enough! Only when this change of mindset is complete is he released from the spell.

Question: Are mindsets a permanent part of your makeup or can you change them?

Mindsets are an important part of your personality, but you *can* change them. Just by knowing about the two mindsets, you can start thinking and reacting in new ways. People tell me they start to catch themselves when they are in the throes of the fixed mindset—passing up a chance for learning, feeling labeled by a failure, or getting discouraged when something requires a lot of effort. And then they switch themselves into the growth mindset—making sure they take the challenge, learn from the failure, or continue their effort. When my graduate students and I first discovered the mindsets, they would catch me in the fixed mindset and scold me.

It's also important to realize that even if people have a fixed mindset, they're not always in that mindset. In fact, in many of our studies, we *put* people into a growth mindset. We tell them that an ability can be learned and that the task will give them a chance to do that. Or we have them read a scientific article that teaches them the growth mindset. The article describes people who did not have natural ability, but who developed exceptional skills. These experiences make our research participants into growth-minded thinkers, at least for the moment—and they act like growth-minded thinkers, too.

Later, there's a chapter all about change. There I describe people who have changed and programs we've developed to bring about change.

Question: Can I be half-and-half? I recognize both mindsets in myself.

Many people have elements of both. I'm talking about it as a simple either–or for the sake of simplicity.

People can also have different mindsets in different areas. I might think that my artistic skills are fixed but that my intelligence can be developed. Or that my personality is fixed, but my creativity can be developed. We've found that whatever mindset people have in a particular area will guide them in that area.

Question: With all your belief in effort, are you saying that when people fail, it's always their fault—they didn't try hard enough?

No! It's true that effort is crucial—no one can succeed for long without it—but it's certainly not the only thing. People have different resources and opportunities. For example, people with money (or rich parents) have a safety net. They can take more risks and keep going longer until they succeed. People with easy access to a good education, people with a network of influential friends, people who know how to be in the right place at the right time—all stand a better chance of having their effort pay off. Rich, educated, connected effort works better.

People with fewer resouces, in spite of their best efforts, can be derailed so much more easily. The hometown plant you've worked in all of your life suddenly shuts down. What now? Your child falls ill and plunges you into debt. There goes the house. Your spouse runs off with the nest egg and leaves you with the children and bills. Forget the night school classes.

Before we judge, let's remember that effort isn't quite everything and that all effort is not created equal.

> *Question: You keep talking about how the growth mindset makes people number one, the best, the most successful. Isn't the growth mindset about personal development, not besting others?*

I use examples of people who made it to the top to show how far the growth mindset can take you: Believing talents can be developed allows people to fulfill their potential.

In addition, examples of laid-back people having a good time would not be as convincing to people with a fixed mindset. It doesn't provide a compelling alternative for them because it makes it look like a choice between fun and excellence.

However, this point is crucial: The growth mindset *does* allow people to love what they're doing—and to continue to love it in the face of difficulties. The growth-minded athletes, CEOs, musicians, or scientists all loved what they did, whereas many of the fixed-minded ones did not.

Many growth-minded people didn't even plan to go to the top. They got there as a result of doing what they love. It's ironic: The top is where the fixed-mindset people hunger to be, but it's where many growth-minded people arrive as a by-product of their enthusiasm for what they do.

This point is also crucial. In the fixed mindset, everything is about the outcome. If you fail—or if you're not the best—it's all been wasted. The growth mindset allows people to value what they're doing *regardless of the outcome.* They're tackling problems, charting new courses, working on important issues. Maybe they haven't found the cure for cancer, but the search was deeply meaningful.

A lawyer spent seven years fighting the biggest bank in his state on behalf of people who felt they'd been cheated. After he lost, he said, "Who am I to say that just because I spent seven years on something I am entitled to success? Did I do it for the success, or did I do it because I thought the effort itself was valid?

"I do not regret it. I had to do it. I would not do it differently."

Question: I know a lot of workaholics on the fast track who seem to have a fixed mindset. They're always trying to prove how smart they are, but they do work hard and they do take on challenges. How does this fit with your idea that people with a fixed mindset go in for low effort and easy tasks?

On the whole, people with a fixed mindset prefer effortless success, since that's the best way to prove their talent. But you're right, there are also plenty of high-powered people who think their traits are fixed and are looking for constant validation. These may be people whose life goal is to win a Nobel Prize or become the richest person on the planet—and they're willing to do what it takes. We'll meet people like this in the chapter on business and leadership.

These people may be free of the belief that high effort equals low ability, but they have the other parts of the fixed mindset. They may constantly put their talent on display. They may feel that their talent makes them superior to other people. And they may be intolerant of mistakes, criticism, or setbacks—something that can hamper their progress.

Incidentally, people with a growth mindset might also like a Nobel Prize or a lot of money. But they are not seeking it as a validation of their worth or as something that will make them better than others.

Question: What if I like my fixed mindset? If I know what my abilities and talents are, I know where I stand, and I know what to expect. Why should I give that up?

If you like it, by all means keep it. This book shows people they have a choice by spelling out the two mindsets and the worlds they create. The point is that people can choose which world they want to inhabit.

The fixed mindset creates the feeling that you can *really* know the permanent truth about yourself. And this can be comforting: You don't have to try for such-and-such because you don't have the talent. You will surely succeed at thus-and-such because you do have the talent.

It's just important to be aware of the drawbacks of this mindset. You may be robbing yourself of an opportunity by underestimating your talent in the first area. Or you may be undermining your chances of success in the second area by assuming that your talent alone will take you there.

By the way, having a growth mindset doesn't force you to pursue something. It just tells you that you can develop your skills. It's still up to you whether you want to.

Question: Can everything about people be changed, and should people try to change everything they can?

The growth mindset is the belief that abilities can be cultivated. But it doesn't tell you how much change is possible or how long change will take. And it doesn't mean that *everything*, like preferences or values, can be changed.

I was once in a taxi, and the driver had an opera on the radio. Thinking to start a conversation, I said, "Do you like opera?" "No," he replied, "I hate it. I've always hated it." "I don't mean to pry," I said, "but why are you listening to it?" He then told me how his father had been an opera buff, listening to his vintage records at every opportunity. My cabdriver, now well into middle age, had tried for many years to cultivate a rapturous response to opera. He played the disks, he read the scores—all to no avail. "Give yourself a break," I advised him. "There are plenty of cultured and intelligent people who can't stand opera. Why don't you just consider yourself one of them?"

The growth mindset also doesn't mean everything that *can* be changed *should* be changed. We all need to accept some of our imperfections, especially the ones that don't really harm our lives or the lives of others.

The fixed mindset stands in the way of development and change. The growth mindset is a starting point for change, but people need to decide for themselves where their efforts toward change would be most valuable.

Question: Are people with the fixed mindset simply lacking in confidence?

No. People with the fixed mindset have just as much confidence as people with the growth mindset—before anything happens, that is. But as you can imagine, their confidence is more fragile since setbacks and even effort can undermine it.

Joseph Martocchio conducted a study of employees who were taking a short computer training course. Half of the employees were put in a fixed mindset. He told them it was all a matter of how much ability they possessed. The other half were put in a growth mindset. He told them that computer skills could be developed through practice. Everyone, steeped in these mindsets, then proceeded with the course.

Although the two groups started off with exactly equal confidence in their computer skills, by the end of the course they looked quite different. Those in the growth mindset gained considerable confidence in their computer skills as they learned, despite the many mistakes they inevitably made. But, because of those mistakes, those with the fixed mindset actually *lost* confidence in their computer skills as they learned!

The same thing happened with Berkeley students. Richard Robins and Jennifer Pals tracked students at the University of California at Berkeley over their years of college. They found that when students had the growth mindset, they gained confidence in themselves as they repeatedly met and mastered the challenges of the university. However, when students had the fixed mindset, their confidence eroded in the face of those same challenges.

That's why people with the fixed mindset have to nurse their confidence and protect it. That's what John McEnroe's excuses were for: to protect his confidence.

Michelle Wie is a teenage golfer who decided to go up against the big boys. She entered the Sony Open, a PGA tournament that features the best male players in the world. Coming from a fixed-mindset perspective, everyone rushed to warn her that she could do serious damage to her confidence if she did poorly—that "taking too many early lumps against superior competition could hurt her long-range development." "It's always negative when you don't win," warned Vijay Singh, a prominent golfer on the tour.

But Wie disagreed. She wasn't going there to groom her confidence. "Once you win junior tournaments, it's easy to win multiple times. What I'm doing now is to prepare for the future." It's the learning experience she was after—what it was like to play with the world's best players in the atmosphere of a tournament.

After the event, Wie's confidence had not suffered one bit. She had exactly what she wanted. "I think I learned that I can play here." It will be a long road to the winner's circle, but she now had a sense of what she was shooting for.

Some years ago, I got a letter from a world-class competitive swimmer.

Dear Professor Dweck:

I've always had a problem with confidence. My coaches always told me to believe in myself 100%. They told me not to let any doubts enter my mind and to think about how I'm better than everyone else. I couldn't do it because I'm always so aware of my defects and the mistakes I make in every meet. Trying to think I was perfect made it even worse. Then I read your work and how it's so important to focus on learning and improving. It turned me around. My defects are things I can work on! Now a mistake doesn't seem so important. I wanted to write you this letter for teaching me how to have confidence. Thank you.

Sincerely,
Mary Williams

A remarkable thing I've learned from my research is that in the growth mindset, you don't always *need* confidence.

What I mean is that even when you think you're not good at something, you can still plunge into it wholeheartedly and stick to it. Actually, sometimes you plunge into something *because* you're not good at it. This is a wonderful feature of the growth mindset. You don't have to think you're already great at something to want to do it and to enjoy doing it.

This book is one of the hardest things I've ever done. I read endless books and articles. The information was overwhelming. I'd never written in a popular way. It was intimidating. Does it seem easy for me? Way back when, that's exactly what I would have wanted you to think. Now I want you to know the effort it took—and the joy it brought.

Grow Your Mindset

- People are all born with a love of learning, but the fixed mindset can undo it. Think of a time you were enjoying something—doing a crossword puzzle, playing a sport, learning a new dance. Then it became hard and you wanted out. Maybe you suddenly felt tired, dizzy, bored, or hungry. Next time this happens, don't fool yourself. It's the fixed mindset. Put yourself in a growth mindset. Picture your brain forming new connections as you meet the challenge and learn. Keep on going.

- It's tempting to create a world in which we're perfect. (Ah, I remember that feeling from grade school.) We can choose partners, make friends, hire people who make us feel faultless. But think about it—do you want to never grow? Next time you're tempted to surround yourself with worshipers, go to church. In the rest of your life, seek constructive criticism.

- Is there something in your past that you think measured you? A test score? A dishonest or callous action? Being fired from a job? Being rejected? Focus on that thing. Feel all the emotions that go with it. Now put it in a growth-mindset perspective. Look honestly at your role in it, but understand that it doesn't define your intelligence or personality. Instead, ask: *What did I (or can I) learn from that experience? How can I use it as a basis for growth?* Carry that with you instead.

- How do you act when you feel depressed? Do you work harder at things in your life or do you let them go? Next time you feel low, put yourself in a growth mindset—think about learning, challenge, confronting obstacles. Think about effort as a positive, constructive force, not as a big drag. Try it out.
- Is there something you've always wanted to do but were afraid you weren't good at? Make a plan to do it.

Chapter 3

THE TRUTH ABOUT ABILITY
AND ACCOMPLISHMENT

Try to picture Thomas Edison as vividly as you can. Think about where he is and what he's doing. Is he alone? I asked people, and they always said things like this:

"He's in his workshop surrounded by equipment. He's working on the phonograph, trying things. He succeeds! [Is he alone?] Yes, he's doing this stuff alone because he's the only one who knows what he's after."

"He's in New Jersey. He's standing in a white coat in a lab-type room. He's leaning over a lightbulb. Suddenly, it works! [Is he alone?] Yes. He's kind of a reclusive guy who likes to tinker on his own."

In truth, the record shows quite a different fellow, working in quite a different way.

Edison was not a loner. For the invention of the lightbulb, he had thirty assistants, including well-trained scientists, often working around the clock in a corporate-funded state-of-the-art laboratory!

It did not happen suddenly. The lightbulb has become the symbol for that single moment when the brilliant solution strikes, but there was no single moment of invention. In fact, the lightbulb was not one invention, but a whole network of time-consuming inventions each requiring one or more chemists, mathematicians, physicists, engineers, and glass-blowers.

Edison was no naïve tinkerer or unworldly egghead. The "Wizard of Menlo Park" was a savvy entrepreneur, fully aware of the commercial potential of his inventions. He also knew how to cozy up to the press—sometimes beating others out as *the* inventor of something because he knew how to publicize himself.

Yes, he was a genius. But he was not always one. His biographer, Paul Israel, sifting through all the available information, thinks he was more or less a regular boy of his time and place. Young Tom was taken with experiments and mechanical things (perhaps more avidly than most), but machines and technology were part of the ordinary midwestern boy's experience.

What eventually set him apart was his mindset and drive. He never stopped being the curious, tinkering boy looking for new challenges. Long after other young men had taken up their roles in society, he rode the rails from city to city learning everything he could about telegraphy, and working his way up the ladder of telegraphers through nonstop self-education and invention. And later, much to the disappointment of his wives, his consuming love remained self-improvement and invention, but only in his field.

There are many myths about ability and achievement, especially about the lone, brilliant person suddenly producing amazing things.

Yet Darwin's masterwork, *The Origin of Species,* took years of teamwork in the field, hundreds of discussions with colleagues and mentors, several preliminary drafts, and half a lifetime of dedication before it reached fruition.

Mozart labored for more than ten years until he produced any work that we admire today. Before then, his compositions were not that original or interesting. Actually, they were often patched-together chunks taken from other composers.

This chapter is about the real ingredients in achievement. It's about why some people achieve less than expected and why some people achieve more.

MINDSET AND SCHOOL ACHIEVEMENT

Let's step down from the celestial realm of Mozart and Darwin and come back to earth to see how mindsets create achievement in real life. It's funny, but seeing one student blossom under the growth mindset has a greater impact on me than all the stories about Mozarts and Darwins. Maybe because it's more about you and me—about what's happened to us and why we are where we are now. And about children and their potential.

Back on earth, we measured students' mindsets as they made the transition to junior high school: Did they believe their intelligence was a fixed trait or something they could develop? Then we followed them for the next two years.

The transition to junior high is a time of great challenge for many students. The work gets much harder, the grading policies toughen up, the teaching becomes less personalized. And all this happens while students are coping with their new adolescent bodies and roles. Grades suffer, but not everyone's grades suffer equally.

No. In our study, only the students with the fixed mindset showed the decline. They showed an immediate drop-off in grades, and slowly but surely did worse and worse over the two years. The students with the growth mindset showed an *increase* in their grades over the two years.

When the two groups had entered junior high, their past records were indistinguishable. In the more benign environment of grade school, they'd earned the same grades and achievement test scores. Only when they hit the challenge of junior high did they begin to pull apart.

Here's how students with the fixed mindset explained their poor grades. Many maligned their abilities: "I am the stupidest" or "I suck in math." And many covered these feelings by blaming someone else: "[The math teacher] is a fat male slut . . . and [the English teacher] is a slob with a pink ass." "Because the teacher is on crack." These interesting analyses of the problem hardly provide a road map to future success.

With the threat of failure looming, students with the growth mindset instead mobilized their resources for learning. They told us that they, too, sometimes felt overwhelmed, but their response was to dig in and do what it takes. They were like George Danzig. Who?

George Danzig was a graduate student in math at Berkeley. One day, as usual, he rushed in late to his math class and quickly copied the two homework problems from the blackboard. When he later went to do them, he found them very difficult, and it took him several days of hard work to crack them open and solve them. They turned out not to be homework problems at all. They were two famous math problems that had never been solved.

The Low-Effort Syndrome

Our students with the fixed mindset who were facing the hard transition saw it as a threat. It threatened to unmask their flaws and turn them from winners into losers. In fact, in the fixed mindset, adolescence is one big test. *Am I smart or dumb? Am I good-looking or ugly? Am I cool or nerdy? Am I a winner or a loser?* And in the fixed mindset, a loser is forever.

It's no wonder that many adolescents mobilize their resources, not for learning, but to protect their egos. And one of the main ways they do this (aside from providing vivid portraits of their teachers) is by not trying. This is when some of the brightest students, just like Nadja Salerno-Sonnenberg, simply stop working. In fact, students with the fixed mindset tell us that their main goal in school—aside from looking smart—is to exert as little effort as possible. They heartily agree with statements like this:

"In school my main goal is to do things as easily as possible so I don't have to work very hard."

This low-effort syndrome is often seen as a way that adolescents assert their independence from adults, but it is also a way that students with the fixed mindset protect themselves. They view the adults as saying, "Now we will measure you and see what you've got." And they are answering, "No you won't."

John Holt, the great educator, says that these are the games all human beings play when others are sitting in judgment of them. "The worst student we had, the worst I have ever encountered, was in his life outside the classroom as mature, intelligent, and interesting a person as anyone at the school. What went wrong? . . . Somewhere along the line, his intelligence became disconnected from his schooling."

For students with the growth mindset, it doesn't make sense to stop trying. For them, adolescence is a time of opportunity: a time to learn new subjects, a time to find out what they like and what they want to become in the future.

Later, I'll describe the project in which we taught junior high students the growth mindset. What I want to tell you now is how teaching them this mindset unleashed their effort. One day, we were introducing the growth mindset to a new group of students. All at once Jimmy—the most hard-core turned-off low-effort kid in the group—looked up with tears in his eyes and said, "You mean I don't have to be dumb?" From that day on, he worked. He started staying up late to do his homework, which he never used to bother with at all. He started handing in assignments early so he could get feedback and revise them. He now believed that working hard was not something that made you vulnerable, but something that made you smarter.

Finding Your Brain

A close friend of mine recently handed me something he'd written, a poem-story that reminded me of Jimmy and his unleashed effort. My friend's second-grade teacher, Mrs. Beer, had had each student draw and cut out a paper horse. She then lined up all the horses above the blackboard and delivered her growth-mindset message: "Your horse is only as fast as your brain. Every time you learn something, your horse will move ahead."

My friend wasn't so sure about the "brain" thing. His father had always told him, "You have too much mouth and too little brains for your own good." Plus, his horse seemed to just sit at the starting gate while "everyone else's brain joined the learning chase," especially the brains of Hank and Billy, the class geniuses, whose horses jumped way ahead of everyone else's. But my friend kept at it. To improve his skills, he kept reading the comics with his mother and he kept adding up the points when he played gin rummy with his grandmother.

> And soon my sleek stallion
> bolted forward like Whirlaway,
> and there was no one
> who was going to stop him.
> Over the weeks and months
> he flew forward overtaking
> the others one by one.
> In the late spring homestretch
> Hank's and Billy's mounts were ahead
> by just a few subtraction exercises, and
> when the last bell of school rang,
> my horse won—"By a nose!"
> Then I knew I had a brain:
> I had the horse to prove it.
>
> —PAUL WORTMAN

Of course, learning shouldn't really be a race. But this race helped my friend discover his brain and connect it up to his schooling.

The College Transition

Another transition, another crisis. College is when all the students who were the brains in high school are thrown together. Like our graduate students, yesterday they were king of the hill, but today who are they?

Nowhere is the anxiety of being dethroned more palpable than in pre-med classes. In the last chapter, I mentioned our study of tense but hopeful undergraduates taking their first college chemistry course. This is the course that would give them—or deny them—entrée to the pre-med curriculum, and it's well known that students will go to almost any lengths to do well in this course.

At the beginning of the semester, we measured students' mindsets, and then we followed them through the course, watching their grades and asking about their study strategies. Once again we found that the students with the growth mindset earned better grades in the course. Even when they did poorly on a particular test, they bounced back on the next ones. When students with the fixed mindset did poorly, they often didn't make a comeback.

In this course, everybody studied. But there are different ways to study. Many students study like this: They read the textbook and their class notes. If the material is really hard, they read them again. Or they might try to memorize everything they can, like a vacuum cleaner. That's how the students with the fixed mindset studied. If they did poorly on the test, they concluded that chemistry was not their subject. After all, "I did everything possible, didn't I?"

Far from it. They would be shocked to find out what students with the growth mindset do. Even I find it remarkable.

The students with growth mindset completely took charge of their learning and motivation. Instead of plunging into unthinking memorization of the course material, they said: "I looked for themes and underlying principles across lectures," and "I went over mistakes until I was certain I understood them." They were studying to learn, not just to ace the test. And, actually, this was why they got higher grades—not because they were smarter or had a better background in science.

Instead of losing their motivation when the course got dry or difficult, they said: "I maintained my interest in the material." "I stayed positive about taking chemistry." "I kept myself motivated to study." Even if they thought the textbook was boring or the instructor was a stiff, they didn't let their motivation evaporate. That just made it all the more important to motivate themselves.

I got an e-mail from one of my undergraduate students shortly after I had taught her the growth mindset. Here's how she used to study before: "When faced with really tough material I tend[ed] to read the material over and over." After learning the growth mindset, she started using better strategies—that worked:

Professor Dweck:

When Heidi [the teaching assistant] told me my exam results today I didn't know whether to cry or just sit down. Heidi will tell you, I looked like I won the lottery (and I feel that way, too)! I can't believe I did SO WELL. I expected to "scrape" by. The encouragement you have given me will serve me well in life. . . .

I feel that I've earned a noble grade, but I didn't earn it alone. Prof. Dweck, you not only teach [your] theory, you SHOW it. Thank you for the lesson. It is a valuable one, perhaps the most valuable I've learned at Columbia. And yeah, I'll be doing THAT [using these strategies] before EVERY exam!

Thank you very, very much (and you TOO Heidi)!

No longer helpless,
June

Because they think in terms of learning, people with the growth mindset are clued in to all the different ways to create learning. It's odd. Our pre-med students with the fixed mindset would do almost anything for a good grade—except take charge of the process to make sure it happens.

Created Equal?

Does this mean that anyone with the right mindset can do well? Are all children created equal? Let's take the second question first. No, some children are different. In her book *Gifted Children*, Ellen Winner offers incredible descriptions of prodigies. These are children who seem to be born with heightened abilities and obsessive interests, and who, through relentless pursuit of these interests, become amazingly accomplished.

Michael was one of the most precocious. He constantly played games involving letters and numbers, made his parents answer endless questions about letters and numbers, and spoke, read, and did math at an unbelievably early age. Michael's mother reports that at four months old, he said, "Mom, Dad, what's for dinner?" At ten months, he astounded people in the supermarket by reading words from the signs. Everyone assumed his mother was doing some kind of ventriloquism thing. His father reports that at three, he was not only doing algebra, but discovering and proving algebraic rules. Each day, when his father got home from work, Michael would pull him toward math books and say, "Dad, let's go do work."

Michael must have started with a special ability, but, for me, the most outstanding feature is his extreme love of learning and challenge. His parents could not tear him away from his demanding activities. The same is true for every prodigy Winner describes. Most often people believe that the "gift" is the ability itself. Yet what feeds it is that constant, endless curiosity and challenge seeking.

Is it ability or mindset? Was it Mozart's musical ability or the fact that he worked till his hands were deformed? Was it Darwin's scientific ability or the fact that he collected specimens nonstop from early childhood?

Prodigies or not, we all have interests that can blossom into abilities. As a child, I was fascinated by people, especially adults. I wondered: *What makes them tick?* In fact, a few years back, one of my cousins reminded me of an episode that took place when we were five years old. We were at my grandmother's house, and he'd had a big fight with his mother over when he could eat his candy. Later, we were sitting outside on the front steps and I said to him: "Don't be so stupid. Adults like to think they're in charge. Just say yes, and then eat your candy when you want to."

Were those the words of a budding psychologist? All I know is that my cousin told me this advice served him well. (Interestingly, he became a dentist.)

Can Everyone Do Well?

Now back to the first question. Is everyone capable of great things with the right mindset? Could you march into the worst high school in your state and teach the students college calculus? If you could, then one thing would be clear: With the right mindset and the right teaching, people are capable of a lot more than we think.

Garfield High School was one of the worst schools in Los Angeles. To say that the students were turned off and the teachers burned out is an understatement. But without thinking twice, Jaime Escalante (of *Stand and Deliver* fame) taught these inner-city Hispanic students college-level calculus. With his growth mindset, he asked "*How* can I teach them?" not "*Can* I teach them?" and "*How* will they learn best?" not "*Can* they learn?"

But not only did he teach them calculus, he (and his colleague, Benjamin Jimenez) took them to the top of the national charts in math. In 1987, only three other public schools in the country had more students taking the Advanced Placement Calculus test. Those three included Stuyvesant High School and the Bronx High School of Science, both elite math-and-science-oriented schools in New York.

What's more, most of the Garfield students earned test grades that were high enough to gain them college credits. In the whole country that year, only a few hundred Mexican American students passed the test at this level. This means there's a lot of intelligence out there being wasted by underestimating students' potential to develop.

Marva Collins

Most often when kids are behind—say, when they're repeating a grade—they're given dumbed-down material on the assumption that they can't handle more. That idea comes from the fixed mindset: These students are dim-witted, so they need the same simple things drummed into them over and over. Well, the results are depressing. Students repeat the whole grade *without learning any more than they knew before.*

Instead, Marva Collins took inner-city Chicago kids who had failed in the public schools and treated them like geniuses. Many of them had been labeled "learning disabled," "retarded," or "emotionally disturbed." Virtually all of them were apathetic. No light in the eyes, no hope in the face.

Collins's second-grade public school class started out with the lowest-level reader there was. By June, they reached the middle of the fifth-grade reader, studying Aristotle, Aesop, Tolstoy, Shakespeare, Poe, Frost, and Dickinson along the way.

Later when she started her own school, *Chicago Sun-Times* columnist Zay Smith dropped in. He saw four-year-olds writing sentences like "See the physician" and "Aesop wrote fables," and talking about "diphthongs" and "diacritical marks." He observed second graders reciting passages from Shakespeare, Longfellow, and Kipling. Shortly before, he had visited a rich suburban high school where many students had never heard of Shakespeare. "Shoot," said one of Collins's students, "you mean those rich high school kids don't know Shakespeare was born in 1564 and died in 1616?"

Students read huge amounts, even over the summer. One student, who had entered as a "retarded" six-year-old, now four years later had read twenty-three books over the summer, including *A Tale of Two Cities* and *Jane Eyre*. The students read deeply and thoughtfully. As the three- and four-year-olds were reading about Daedalus and Icarus, one four-year-old exclaimed, "Mrs. Collins, if we do not learn and work hard, we will take an Icarian flight to nowhere." Heated discussions of *Macbeth* were common.

Alfred Binet believed you could change the quality of someone's mind. Clearly you can. Whether you measure these children by the breadth of their knowledge or by their performance on standardized tests, their minds had been transformed.

Benjamin Bloom, an eminent educational researcher, studied 120 outstanding achievers. They were concert pianists, sculptors, Olympic swimmers, world-class tennis players, mathematicians, and research neurologists. Most were not that remarkable as children and didn't show clear talent before their training began in earnest. Even by early adolescence, you usually couldn't predict their future accomplishment from their current ability. Only their continued motivation and commitment, along with their network of support, took them to the top.

Bloom concludes, "After forty years of intensive research on school learning in the United States as well as abroad, my major conclusion is: What any person in the world can learn, *almost* all persons can learn, *if* provided with the appropriate prior and current conditions of learning." He's not counting the 2 to 3 percent of children who have severe impairments, and he's not counting the top 1 to 2 percent of children at the other extreme that include children like Michael. He *is* counting everybody else.

Ability Levels and Tracking

But aren't students sorted into different ability levels for a reason? Haven't their test scores and past achievement shown what their ability is? Remember, test scores and measures of achievement tell you where a student is, but they don't tell you where a student could end up.

Falko Rheinberg, a researcher in Germany, studied schoolteachers with different mindsets. Some of the teachers had the fixed mindset. They believed that students entering their class with different achievement levels were deeply and permanently different:

"According to my experience students' achievement mostly remains constant in the course of a year."

"If I know students' intelligence I can predict their school career quite well."

"As a teacher I have no influence on students' intellectual ability."

Like my sixth-grade teacher, Mrs. Wilson, these teachers preached and practiced the fixed mindset. In their classrooms, the students who started the year in the high-ability group ended the year there, and those who started the year in the low-ability group ended the year there.

But some teachers preached and practiced a growth mindset. They focused on the idea that all children could develop their skills, and in their classrooms a weird thing happened. It didn't matter whether students started the year in the high- or the low-ability group. Both groups ended the year way up high. It's a powerful experience to see these findings. The group differences had simply disappeared under the guidance of teachers who taught for improvement, for these teachers had found a way to reach their "low-ability" students.

How teachers put a growth mindset into practice is the topic of a later chapter, but here's a preview of how Marva Collins, the renowned teacher, did it. On the first day of class, she approached Freddie, a left-back second grader, who wanted no part of school. "Come on, peach," she said to him, cupping his face in her hands, "we have work to do. You can't just sit in a seat and grow smart. . . . I promise, you are going to *do*, and you are going to *produce*. I am not going to let you fail."

Summary

The fixed mindset limits achievement. It fills people's minds with interfering thoughts, it makes effort disagreeable, and it leads to inferior learning strategies. What's more, it makes other people into judges instead of allies. Whether we're talking about Darwin or college students, important achievements require a clear focus, all-out effort, and a bottomless trunk full of strategies. Plus allies in learning. This is what the growth mindset gives people, and that's why it helps their abilities grow and bear fruit.

IS ARTISTIC ABILITY A GIFT?

Despite the widespread belief that intelligence is born, not made, when we really think about it, it's not so hard to imagine that people can develop their intellectual abilities. The intellect is so multifaceted. You can develop verbal skills or mathematical-scientific skills or logical thinking skills, and so on. But when it comes to artistic ability, it seems more like a God-given gift. For example, people seem to naturally draw well or poorly.

Even I believed this. While some of my friends seemed to draw beautifully with no effort and no training, my drawing ability was arrested in early grade school. Try as I might, my attempts were primitive and disappointing. I was artistic in other ways. I can design, I'm great with colors, I have a subtle sense of composition. Plus I have really good eye–hand coordination. Why couldn't I draw? I must not have the gift.

I have to admit that it didn't bother me all that much. After all, when do you really *have* to draw? I found out one evening as the dinner guest of a fascinating man. He was an older man, a psychiatrist, who had escaped from the Holocaust. As a ten-year-old child in Czechoslovakia, he and his younger brother came home from school one day to find their parents gone. They had been taken. Knowing there was an uncle in England, the two boys walked to London and found him.

A few years later, lying about his age, my host joined the Royal Air Force and fought for Britain in the war. When he was wounded, he married his nurse, went to medical school, and established a thriving practice in America.

Over the years, he developed a great interest in owls. He thought of them as embodying characteristics he admired, and he liked to think of himself as owlish. Besides the many owl statuettes that adorned his house, he had an owl-related guest book. It turned out that whenever he took a shine to someone, he asked them to draw an owl and write something to him in this book. As he extended this book to me and explained its significance, I felt both honored and horrified. Mostly horrified. All the more because my creation was not to be buried somewhere in the middle of the book, but was to adorn its very last page.

I won't dwell on the intensity of my discomfort or the poor quality of my artwork, although both were painfully clear. I tell this story as a prelude to the astonishment and joy I felt when I read *Drawing on the Right Side of the Brain.* On the opposite page are the before-and-after self-portraits of people who took a short course in drawing from the author, Betty Edwards. That is, they are the self-portraits drawn by the students when they entered her course and *five days later* when they had completed it.

Aren't they amazing? At the beginning, these people didn't look as though they had much artistic ability. Most of their pictures reminded me of my owl. But only a few days later, everybody could really draw! And Edwards swears that this is a typical group. It seems impossible.

Edwards agrees that most people view drawing as a magical ability that only a select few possess, and that only a select few will ever possess. But this is because people don't understand the components—the *learnable* components—of drawing. Actually, she informs us, they are not drawing skills at all, but *seeing* skills. They are the ability to perceive edges, spaces, relationships, lights and shadows, and the whole. Drawing requires us to learn each component skill and then combine them into

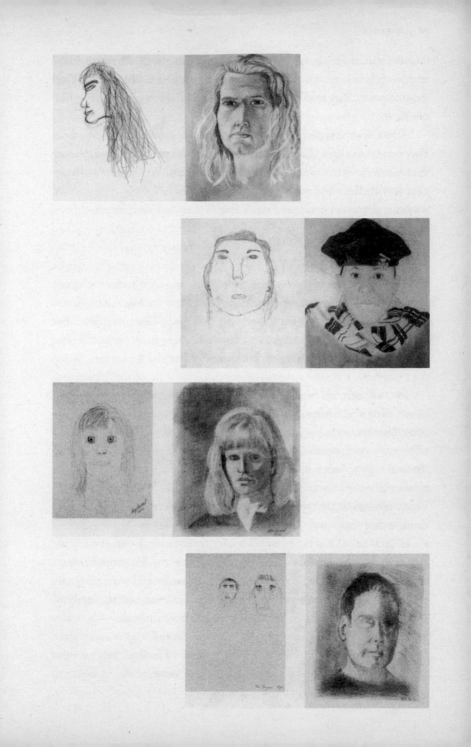

one process. Some people simply pick up these skills in the natural course of their lives, whereas others have to work to learn them and put them together. But as we can see from the "after" self-portraits, everyone can do it.

Here's what this means: *Just because some people can do something with little or no training, it doesn't mean that others can't do it (and sometimes do it even better) with training.* This is so important, because many, many people with the fixed mindset think that someone's early performance tells you all you need to know about their talent and their future.

Jackson Pollock

It would have been a real shame if people discouraged Jackson Pollock for that reason. Experts agree that Pollock had little native talent for art, and when you look at his early products, it showed. They also agree that he became one of the greatest American painters of the twentieth century and that he revolutionized modern art. How did he go from point A to point B?

Twyla Tharp, the world-famous choreographer and dancer, wrote a book called *The Creative Habit.* As you can guess from the title, she argues that creativity is not a magical act of inspiration. It's the result of hard work and dedication. *Even for Mozart.* Remember the movie *Amadeus?* Remember how it showed Mozart easily churning out one masterpiece after another while Salieri, his rival, is dying of envy? Well, Tharp worked on that movie and she says: Hogwash! Nonsense! "There are no 'natural' geniuses."

Dedication is how Jackson Pollock got from point A to point B. Pollock was wildly in love with the idea of being an artist. He thought about art all the time, and he did it all the time. Because he was so gung-ho, he got others to take him seriously and mentor him until he mastered all there was to master and began to produce startlingly original works. His "poured" paintings, each completely unique, allowed him to draw from his unconscious mind and convey a huge range of feeling. Several years ago, I was privileged to see a show of these paintings at the Museum of

Modern Art in New York. I was stunned by the power and beauty of each work.

Can anyone do *anything*? I don't really know. However, I think we can now agree that people can do a lot more than first meets the eye.

THE DANGER OF PRAISE AND POSITIVE LABELS

If people have such potential to achieve, how can they gain faith in their potential? How can we give them the confidence they need to go for it? How about praising their ability in order to convey that they have what it takes? In fact, more than 80 percent of parents told us it was necessary to praise children's ability so as to foster their confidence and achievement. You know, it makes a lot of sense.

But then we began to worry. We thought about how people with the fixed mindset already focus too much on their ability: "Is it high enough?" "Will it look good?" Wouldn't praising people's ability focus them on it even more? Wouldn't it be telling them that that's what we value and, even worse, that we can read their deep, underlying ability from their performance? Isn't that teaching them the fixed mindset?

Adam Guettel has been called the crown prince and savior of musical theater. He is the grandson of Richard Rodgers, the man who wrote the music to such classics as *Oklahoma!* and *Carousel*. Guettel's mother gushes about her son's genius. So does everyone else. "The talent is there and it's major," raved a review in *The New York Times*. The question is whether this kind of praise encourages people.

What's great about research is that you can ask these kinds of questions and then go get the answers. So we conducted studies with hundreds of students, mostly early adolescents. We first gave each student a set of ten fairly difficult problems from a nonverbal IQ test. They mostly did pretty well on these, and when they finished we praised them.

We praised some of the students for their ability. They were told: "Wow, you got [say] eight right. That's a really good score. You must be smart at this." They were in the Adam Guettel *you're-so-talented* position.

We praised other students for their effort: "Wow, you got [say] eight right. That's a really good score. You must have worked really hard." They were not made to feel that they had some special gift; they were praised for doing what it takes to succeed.

Both groups were exactly equal to begin with. But right after the praise, they began to differ. As we feared, the ability praise pushed students right into the fixed mindset, and they showed all the signs of it, too: When we gave them a choice, they rejected a challenging new task that they could learn from. They didn't want to do anything that could expose their flaws and call into question their talent.

When Guettel was thirteen, he was all set to star in a Metropolitan Opera broadcast and TV movie of *Amahl and the Night Visitors.* He bowed out, saying that his voice had broken. "I kind of faked that my voice was changing. . . . I didn't want to handle the pressure."

In contrast, when students were praised for effort, 90 percent of them wanted the challenging new task that they could learn from.

Then we gave students some hard new problems, which they didn't do so well on. The ability kids now thought they were not smart after all. If success had meant they were intelligent, then less-than-success meant they were deficient.

Guettel echoes this. "In my family, to be good is to fail. To be *very* good is to fail. . . . The only thing *not* a failure is to be great."

The effort kids simply thought the difficulty meant "Apply more effort." They didn't see it as a failure, and they didn't think it reflected on their intellect.

What about the students' enjoyment of the problems? After the success, everyone loved the problems, but after the difficult problems, the ability students said it wasn't fun anymore. It can't be fun when your claim to fame, your special talent, is in jeopardy.

Here's Adam Guettel: "I wish I could just have fun and relax and not have the responsibility of that potential to be some kind of *great man.*" As with the kids in our study, the burden of talent was killing his enjoyment.

The effort-praised students still loved the problems, and many of them said that the hard problems were the most fun.

We then looked at the students' performance. After the experience with difficulty, the performance of the ability-praised students plum-meted, even when we gave them some more of the easier problems. Los-ing faith in their ability, they were doing worse than when they started. The effort kids showed better and better performance. They had used the hard problems to sharpen their skills, so that when they returned to the easier ones, they were way ahead.

Since this was a kind of IQ test, you might say that praising ability lowered the students' IQs. And that praising their effort raised them.

Guettel was not thriving. He was riddled with obsessive-compulsive tics and bitten, bleeding fingers. "Spend a minute with him—it takes only one—and a picture of the terror behind the tics starts to emerge," says an interviewer. Guettel has also fought serious, recurrent drug prob-lems. Rather than empowering him, the "gift" has filled him with fear and doubt. Rather than fulfilling his talent, this brilliant composer has spent most of his life running from it.

One thing is hopeful—his recognition that he has his own life course to follow that is not dictated by other people and their view of his talent. One night he had a dream about his grandfather. "I was walking him to an elevator. I asked him if I was any good. He said, rather kindly, 'You have your own voice.' "

Is that voice finally emerging? For the score of *The Light in the Piazza,* an intensely romantic musical, Guettel won the 2005 Tony Award. Will he take it as praise for talent or praise for effort? I hope it's the latter.

There was one more finding in our study that was striking and de-pressing at the same time. We said to each student: "You know, we're going to go to other schools, and I bet the kids in those schools would like to know about the problems." So we gave students a page to write out their thoughts, but we also left a space for them to write the scores they had received on the problems.

Would you believe that almost 40 percent of the ability-praised stu-dents *lied* about their scores? And always in one direction. In the fixed mindset, imperfections are shameful—especially if you're talented—so they lied them away.

What's so alarming is that we took ordinary children and made them into liars, simply by telling them they were smart.

Right after I wrote these paragraphs, I met with a young man who tutors students for their College Board exams. He had come to consult with me about one of his students. This student takes practice tests and then lies to him about her score. He is supposed to tutor her on what she doesn't know, but she can't tell him the truth about what she doesn't know! And she is paying money for this.

So telling children they're smart, in the end, made them feel dumber and act dumber, but claim they were smarter. I don't think this is what we're aiming for when we put positive labels—"gifted," "talented," "brilliant"—on people. We don't mean to rob them of their zest for challenge and their recipes for success. But that's the danger.

Here is a letter from a man who'd read some of my work:

Dear Dr. Dweck,

It was painful to read your chapter . . . as I recognized myself therein.

As a child I was a member of The Gifted Child Society and continually praised for my intelligence. Now, after a lifetime of not living up to my potential (I'm 49), I'm learning to apply myself to a task. And also to see failure not as a sign of stupidity but as lack of experience and skill. Your chapter helped see myself in a new light.

Seth Abrams

This is the danger of positive labels. There are alternatives, and I will return to them later in the chapter on parents, teachers, and coaches.

NEGATIVE LABELS AND HOW THEY WORK

I was once a math whiz. In high school, I got a 99 in algebra, a 99 in geometry, and a 99 in trigonometry, and I was on the math team. I scored up there with the boys on the air force test of visual-spatial ability, which is why I got recruiting brochures from the air force for many years to come.

Then I got a Mr. Hellman, a teacher who didn't believe girls could do math. My grades declined, and I never took math again.

I actually agreed with Mr. Hellman, but I didn't think it applied to *me*. *Other* girls couldn't do math. Mr. Hellman thought it applied to me, too, and I succumbed.

Everyone knows negative labels are bad, so you'd think this would be a short section. But it isn't a short section, because psychologists are learning *how* negative labels harm achievement.

No one knows about negative ability labels like members of stereotyped groups. For example, African Americans know about being stereotyped as lower in intelligence. And women know about being stereotyped as bad at math and science. But I'm not sure even they know how creepy these stereotypes are.

Research by Claude Steele and Joshua Aronson shows that even checking a box to indicate your race or sex can trigger the stereotype in your mind and lower your test score. Almost anything that reminds you that you're black or female before taking a test in the subject you're supposed to be bad at will lower your test score—a lot. In many of their studies, blacks are equal to whites in their performance, and females are equal to males, when no stereotype is evoked. But just put more males in the room with a female before a math test, and down goes the female's score.

This is why. When stereotypes are evoked, they fill people's minds with distracting thoughts—with secret worries about confirming the stereotype. People usually aren't even aware of it, but they don't have enough mental power left to do their best on the test.

This doesn't happen to everybody, however. It mainly happens to people who are in a fixed mindset. It's when people are thinking in terms of fixed traits that the stereotypes get to them. Negative stereotypes say: "You and your group are permanently inferior." Only people in the fixed mindset resonate to this message.

So in the fixed mindset, both positive and negative labels can mess with your mind. When you're given a positive label, you're afraid of losing it, and when you're hit with a negative label, you're afraid of deserving it.

When people are in a growth mindset, the stereotype doesn't disrupt their performance. The growth mindset takes the teeth out of the stereotype and makes people better able to fight back. They don't believe in permanent inferiority. And if they *are* behind—well, then they'll work harder and try to catch up.

The growth mindset also makes people able to take what they can and what they need even from a threatening environment. We asked African American students to write an essay for a competition. They were told that when they finished, their essays would be evaluated by Edward Caldwell III, a distinguished professor with an Ivy League pedigree. That is, a representative of the white establishment.

Edward Caldwell III's feedback was quite critical, but also helpful—and students' reactions varied greatly. Those with a fixed mindset viewed it as a threat, an insult, or an attack. They rejected Caldwell and his feedback.

Here's what one student with the fixed mindset thought: "He's mean, he doesn't grade right, or he's obviously biased. He doesn't like me."

Said another: "He is a pompous asshole. . . . It appears that he was searching for anything to discredit the work."

And another, deflecting the feedback with blame: "He doesn't understand the conciseness of my points. He thought it was vague because he was impatient when he read it. He dislikes creativity."

None of them will learn anything from Edward Caldwell's feedback.

The students with the growth mindset may also have viewed him as a dinosaur, but he was a dinosaur who could teach them something.

"Before the evaluation, he came across as arrogant and overdemanding. [After the evaluation?] 'Fair' seems to be the first word that comes to mind. . . . It seems like a new challenge."

"He sounded like an arrogant, intimidating, and condescending man. [What are your feelings about the evaluation?] The evaluation was seemingly honest and specific. In this sense, the evaluation could be a stimulus . . . to produce better work."

"He seems to be proud to the point of arrogance. [The evaluation?]

He was intensely critical. . . . His comments were helpful and clear, however. I feel I will learn much from him."

The growth mindset allowed African American students to recruit Edward Caldwell III for their own goals. They were in college to get an education and, pompous asshole or not, they were going to get it.

Do I Belong Here?

Aside from hijacking people's abilities, stereotypes also do damage by making people feel they don't belong. Many minorities drop out of college and many women drop out of math and science because they just don't feel they fit in.

To find out how this happens, we followed college women through their calculus course. This is often when students decide whether math, or careers involving math, are right for them. Over the semester, we asked the women to report their feelings about math and their sense of belonging in math. For example, when they thought about math, did they feel like a full-fledged member of the math community or did they feel like an outsider; did they feel comfortable or did they feel anxious; did they feel good or bad about their math skills?

The women with the growth mindset—those who thought math ability could be improved—felt a fairly strong and stable sense of belonging. And they were able to maintain this even when they thought there was a lot of negative stereotyping going around. One student described it this way: "In a math class, [female] students were told they were wrong when they were not (they were in fact doing things in novel ways). It was absurd, and reflected poorly on the instructor not to 'see' the students' good reasoning. It was alright because we were working in groups and we were able to give & receive support among us students. . . . We discussed our interesting ideas among ourselves."

The stereotyping was disturbing to them (as it should be), but they could still feel comfortable with themselves and confident about themselves in a math setting. They could fight back.

But women with the fixed mindset, as the semester wore on, felt a shrinking sense of belonging. And the more they felt the presence of stereotyping in their class, the more their comfort with math withered. One student said that her sense of belonging fell because "I was disrespected by the professor with his comment, 'that was a good guess,' whenever I made a correct answer in class."

The stereotype of low ability was able to invade them—to define them—and take away their comfort and confidence. I'm not saying it's their fault by any means. Prejudice is a deeply ingrained societal problem, and I do not want to blame the victims of it. I am simply saying that a growth mindset helps people to see prejudice for what it is—*someone else's* view of them—and to confront it with their confidence and abilities intact.

Trusting People's Opinions

Many females have a problem not only with stereotypes, but with other people's opinions of them in general. They trust them too much.

One day, I went into a drugstore in Hawaii to buy dental floss and deodorant, and, after fetching my items, I went to wait in line. There were two women together in front of me waiting to pay. Since I am an incurable time stuffer, at some point I decided to get my money ready for when my turn came. So I walked up, put the items way on the side of the counter, and started to gather up the bills that were strewn throughout my purse. The two women went berserk. I explained that in no way was I trying to cut in front of them. I was just preparing for when my turn came. I thought the matter was resolved, but when I left the store, they were waiting for me. They got in my face and yelled, *"You're a bad-mannered person!"*

My husband, who had seen the whole thing from beginning to end, thought they were nuts. But they had a strange and disturbing effect on me, and I had a hard time shaking off their verdict.

This vulnerability afflicts many of the most able, high-achieving females. Why should this be? When they're little, these girls are often so perfect, and they delight in everyone's telling them so. They're so well behaved, they're so cute, they're so helpful, and they're so precocious. Girls learn to trust people's estimates of them. "Gee, everyone's so nice to me; if they criticize me, it must be true." Even females at the top universities in the country say that other people's opinions are a good way to know their abilities.

Boys are constantly being scolded and punished. When we observed in grade school classrooms, we saw that boys got *eight* times more criticism than girls for their conduct. Boys are also constantly calling each other slobs and morons. The evaluations lose a lot of their power.

A male friend once called me a slob. He was over to dinner at my house and, while we were eating, I dripped some food on my blouse. "That's because you're such a slob," he said. I was shocked. It was then that I realized no one had ever said anything like that to me. Males say it to each other all the time. It may not be a kind thing to say, even in jest, but it certainly makes them think twice before buying into other people's evaluations.

Even when women reach the pinnacle of success, other people's attitudes can get them. Frances Conley is one of the most eminent neurosurgeons in the world. In fact, she was the first woman ever given tenure in neurosurgery at an American medical school. Yet careless comments from male colleagues—even assistants—could fill her with self-doubt. One day during surgery, a man condescendingly called her "honey." Instead of returning the compliment, she questioned herself. "Is a honey," she wondered, "especially *this* honey, good enough and talented enough to be doing this operation?"

The fixed mindset, plus stereotyping, plus women's trust in people's assessments: I think we can begin to understand why there's a gender gap in math and science.

That gap is painfully evident in the world of high tech. Julie Lynch, a budding techie, was already writing computer code when she was in junior high school. Her father and two brothers worked in technology, and she loved it, too. Then her computer programming teacher criticized her. She had written a computer program and the program ran just fine, but he didn't like a shortcut she had taken. Her interest evaporated. Instead, she went on to study recreation and public relations.

Math and science need to be made more hospitable places for women. And women need all the growth mindset they can get to take their rightful places in these fields.

When Things Go Right

But let's look at the times the process goes right.

The Polgar family has produced three of the most successful female chess players ever. How? Says Susan, one of the three, "My father believes that innate talent is nothing, that [success] is 99 percent hard work. I agree with him." The youngest daughter, Judit, is now considered the best woman chess player of all time. She was not the one with the most talent. Susan reports, "Judit was a slow starter, but very hardworking."

A colleague of mine has two daughters who are math whizzes. One is a graduate student in math at a top university. The other was the first girl to rank number one in the country on an elite math test, won a nationwide math contest, and is now a neuroscience major at a top university. What's their secret? Is it passed down in the genes? I believe it's passed down in the mindset. It's the most growth-mindset family I've ever seen.

In fact, their father applied the growth mindset to *everything*. I'll never forget a conversation we had some years ago. I was single at the time, and he asked me what my plan was for finding a partner. He was aghast when I said I didn't have a plan. "You wouldn't expect your *work* to get done by itself," he said. "Why is this any different?" It was inconceivable to him that you could have a goal and not take steps to make it happen.

In short, the growth mindset lets people—even those who are targets of negative labels—use and develop their minds fully. Their heads are not filled with limiting thoughts, a fragile sense of belonging, and a belief that other people can define them.

Grow Your Mindset

- Think about your hero. Do you think of this person as someone with extraordinary abilities who achieved with little effort?

Now go find out the truth. Find out the tremendous effort that went into their accomplishment—and admire them *more*.

- Think of times other people outdid you and you just assumed they were smarter or more talented. Now consider the idea that they just used better strategies, taught themselves more, practiced harder, and worked their way through obstacles. You can do that, too, if you want to.

- Are there situations where you get stupid—where you disengage your intelligence? Next time you're in one of those situations, get yourself into a growth mindset—think about learning and improvement, not judgment—and hook it back up.

- Do you label your kids? *This one is the artist and that one is the scientist.* Next time, remember that you're not helping them— even though you may be praising them. Remember our study where praising kids' ability lowered their IQ scores. Find a growth-mindset way to compliment them.

- More than half of our society belongs to a negatively stereotyped group. First you have all the women, and then you have all the other groups who are not supposed to be good at something or other. Give them the gift of the growth mindset. Create an environment that teaches the growth mindset to the adults and children in your life, especially the ones who are targets of negative stereotypes. Even when the negative label comes along, they'll remain in charge of their learning.

Chapter 4

SPORTS: THE MINDSET OF A CHAMPION

In sports, everybody believes in talent. Even—or especially—the experts. In fact, sports is where the idea of "a natural" comes from—someone who looks like an athlete, moves like an athlete, and is an athlete, all without trying. So great is the belief in natural talent that many scouts and coaches search only for naturals, and teams will vie with each other to pay exorbitant amounts to recruit them.

Billy Beane was a natural. Everyone agreed he was the next Babe Ruth.

But Billy Beane lacked one thing. The mindset of a champion.

As Michael Lewis tells us in *Moneyball*, by the time Beane was a sophomore in high school, he was the highest scorer on the basketball team, the quarterback of the football team, and the best hitter on the baseball team, batting .500 in one of the toughest leagues in the country. His talent was real enough.

But the minute things went wrong, Beane searched for something to break. "It wasn't merely that he didn't like to fail; it was as if he didn't know how to fail."

As he moved up in baseball from the minor leagues to the majors, things got worse and worse. Each at-bat became a nightmare, another opportunity for humiliation, and with every botched at-bat, he went to pieces. As one scout said, "Billy was of the opinion that he should never make an out." Sound familiar?

Did Beane try to fix his problems in constructive ways? No, of course not, because this is a story of the fixed mindset. Natural talent should not need effort. Effort is for the others, the less endowed. Natural talent does not ask for help. It is an admission of weakness. In short, the natural does not analyze his deficiencies and coach or practice them away. The very idea of deficiencies is terrifying.

Being so imbued with the fixed mindset, Beane was trapped. Trapped by his huge talent. Beane the player never recovered from the fixed mindset, but Beane the incredibly successful major-league executive did. How did this happen?

There was another player who lived and played side by side with Beane in the minors and in the majors, Lenny Dykstra. Dykstra did not have a fraction of Beane's physical endowment or "natural ability," but Beane watched him in awe. As Beane later described, "He had no concept of failure. . . . And I was the opposite."

Beane continues, "I started to get a sense of what a baseball player was and I could see it wasn't me. It was Lenny."

As he watched, listened, and mulled it over, it dawned on Beane that mindset was more important than talent. And not long after that, as part of a group that pioneered a radically new approach to scouting and managing, he came to believe that scoring runs—the whole point of baseball—was much more about process than about talent.

Armed with these insights, Beane, as general manager of the 2002 Oakland Athletics, led his team to a season of 103 victories—winning the division championship and almost breaking the American League record for consecutive wins. The team had the second lowest payroll in baseball! They didn't buy talent, they bought mindset.

THE IDEA OF THE NATURAL

Now You See It, Now You Don't

Physical endowment is not like intellectual endowment. It's visible. Size, build, agility are all visible. Practice and training are also visible, and they produce visible results. You would think that this would dispel the myth of the natural. You could *see* Muggsy Bogues at five foot three playing NBA basketball, and Doug Flutie, the small quarterback who has played for the New England Patriots and the San Diego Chargers. You could see Pete Gray, the one-armed baseball player who made it to the major leagues. Ben Hogan, one of the greatest golfers of all time, who was completely lacking in grace. Glenn Cunningham, the great runner, who had badly burned and damaged legs. Larry Bird and his lack of swiftness. You can *see* the small or graceless or even "disabled" ones who make it, and the god-like specimens who don't. Shouldn't this tell people something?

Boxing experts relied on physical measurements, called "tales of the tape," to identify naturals. They included measurements of the fighter's fist, reach, chest expansion, and weight. Muhammad Ali failed these measurements. He was not a natural. He had great speed but he didn't have the physique of a great fighter, he didn't have the strength, and he didn't have the classical moves. In fact, he boxed all wrong. He didn't block punches with his arms and elbows. He punched in rallies like an amateur. He kept his jaw exposed. He pulled back his torso to evade the impact of oncoming punches, which Jose Torres said was "like someone in the middle of a train track trying to avoid being hit by an oncoming train, not by moving to one or the other side of the track, but by running backwards."

Sonny Liston, Ali's adversary, *was* a natural. He had it all—the size, the strength, and the experience. His power was legendary. It was unimaginable that Ali could beat Sonny Liston. The matchup was so ludicrous that the arena was only half full for the fight.

But aside from his quickness, Ali's brilliance was his mind. His brains, not his brawn. He sized up his opponent and went for his mental jugular. Not only did he study Liston's fighting style, but he closely observed what kind of person Liston was out of the ring: "I read everything I could where he had been interviewed. I talked with people who had been around him or had talked with him. I would lay in bed and put all of the things together and think about them, and try to get a picture of how his mind worked." And then he turned it against him.

Why did Ali appear to "go crazy" before each fight? Because, Torres says, he knew that a knockout punch is the one they don't see coming. Ali said, "Liston had to believe that I was crazy. That I was capable of doing anything. He couldn't see nothing to me at all but mouth and that's all I wanted him to see!"

Float like a butterfly,
Sting like a bee
Your hands can't hit
What your eyes can't see.

Ali's victory over Liston is boxing history. A famous boxing manager reflects on Ali:

"He was a paradox. His physical performances in the ring were absolutely wrong. . . . Yet, his brain was always in perfect working condition." "He showed us all," he continued with a broad smile written across his face, "that all victories come from here," hitting his forehead with his index finger. Then he raised a pair of fists, saying: "Not from here."

This didn't change people's minds about physical endowment. No, we just look back at Ali now, with our hindsight, and see the body of a great boxer. It was gravy that his mind was so sharp and that he made up amusing poems, but we still think his greatness resided in his physique. And we don't understand how the experts failed to see that greatness right from the start.

Michael Jordan

Michael Jordan wasn't a natural, either. He was the hardest-working athlete, perhaps in the history of sport.

It is well known that Michael Jordan was cut from the high school varsity team—we laugh at the coach who cut him. He wasn't recruited by the college he wanted to play for (North Carolina State). Well, weren't *they* foolish? He wasn't drafted by the first two NBA teams that could have chosen him. What a blooper! Because now we know he was the greatest basketball player ever, and we think it should have been obvious from the start. When we look at him we see *MICHAEL JORDAN*. But at that point he was only Michael Jordan.

When Jordan was cut from the varsity team, he was devastated. His mother says, "I told him to go back and discipline himself." Boy, did he listen. He used to leave the house at six in the morning to go practice before school. At the University of North Carolina, he constantly worked on his weaknesses—his defensive game and his ball handling and shooting. The coach was taken aback by his willingness to work harder than anyone else. Once, after the team lost the last game of the season, Jordan went and practiced his shots for hours. He was preparing for the next year. Even at the height of his success and fame—after he had made himself into an athletic genius—his dogged practice remained legendary. Former Bulls assistant coach John Bach called him "a genius who constantly wants to upgrade his genius."

For Jordan, success stems from the mind. "The mental toughness and the heart are a lot stronger than some of the physical advantages you might have. I've always said that and I've always believed that." But other people don't. They look at Michael Jordan and they see the physical perfection that led inevitably to his greatness.

The Babe

What about Babe Ruth? Now, he was clearly no vessel of human physical perfection. Here was the guy with the famous appetites and a giant stomach bulging out of his Yankee uniform. Wow, doesn't that make him even more of a natural? Didn't he just carouse all night and then kind of saunter to the plate the next day and punch out home runs?

The Babe was not a natural, either. At the beginning of his professional career, Babe Ruth was not that good a hitter. He had a lot of power, power that came from his total commitment each time he swung the bat. When he connected, it was breathtaking, but he was highly inconsistent.

It's true that he could consume astounding amounts of liquor and unheard-of amounts of food. After a huge meal, he could eat one or more whole pies for dessert. But he could also discipline himself when he had to. Many winters, he worked out the entire off-season at the gym to become more fit. In fact, after the 1925 season, when it looked as though he was washed up, he really committed himself to getting in shape, and it worked. From 1926 through 1931, he batted .354, averaging 50 home runs a year and 155 runs batted in. Robert Creamer, his biographer, says, "Ruth put on the finest display of sustained hitting that baseball has ever seen. . . . From the ashes of 1925, Babe Ruth rose like a rocket." Through discipline.

He also loved to practice. In fact, when he joined the Boston Red Sox, the veterans resented him for wanting to take batting practice every day. He wasn't just a rookie; he was a rookie *pitcher*. Who did he think he was, trying to take batting practice? One time, later in his career, he was disciplined and was banned from a game. That was one thing. But they wouldn't let him practice, either, and that *really* hurt.

Ty Cobb argued that being a pitcher helped Ruth develop his hitting. Why would being a pitcher help his batting? "He could experiment at the plate," Cobb said. "No one cares much if a pitcher strikes out or looks bad at bat, so Ruth could take that big swing. If he missed, it didn't matter. . . . As time went on, he learned more and more about how to control that big swing and put the wood on the ball. By the time he became a fulltime outfielder, he was ready."

Yet we cling fast to what Stephen Jay Gould calls "the common view that ballplayers are hunks of meat, naturally and effortlessly displaying the talents that nature provided."

The Fastest Women on Earth

What about Wilma Rudolph, hailed as the fastest woman on earth after she won three gold medals for sprints and relay in the 1960 Rome Olympics? She was far from a physical wonder as a youngster. She was a premature baby, the twentieth of twenty-two children born to her parents, and a constantly sick child. At four years of age, she nearly died of a long struggle with double pneumonia, scarlet fever, and polio(!), emerging with a mostly paralyzed left leg. Doctors gave her little hope of ever using it again. For eight years, she vigorously pursued physical therapy, until at age twelve she shed her leg brace and began to walk normally.

If this wasn't a lesson that physical skills could be developed, what was? She immediately went and applied that lesson to basketball and track, although she lost every race she entered in her first official track meet. After her incredible career, she said, "I just want to be remembered as a hardworking lady."

What about Jackie Joyner-Kersee, hailed as the greatest female athlete of all time? Between 1985 and the beginning of 1996, she won every heptathlon she competed in. What exactly is a heptathlon? It's a grueling two-day, seven-part event consisting of a 100-meter hurdles race, the high jump, the javelin throw, a 200-meter sprint, the long jump, the shotput, and an 800-meter run. No wonder the winner gets to be called the best female athlete in the world. Along the way, Joyner-Kersee earned the six highest scores in the history of the sport, set world records, and won two world championships as well as two Olympic gold medals (six if we count the ones in other events).

Was she a natural? Talent she had, but when she started track, she finished in last place for quite some time. The longer she worked, the faster she got, but she still didn't win any races. Finally, she began to win. What changed? "Some might attribute my transformation to the laws of heredity. . . . But I think it was my reward for all those hours of work on the bridle path, the neighborhood sidewalks and the schoolhouse corridors."

Sharing the secret of her continued success, she says, "There is something about seeing myself improve that motivates and excites me. It's that way now, after six Olympic medals and five world records. And it was the way I was in junior high, just starting to enter track meets."

Her last two medals (a world-championship and an Olympic medal) came during an asthma attack and a severe, painful hamstring injury. It was not natural talent taking its course. It was mindset having its say.

Naturals Shouldn't Need Effort

Did you know there was once a strong belief that you couldn't physically train for golf, and that if you built your strength you would lose your "touch"? Until Tiger Woods came along with his workout regimes and fierce practice habits and won every tournament there was to win.

In some cultures, people who tried to go beyond their natural talent through training received sharp disapproval. You were supposed to accept your station in life. These cultures would have hated Maury Wills. Wills was an eager baseball player in the 1950s and '60s with a dream to be a major leaguer. His problem was that his hitting wasn't good enough, so when the Dodgers signed him, they sent him down to the minor leagues. He proudly announced to his friends, "In two years, I'm going to be in Brooklyn playing with Jackie Robinson."

He was wrong. Despite his optimistic prediction and grueling daily practice, he languished in the minors for eight and a half years. At the seven-and-a-half-year mark, the team manager made a batting suggestion, telling Wills, "You're in a seven-and-a-half-year slump, you have nothing to lose." Shortly thereafter, when the Dodger shortstop broke his toe, Wills was called up. He had his chance.

His batting was *still* not good enough. Not ready to give up, he went to the first-base coach for help; they worked together several hours a day aside from Wills's regular practice. Still not good enough. Even the gritty Wills was now ready to quit, but the first-base coach refused to let him. Now that the mechanics were in place, Wills needed work on his mind.

He began to hit—and, with his great speed, he began to steal bases. He studied the throws of the opposing pitchers and catchers, figuring out the best moment to steal a base. He developed sudden, powerful takeoffs and effective slides. His stealing began to distract the pitchers, throw off the catchers, and thrill the fans. Wills went on to break Ty Cobb's record for stolen bases, a record unchallenged for forty-seven years. That season, he was voted the most valuable player in the National League.

Sports IQ

You would think the sports world would *have* to see the relation between practice and improvement—and between the mind and performance—

and stop harping so much on innate physical talent. Yet it's almost as if they refuse to see. Perhaps it's because, as Malcolm Gladwell suggests, people prize natural endowment over earned ability. As much as our culture talks about individual effort and self-improvement, deep down, he argues, we revere the naturals. We like to think of our champions and idols as superheroes who were born different from us. We don't like to think of them as relatively ordinary people who made themselves extraordinary. Why not? To me that is so much more amazing.

Even when experts are willing to recognize the role of the mind, they continue to insist that it's all innate!

This really hit me when I came upon an article about Marshall Faulk, the great running back for the St. Louis Rams football team. Faulk had just become the first player to gain a combined two thousand rushing and receiving yards in four consecutive seasons.

The article, written on the eve of the 2002 Super Bowl, talked about Faulk's uncanny skill at knowing where every player on the field is, even in the swirling chaos of twenty-two running and falling players. He not only knows where they are, but he also knows what they are doing, and what they are *about* to do. According to his teammates, he's never wrong.

Incredible. How does he do it? As Faulk tells it, he spent years and years watching football. In high school he even got a job as a ballpark vendor, which he hated, in order to watch pro football. As he watched, he was always asking the question *Why?:* "Why are we running this play?" "Why are we attacking it this way?" "Why are they doing that?" "Why are they doing this?" "That question," Faulk says, "basically got me involved in football in a more in-depth way." As a pro, he never stopped asking why and probing deeper into the workings of the game.

Clearly, Faulk himself sees his skills as the product of his insatiable curiosity and study.

How do players and coaches see it? As a gift. "Marshall has the highest football IQ of any position player I've ever played with," says a veteran teammate. Other teammates describe his ability to recognize defensive alignments flawlessly as a "savant's gift." In awe of his array of skills, one coach explained: "It takes a very innate football intelligence to do all that."

"CHARACTER"

But aren't there some naturals, athletes who really seem to have "it" from the start? Yes, and as it was for Billy Beane and John McEnroe, sometimes it's a curse. With all the praise for their talent and with how little they've needed to work or stretch themselves, they can easily fall into a fixed mindset. Bruce Jenner, 1976 Olympic gold medalist in the decathlon, says, "If I wasn't dyslexic, I probably wouldn't have won the Games. If I had been a better reader, then that would have come easily, sports would have come easily . . . and I never would have realized that the way you get ahead in life is hard work."

The naturals, carried away with their superiority, don't learn how to work hard or how to cope with setbacks. This is the story of Pedro Martinez, the brilliant pitcher then with the Boston Red Sox, who self-destructed when they needed him most. But it's an even larger story too, a story about character.

A group of sportswriters from *The New York Times* and *The Boston Globe* were on the Delta shuttle to Boston. So was I. They were headed to Game 3 of the 2003 American League play-off series between the New York Yankees and the Boston Red Sox. They were talking about character, and they all agreed—the Boston writers reluctantly—that the Yankees had it.

Among other things, they remembered what the Yankees had done for New York two years before. It was October 2001, and New Yorkers had just lived through September 11. I was there and we were devastated. We needed some hope. The city needed the Yankees to go for it—to go for the World Series. But the Yankees had lived through it, too, and they were injured and exhausted. They seemed to have nothing left. I don't know where they got it from, but they dug down deep and they polished off one team after another, each win bringing us a little bit back to life, each one giving us a little more hope for the future. Fueled by our need, they became the American League East champs, then the American League champs, and then they were in the World Series, where they made a valiant run and almost pulled it off. Everyone hates the Yankees.

It's the team the whole country roots against. I grew up hating the Yankees, too, but after that I had to love them. This is what the sportswriters meant by character.

Character, the sportswriters said. They know it when they see it—it's the ability to dig down and find the strength even when things are going against you.

The very next day, Pedro Martinez, the dazzling but over-pampered Boston pitcher, showed what character meant. By showing what it isn't.

No one could have wanted this American League Championship more than the Boston Red Sox. They hadn't won a World Series in eighty-five years, ever since the curse of the Bambino—that is, ever since Sox owner Harry Frazee sold Babe Ruth to the Yankees for money to finance a Broadway show. It was bad enough that he was selling the best left-handed pitcher in baseball (which Ruth was at the time), but he was selling him to the despised enemy.

The Yankees went on to dominate baseball, winning, it seemed, endless World Series. Meanwhile Boston made it to four World Series and several play-offs, but they always lost. And they always lost in the most tragic way possible. By coming achingly near to victory and then having a meltdown. Here, finally, was another chance to fight off the curse *and* defeat their archrivals. If they won, they would make that trip to the World Series and the Yankees would stay home. Pedro Martinez was their hope. In fact, earlier in the season, he had cursed the curse.

Yet after pitching a beautiful game, Martinez was losing his lead and falling behind. What did he do then? He hit a batter with the ball (Karim Garcia), threatened to bean another (Jorge Posada), and hurled a seventy-two-year-old man to the ground (Yankee coach Don Zimmer).

As *New York Times* writer Jack Curry wrote: "We knew we were going to have Pedro vs. Roger [Clemens] on a memorable afternoon at Fenway Park. . . . But no one expected to watch Pedro against Garcia, Pedro against Posada, Pedro against Zimmer."

Even the Boston writers were aghast. Dan Shaughnessy, of the *Globe,* asked: "Which one would you rather have now, Red Sox fans? Roger Clemens, who kept his composure and behaved like a professional Saturday night, winning the game for his team despite his obvious anger? Or Martinez, the baby who hits a guy after he blows the lead, then points at his head and at Yankees catcher Jorge Posada, threatening, 'You're next'? . . . Red Sox fans don't like to hear this, but Martinez was an embarrassment Saturday, and a disgrace to baseball. He gets away with it because he's Pedro. And the Sox front office enables him. Could Martinez one time stand up and admit he's wrong?"

Like Billy Beane, Pedro Martinez did not know how to tolerate frustration, did not know how to dig down and turn an important setback into an important win. Nor, like Billy Beane, could he admit his faults and learn from them. Because he threw his tantrum instead of doing the job, the Yankees won the game and went on to win the play-off by one game.

The sportswriters on the plane agreed that character is all. But they confessed that they didn't understand where it comes from. Yet I think by now we're getting the idea that character grows out of mindset.

We now know that there is a mindset in which people are enmeshed in the idea of their own talent and specialness. When things go wrong, they lose their focus and their ability, putting everything they want—and in this case, everything the team and the fans so desperately want—in jeopardy.

We also know that there is a mindset that helps people cope well with setbacks, points them to good strategies, and leads them to act in their best interest.

Wait. The story's not over. One year later, the Sox and the Yankees went head-to-head again. Whoever won four games out of the seven would be the American League Champions and would take that trip to the World Series. The Yankees won the first three games, and Boston's humiliating fate seemed sealed once again.

But that year Boston had put their prima donnas on notice. They traded one, tried to trade another (no one wanted him), and sent out the message: This is a team, not a bunch of stars. We work hard for each other.

Four games later, the Boston Red Sox were the American League Champions. And then the World Champions. It was the first time since

1904 that Boston had beaten the Yankees in a championship series, showing two things. First, that the curse was over. And second, that character can be learned.

More About Character

Let's take it from the top with Pete Sampras and the growth mindset. In 2000, Sampras was at Wimbledon, trying for his thirteenth Grand Slam tennis victory. If he won, he would break Roy Emerson's record of twelve wins in top tournaments. Although Sampras managed to make it to the finals, he had not played that well in the tournament and was not optimistic about his chances against the young, powerful Patrick Rafter.

Sampras lost the first set, and was about to lose the second set. He was down 4–1 in the tiebreaker. Even he said, "I really felt like it was slipping away." What would McEnroe have done? What would Pedro Martinez have done? What did Sampras do?

As William Rhoden puts it, "He . . . searched for a frame of reference that could carry him through." Sampras says, "When you're sitting on the changeover you think of past matches that you've lost the first set . . . came back and won the next three. There's time. You reflect on your past experiences, being able to get through it."

Suddenly, Sampras had a five-point run. Then two more. He had won the second set and he was alive.

"Last night," Rhoden says, "Sampras displayed all the qualities of the hero: the loss in the first set, vulnerability near defeat, then a comeback and a final triumph."

Jackie Joyner-Kersee talked herself through an asthma attack during her last world championship. She was in the 800-meter race, the last event of the heptathlon, when she felt the attack coming on. "Just keep pumping your arms," she instructed herself. "It's not that bad, so keep going. You can make it. You're not going to have a full-blown attack. You have enough air. You've got this thing won. . . . Just run as hard as you can in this last 200 meters, Jackie." She instructed herself all the way to victory. "I have to say this is my greatest triumph, considering the competition and the ups and downs I was going through. . . . If I really wanted it, I had to pull it together."

In her last Olympics, the dreaded thing happened. A serious hamstring injury forced her to drop out of the heptathlon. She was devastated. She was no longer a contender in her signature event, but would she be a contender in the long jump a few days later? Her first five jumps said no. They were nowhere near medal level. But the sixth jump won her a bronze medal, more precious than her gold ones. "The strength for that sixth jump came from my assorted heartbreaks over the years . . . I'd collected all my pains and turned them into one mighty performance."

Joyner-Kersee, too, displayed all the qualities of a hero: the loss, the vulnerability near defeat, then a comeback and a final triumph.

Character, Heart, Will, and the Mind of a Champion

It goes by different names, but it's the same thing. It's what makes you practice, and it's what allows you to dig down and pull it out when you most need it.

Remember how McEnroe told us all the things that went wrong to make him lose each match he lost? There was the time it was cold and the time it was hot, the time he was jealous and the times he was upset, and the many, many times he was distracted. But, as Billie Jean King tells us, the mark of a champion is the ability to win when things are not quite right—when you're not playing well and your emotions are not the right ones. Here's how she learned what being a champion meant.

King was in the finals at Forest Hills playing against Margaret Smith (later Margaret Smith Court), who was at the peak of her greatness. King had played her more than a dozen times and had beaten her only once. In the first set, King played fabulously. She didn't miss a volley and built a nice lead. Suddenly, the set was over. Smith had won it.

In the second set, King again built a commanding lead and was serving to win the set. Before she knew it, Smith had won the set and the match.

At first, King was perplexed. She had never built such a commanding lead in such an important match. But then she had a *Eureka!* moment. All at once, she understood what a champion was: someone who could raise their level of play when they needed to. When the match is on the line, they suddenly "get around three times tougher."

Jackie Joyner-Kersee had her *Eureka!* moment too. She was fifteen years old and competing in the heptathlon at the AAU Junior Olympics. Everything now depended on the last event, the 800-meter race, an event she dreaded. She was exhausted and she was competing against an expert distance runner whose times she had never matched. She did this time. "I felt a kind of high. I'd proven that I could win if I wanted it badly enough. . . . That win showed me that I could not only compete with the best athletes in the country, I could *will* myself to win."

Often called the best woman soccer player in the world, Mia Hamm says she was always asked, "Mia, what is the most important thing for a soccer player to have?" With no hesitation, she answered, "Mental toughness." And she didn't mean some innate trait. When eleven players want to knock you down, when you're tired or injured, when the referees are against you, you can't let any of it affect your focus. How do you do that? You have to *learn* how. "It is," said Hamm, "one of the most difficult aspects of soccer and the one I struggle with every game and every practice."

By the way, did Hamm think she was the greatest player in the world? No. "And because of that," she said, "someday I just might be."

In sports, there are always do-or-die situations, when a player must come through or it's all over. Jack Nicklaus, the famed golfer, was in these situations many times in his long professional career on the PGA Tour—where the tournament rested on his making a must-have shot. If you had to guess, how many of these shots do you think he missed? The answer is one. One!

That's the championship mentality. It's how people who are not as talented as their opponents win games. John Wooden, the legendary basketball coach, tells one of my favorite stories. Once, while Wooden was still a high school coach, a player was unhappy because he wasn't included in the big games. The player, Eddie Pawelski, begged Wooden to give him a chance, and Wooden relented. "All right Eddie," he said, "I'll give you a chance. I'll start you against Fort Wayne Central tomorrow night."

"Suddenly," Wooden tells us, "I wondered where those words came from." Three teams were locked in a battle for number one in Indiana—one was his team and another was Fort Wayne Central, tomorrow night's team.

The next night, Wooden started Eddie. He figured that Eddie would last at most a minute or two, especially since he was up against Fort Wayne's Armstrong, the toughest player in the state.

"Eddie literally took him apart," Wooden reports. "Armstrong got the lowest point total of his career. Eddie scored 12, and our team showed the best balance of all season. . . . But in addition to his scoring, his defense, rebounding, and play-making were excellent." Eddie never sat out again and was named most valuable player for the next two years.

All of these people had character. None of them thought they were special people, born with the right to win. They were people who worked hard, who learned how to keep their focus under pressure, and who stretched beyond their ordinary abilities when they had to.

Staying on Top

Character is what allows you to reach the top *and stay there.* Darryl Strawberry, Mike Tyson, and Martina Hingis reached the top, but they didn't stay there. Isn't that because they had all kinds of personal problems and injuries? Yes, but so have many other champions. Ben Hogan was hit by a bus and was physically destroyed, but he made it back to the top.

"I believe ability can get you to the top," says coach John Wooden, "but it takes character to keep you there. . . . It's so easy to . . . begin thinking you can just 'turn it on' automatically, without proper preparation. It takes real character to keep working as hard or even harder once you're there. When you read about an athlete or team that wins over and over and over, remind yourself, 'More than ability, they have character.' "

Let's take an even deeper look at what character means, and how the growth mindset creates it. Stuart Biddle and his colleagues measured adolescents' and young adults' mindset about athletic ability. Those with the fixed mindset were the people who believed that:

"You have a certain level of ability in sports and you cannot really do much to change that level."

"To be good at sports you need to be naturally gifted."

In contrast, the people with the growth mindset agreed that:

"How good you are at sports will *always* improve if you work harder at it."

"To be successful in sports, you need to learn techniques and skills and practice them regularly."

Those with the growth mindset were the ones who showed the most character or heart. They were the ones who had the minds of champions. What do I mean? Let's look at the findings from these sports researchers and see.

WHAT IS SUCCESS?

Finding #1: Those with the growth mindset found success in doing their best, in learning and improving. And this is exactly what we find in the champions.

"For me the joy of athletics has never resided in winning," Jackie Joyner-Kersee tells us, ". . . I derive just as much happiness from the process as from the results. I don't mind losing as long as I see improvement or I feel I've done as well as I possibly could. If I lose, I just go back to the track and work some more."

This idea—that personal success is when you work your hardest to become your best—was central to John Wooden's life. In fact, he says, "there were many, many games that gave me as much pleasure as any of the ten national championship games we won, simply because we prepared fully and played near our highest level of ability."

Tiger Woods and Mia Hamm are two of the fiercest competitors who ever lived. They love to win, but what counted most for them is the effort they made even when they didn't win. They could be proud of that. McEnroe and Beane could not.

After the '98 Masters tournament, Woods was disappointed that he did not repeat his win of the previous year, but he felt good about his top-ten finish: "I squeezed the towel dry this week. I'm very proud of the way I hung in there." Or after a British Open, where he finished third: "Sometimes you get even more satisfaction out of creating a score when things aren't completely perfect, when you're not feeling so well about your swing."

Tiger is a hugely ambitious man. He wants to be the best, even the best ever. "But the best me—that's a little more important."

Mia Hamm tells us, "After every game or practice, if you walk off the field knowing that you gave everything you had, you will always be a winner." Why did the country fall in love with her team? "They saw that we truly love what we do and that we gave everything we had to each other and to each game."

For those with the fixed mindset, success is about establishing their superiority, pure and simple. Being that somebody who is worthier than the nobodies. "There was a time—I'll admit it," McEnroe says, "when my head was so big it could barely fit through the door." Where's the talk about effort and personal best? There is none. "Some people don't want to rehearse; they just want to perform. Other people want to practice a hundred times first. I'm in the former group." Remember, in the fixed mindset, effort is not a cause for pride. It is something that casts doubt on your talent.

WHAT IS FAILURE?

Finding #2: Those with the growth mindset found setbacks motivating. They're informative. They're a wake-up call.

Only once did Michael Jordan try to coast. It was the year he returned to the Bulls after his stint in baseball, and he learned his lesson. The Bulls were eliminated in the play-offs. "You can't leave and think you can come back and dominate this game. I will be physically and mentally prepared from now on." Truer words are rarely spoken. The Bulls won the NBA title the next three years.

Michael Jordan embraced his failures. In fact, in one of his favorite ads for Nike, he says: "I've missed more than nine thousand shots. I've lost almost three hundred games. Twenty-six times, I've been trusted to take the game-winning shot, and missed." You can be sure that each time, he went back and practiced the shot a hundred times.

Here's how Kareem Abdul-Jabbar, the great basketball player, re-acted when college basketball outlawed his signature shot, the dunk (later reinstated). Many thought that would stop his ascent to greatness. Instead, he worked twice as hard on developing other shots: his bank shot off the glass, his skyhook, and his turnaround jumper. He had ab-sorbed the growth mindset from Coach Wooden, and put it to good use.

In the fixed mindset, setbacks label you.

John McEnroe could never stand the thought of losing. Even worse was the thought of losing to someone who was a friend or relative. That would make him less special. For example, he hoped desperately for his best friend, Peter, to lose in the finals at Maui after Peter had beaten him in an earlier round. He wanted it so badly he couldn't watch the match. Another time, he played his brother Patrick in a finals in Chicago, and said to himself, "God, if I lose to Patrick, that's it. I'm jumping off the Sears tower."

Here's how failure motivated him. In 1979, he played mixed doubles at Wimbledon. He didn't play mixed doubles again for twenty years. Why? He and his partner lost in three straight sets. Plus, McEnroe lost his serve twice, while no one else lost theirs even once. "That was the ultimate em-barrassment. I said, 'That's it. I'm never playing again. I can't handle this.' "

In 1981, McEnroe bought a beautiful black Les Paul guitar. That week, he went to see Buddy Guy play at the Checkerboard Lounge in Chicago. Instead of feeling inspired to take lessons or practice, McEn-roe went home and smashed his guitar to pieces.

Here's how failure motivated Sergio Garcia, another golden boy with mindset issues. Garcia had taken the golf world by storm with his great shots and his charming, boyish ways; he seemed like a younger Tiger. But when his performance took a dive, so did his charm. He fired cad-die after caddie, blaming them for everything that went wrong. He once blamed his shoe when he slipped and missed a shot. To punish the shoe, he threw it and kicked it. Unfortunately, he almost hit an official. These are the ingenious remedies for failure in the fixed mindset.

TAKING CHARGE OF SUCCESS

Finding #3: People with the growth mindset in sports (as in pre-med chemistry) took charge of the processes that bring success—and that maintain it.

How come Michael Jordan's skill didn't seem to decline with age? He did lose some stamina and agility with age, but to compensate, he worked even harder on conditioning and on his moves, like the turn-around jump shot and his celebrated fallaway jumper. He came into the league as a slam-dunker and he left as the most complete player ever to grace the game.

Woods, too, takes charge of the process. Golf is like a wayward lover. When you think you've conquered her, she will certainly desert you. Butch Harmon, the renowned coach, says "the golf swing is just about the farthest thing from a perfectible discipline in athletics. . . . The most reliable swings are only relatively repeatable. They never stop being works in progress." That's why even the biggest golf star wins only a fraction of the time, and may not win for long periods of time (which happened to Woods in the 2003 and 2004 seasons). And that's also why taking charge of the process is so crucial.

With this in mind, Tiger's dad made sure to teach him how to manage his attention and his course strategy. Mr. Woods would make loud noises or throw things just as little Tiger was about to swing. This helped him become less distractible. (Do we know someone else who could have profited from this training?) When Tiger was three years old, his dad was already teaching him to think about course management. After Tiger drove the ball behind a big clump of trees, Mr. Woods asked the toddler what his plan was.

Woods carries on what his dad started by taking control of all parts of his game. He experiments constantly with what works and what doesn't, but he also has a long-term plan that guides him: "I know my game. I know what I want to achieve, I know how to get there."

Like Michael Jordan, Woods manages his motivation. He does this by making his practice into fun: "I love working on shots, carving them this way and that, and proving to myself that I can hit a certain shot on command." And he does it by thinking of a rival out there somewhere who will challenge him: "He's twelve. I have to give myself a reason to work so hard. He's out there somewhere. He's twelve."

Mark O'Meara, Woods's golf partner and friend, had a choice. It's not easy to play beside someone as extraordinary as Woods. O'Meara's choice was this: He could feel jealous of and diminished by Woods's superior play, or he could learn from it. He chose the latter path. O'Meara was one of those talented players who never seemed to fulfill his potential. His choice—to take charge of his game—turned him around.

At the age of twenty-one, Woods had won the Masters Tournament. That night, he slept with his arms around his prize, the famous green jacket. One year later, he put a green jacket on Mark O'Meara.

From McEnroe, we hear little talk of taking control. When he was on top, we hear little mention of working on his game to stay on top. When he was doing poorly, we hear little self-reflection or analysis (except to pin the blame). For example, when he didn't do as well as expected for part of '82, we hear that "little things happened that kept me off my game for weeks at a time and prevented me from dominating the tour."

Always a victim of outside forces. Why didn't he take charge and learn how to perform well in spite of them? That's not the way of the fixed mindset. In fact, rather than combating those forces or fixing his problems, he tells us he wished he played a team sport, so he could conceal his flaws: "If you're not at your peak, you can hide it so much easier in a team sport."

McEnroe also admits that his on-court temper tantrums were often a cover for choking and only made things worse. So what did he do? Nothing. He wished someone else would do it for him. "When you can't control yourself, you want someone to do it for you—that's where I acutely missed being part of a team sport. . . . People would have worked with me, coached me."

Or: "The system let me get away with more and more . . . I really liked it less and less." He got mad at the system! Hi there, John. This was *your* life. Ever think of taking responsibility?

No, because in the fixed mindset, you don't take control of your abilities and your motivation. You look for your talent to carry you through, and when it doesn't, well then, what else could you have done? You are not a work in progress, you're a finished product. And finished products have to protect themselves, lament, and blame. Everything but take charge.

WHAT DOES IT MEAN TO BE A STAR?

Does a star have less responsibility to the team than other players? Is it just their role to be great and win games? Or does a star have *more* responsibility than others? What does Michael Jordan think?

"In our society sometimes it's hard to come to grips with filling a role instead of trying to be a superstar," says Jordan. A superstar's talent can win games, but it's teamwork that wins championships.

Coach John Wooden claims he was tactically and strategically average. So how did he win ten national championships? One of the main reasons, he tells us, is because he was good at getting players to fill roles as part of a *team*. "I believe, for example, I could have made Kareem [Abdul-Jabbar] the greatest scorer in college history. I could have done that by developing the team around that ability of his. Would we have won three national championships while he was at UCLA? Never."

In the fixed mindset, athletes want to validate their talent. This means acting like a superstar, not "just" a team member. But, as with Pedro Martinez, this mindset works against the important victories they want to achieve.

A telling tale is the story of Patrick Ewing, who could have been a basketball champion. The year Ewing was a draft pick—by far the most exciting pick of the year—the Knicks won the lottery and to their joy got to select Ewing for their team. They now had "twin towers," the seven-foot Ewing and the seven-foot Bill Cartwright, their high-scoring center. They had a chance to do it all.

They just needed Ewing to be the power forward. He wasn't happy with that. Center is the star position. And maybe he wasn't sure he could hit the outside shots that a power forward has to hit. What if he had really given his all to learn that position? (Alex Rodriguez, the best shortstop in baseball, agreed to play third base when he joined the Yankees. He had to retrain himself and, for a while, he wasn't all he had been.) Instead, Cartwright was sent to the Bulls, and Ewing's Knicks never won a championship.

Then there is the tale of the football player Keyshawn Johnson, another immensely talented player who was devoted to validating his own greatness. When asked before a game how he compared to a star player on the opposing team, he replied, "You're trying to compare a flashlight to a star. Flashlights only last so long. A star is in the sky forever."

Was he a team player? "I am a team player, but I'm an individual first. . . . I have to be the No. 1 guy with the football. Not No. 2 or No. 3. If I'm not the No. 1 guy, I'm no good to you. I can't really help you." What does *that* mean? For his definition of *team player*, Johnson was traded by the Jets, and, after that, deactivated by the Tampa Bay Buccaneers.

I've noticed an interesting thing. When some star players are interviewed after a game, they say *we*. They are part of the team and they think of themselves that way. When others are interviewed, they say *I* and they refer to their teammates as something apart from themselves— as people who are privileged to participate in their greatness.

Every Sport Is a Team Sport

You know, just about every sport is in some sense a team sport. No one does it alone. Even in individual sports, like tennis or golf, great athletes have a team—coaches, trainers, caddies, managers, mentors. This really hit me when I read about Diana Nyad, the woman who holds the world's record for open-water swimming. What could be more of a lone sport than swimming? All right, maybe you need a little rowboat to follow you and make sure you're okay.

When Nyad hatched her plan, the open-water swimming record for both men and women was sixty miles. She wanted to swim one hundred. After months of arduous training, she was ready. But with her went a team of guides (for measuring the winds and the current, and watching for obstacles), divers (looking for sharks), NASA experts (for guidance on nutrition and endurance—she needed eleven hundred calories per hour and she lost twenty-nine pounds on the trip!), and trainers who talked her through uncontrollable shivers, nausea, hallucinations, and despair. Her new record—102.5 miles—stands to this day. It is her name in the record books, but it took fifty-one other people to do it.

HEARING THE MINDSETS

You can already hear the mindsets in young athletes. Listen for them.

It's 2004. Iciss Tillis is a college basketball star, a six-foot-five forward for the Duke University women's basketball team. She has a picture of her father, James "Quick" Tillis, taped to her locker as a motivator. "But the picture is not a tribute," says sportswriter Viv Bernstein. "It is a reminder of all Tillis hopes she will never be."

Quick Tillis was a contender in the 1980s. In '81, he boxed for the world heavyweight title; in '85, he was in the movie *The Color Purple* (as a boxer); and in '86, he was the first boxer to go the distance (ten rounds) with Mike Tyson. But he never made it to the top.

Iciss Tillis, who is a senior, says, "This is the year to win a national championship. I just feel like I'd be such a failure . . . [I'd] feel like I'm regressing back and I'm going to end up like my dad: a nobody."

Uh-oh, it's the somebody–nobody syndrome. *If I win, I'll be somebody; if I lose I'll be nobody.*

Tillis's anger at her father may be justified—he abandoned her as a child. But this thinking is getting in her way. "Perhaps nobody else has that combination of size, skill, quickness, and vision in the women's college game," says Bernstein. "Yet few would rate Tillis ahead of the top two players in the country: Connecticut's Diana Taurasi and [Duke's Alana] Beard." Tillis's performance often fails to match her ability.

She's frustrated that people have high expectations for her and want her to play better. "I feel like I have to come out and have a triple-double [double digits in points scored, rebounds, and assists], dunk the ball over-the-head 360 [leave your feet, turn completely around in the air, and slam the ball into the basket] and maybe people will be like, 'Oh, she not that bad.' "

I don't think people want the impossible. I think they just want to see her use her wonderful talent to the utmost. I think they want her to develop the skills she needs to reach her goals.

Worrying about being a nobody is not the mindset that motivates and sustains champions. (Hard as it is, perhaps Tillis should admire the fact that her father went for it, instead of being contemptuous that he didn't quite make it.) Somebodies are not determined by whether they won or lost. Somebodies are people who go for it with all they have. If you go for it with all you have, Iciss Tillis—not just in the games, but in practice too—you will already be a somebody.

Here's the other mindset. It's six-foot-three Candace Parker, then a seventeen-year-old senior at Naperville Central High near Chicago, who was going to Tennessee to play for the Lady Vols and their great coach, Pat Summitt.

Candace has a very different father from Iciss, a dad who is teaching her a different lesson: "If you work hard at something, you get out what you put in."

Several years before, when he was coach of her team, her dad lost his cool with her during a tournament game. She was not going for the rebounds, she was shooting lazy shots from the outside instead of using her height near the basket, and she was not exerting herself on defense. "Now let's go out and try harder!" So what happened? She went out and scored twenty points in the second half, and had ten rebounds. They blew the other team away. "He lit a fire under me. And I knew he was right."

Candace lights the same fire under *herself* now. Rather than being content to be a star, she looks to improve all the time. When she returned from knee surgery, she knew what she needed to work on—her timing, nerves, and wind. When her three-point shot went bad, she asked her father to come to the gym to work on it with her. "Whether it be in basketball or everyday life," she says, "nothing is promised."

Only weeks later, the mindset prophecies were already coming true. Two things happened. One, sadly, is that Tillis's team was knocked out of the championship. The other was that Candace Parker became the first woman ever to win the basketball dunking championship—against five men.

Character, heart, the mind of a champion. It's what makes great athletes and it's what comes from the growth mindset with its focus on self-development, self-motivation, and responsibility.

Even though the finest athletes are wildly competitive and want to be the best, greatness does not come from the ego of the fixed mindset, with its somebody–nobody syndrome. Many athletes with the fixed mindset may have been "naturals"—but you know what? As John Wooden says, we can't remember most of them.

Grow Your Mindset

- Are there sports you always assumed you're bad at? Well, maybe you are, but then maybe you aren't. It's not something you can know until you've put in a lot of effort. Some of the world's best athletes didn't start out being that hot. If you have a passion for a sport, put in the effort and see.

- Sometimes being exceptionally endowed is a curse. These athletes may stay in a fixed mindset and not cope well with adversity. Is there a sport that came easily to you until you hit a wall? Try on the growth mindset and go for it again.

- "Character" is an important concept in the sports world, and it comes out of a growth mindset. Think about times you've needed to reach deep down inside in difficult sports matches. Think about the growth-mindset champions from this chapter and how they do it. What could you do next time to make sure you're in a growth mindset in the pinch?

- Athletes with a growth mindset find success in learning and improving, not just winning. The more you can do this, the more rewarding sports will be for you—and for those who play them with you!

Chapter 5

BUSINESS: MINDSET AND LEADERSHIP

ENRON AND THE TALENT MINDSET

In 2001 came the announcement that shocked the corporate world. Enron—the corporate poster child, the company of the future—had gone belly-up. What happened? How did such spectacular promise turn into such a spectacular disaster? Was it incompetence? Was it corruption?

It was mindset. According to Malcolm Gladwell, writing in *The New Yorker*, American corporations had become obsessed with talent. Indeed, the gurus at McKinsey & Company, the premier management consulting firm in the country, were insisting that corporate success today *requires* the "talent mind-set." Just as there are naturals in sports, they maintained, there are naturals in business. Just as sports teams write huge checks to sign outsized talent, so, too, should corporations spare no expense in recruiting talent, for this is the secret weapon, the key to beating the competition.

As Gladwell writes, "This 'talent mind-set' is the new orthodoxy of American management." It created the blueprint for the Enron culture—and sowed the seeds of its demise.

Enron recruited big talent, mostly people with fancy degrees, which is not in itself so bad. It paid them big money, which is not that terrible. But by putting complete faith in talent, Enron did a fatal thing: It created a culture that worshiped talent, thereby forcing its employees to look and act extraordinarily talented. Basically, it forced them into the fixed mindset. And we know a lot about that. We know from our studies that people with the fixed mindset do not admit and correct their deficiencies.

Remember the study where we interviewed students from the University of Hong Kong, where everything is in English? Students with the fixed mindset were so worried about appearing deficient that they refused to take a course that would improve their English. They did not live in a psychological world where they could take this risk.

And remember how we put students into a fixed mindset by praising their intelligence—much as Enron had done with its star employees? Later, after some hard problems, we asked the students to write a letter to someone in another school describing their experience in our study. When we read their letters, we were shocked: Almost 40 percent of them had lied about their scores—always in the upward direction. The fixed mindset had made a flaw intolerable.

Gladwell concludes that when people live in an environment that esteems them for their innate talent, they have grave difficulty when their image is threatened: "They will not take the remedial course. They will not stand up to investors and the public and admit that they were wrong. They'd sooner lie."

Obviously, a company that cannot self-correct cannot thrive.

If Enron was done in by its fixed mindset, does it follow that companies that thrive have a growth mindset? Let's see.

ORGANIZATIONS THAT GROW

Jim Collins set out to discover what made some companies move from being good to being great. What was it that allowed them to make the leap to greatness—and stay there—while other, comparable companies just held steady at good?

To answer this question, he and his research team embarked on a five-year study. They selected eleven companies whose stock returns had skyrocketed relative to other companies in their industry, and who had maintained this edge for at least fifteen years. They matched each company to another one in the same industry that had similar resources, but did not make the leap. He also studied a third group of companies: ones that had made a leap from good to great but did not sustain it.

What distinguished the thriving companies from the others? There were several important factors, as Collins reports in his book, *Good to Great*, but one that was absolutely key was the type of leader who *in every case* led the company into greatness. These were not the larger-than-life, charismatic types who oozed ego and self-proclaimed talent. They were self-effacing people who constantly asked questions and had the ability to confront the most brutal answers—that is, to look failures in the face, even their own, while maintaining faith that they would succeed in the end.

Does this sound familiar? Collins wonders why his effective leaders have these particular qualities. And why these qualities go together the way they do. And how these leaders came to acquire them. But we know. They have the growth mindset. They believe in human development. And these are the hallmarks:

They're not constantly trying to prove they're better than others. For example, they don't highlight the pecking order with themselves at the top, they don't claim credit for other people's contributions, and they don't undermine others to feel powerful.

Instead, they are constantly trying to *improve.* They surround themselves with the most able people they can find, they look squarely at their own mistakes and deficiencies, and they ask frankly what skills they and the company will need in the future. And because of this, they can move forward with confidence that's grounded in the facts, not built on fantasies about their talent.

Collins reports that Alan Wurtzel, the CEO of the giant electronics chain Circuit City, held debates in his boardroom. Rather than simply trying to impress his board of directors, he used them to learn. With his executive team as well, he questioned, debated, prodded until he slowly gained a clearer picture of where the company was and where it needed to go. "They used to call me the prosecutor, because I would hone in on a question," Wurtzel told Collins. "You know, like a bulldog. I wouldn't let go until I understood. Why, why, why?"

Wurtzel considered himself a "plow horse," a hardworking, no-nonsense normal kind of guy, but he took a company that was close to bankruptcy and over the next fifteen years turned it into one that delivered the highest total return to its stockholders of any firm on the New York Stock Exchange.

A STUDY OF MINDSET AND MANAGEMENT DECISIONS

Robert Wood and Albert Bandura did a fascinating study with graduate students in business, many of whom had management experience. In their study, they *created* Enron-type managers and Wurtzel-type managers by putting people into different mindsets.

Wood and Bandura gave these budding business leaders a complex management task in which they had to run a simulated organization, a furniture company. In this computerized task, they had to place employees in the right jobs and decide how best to guide and motivate these workers. To discover the best ways, they had to keep revising their decisions based on the feedback they got about employee productivity.

The researchers divided the business students into two groups. One group was given a fixed mindset. They were told that the task measured their basic, underlying capabilities. The higher their capacity, the better their performance. The other group was given a growth mindset. They were told that management skills were developed through practice and that the task would give them an opportunity to cultivate these skills.

The task was hard because students were given high production standards to meet, and—especially in their early attempts—they fell short. As at Enron, those with the fixed mindset did not profit from their mistakes.

But those with the growth mindset kept on learning. Not worried about measuring—or protecting—their fixed abilities, they looked directly at their mistakes, used the feedback, and altered their strategies accordingly. They became better and better at understanding how to deploy and motivate their workers, and their productivity kept pace. In fact, they ended up way more productive than those with the fixed mindset. What's more, throughout this rather grueling task, they maintained a healthy sense of confidence. They operated like Alan Wurtzel.

LEADERSHIP AND THE FIXED MINDSET

In contrast to Alan Wurtzel, the leaders of Collins's comparison companies had every symptom of the fixed mindset writ large.

Fixed-mindset leaders, like fixed-mindset people in general, live in a world where some people are superior and some are inferior. They must repeatedly affirm that they are superior, and the company is simply a platform for this.

Collins's comparison leaders were typically concerned with their "reputation for personal greatness"—so much so that they often set the company up to fail when their regime ended. As Collins puts it, "After all, what better testament to your own personal greatness than that the place falls apart after you leave?"

In more than two-thirds of these leaders, the researchers saw a "gargantuan personal ego" that either hastened the demise of the company or kept it second-rate. Once such leader was Lee Iacocca, head of Chrysler, who achieved a miraculous turnaround for his company, then spent so much time grooming his fame that in the second half of his tenure, the company plunged back into mediocrity.

Many of these comparison companies operated on what Collins calls a "genius with a thousand helpers" model. Instead of building an extraordinary management team like the good-to-great companies, they operated on the fixed-mindset premise that great geniuses do not need great teams. They just need little helpers to carry out their brilliant ideas.

Don't forget that these great geniuses don't *want* great teams, either. Fixed-mindset people want to be the only big fish so that when they compare themselves to those around them, they can feel a cut above the rest. In not one autobiography of a fixed-mindset CEO did I read much about mentoring or employee development programs. In every growth-mindset autobiography, there was deep concern with personnel development and extensive discussion of it.

Finally, as with Enron, the geniuses refused to look at their deficiencies. Says Collins: The good-to-great Kroger grocery chain looked bravely at the danger signs in the 1970s—signs that the old-fashioned grocery store was becoming extinct. Meanwhile, its counterpart, A&P, once the largest retailing organization in the world, shut its eyes. For example, when A&P opened a new kind of store, a superstore, and it seemed to be more successful than the old kind, they closed it down. It was not what they wanted to hear. In contrast, Kroger eliminated or changed every single store that did not fit the new superstore model and by the end of the 1990s it had become the number one grocery chain in the country.

CEOs and the Big Ego

How did *CEO* and *gargantuan ego* become synonymous? If it's the more self-effacing growth-minded people who are the true shepherds of industry, why are so many companies out looking for larger-than-life leaders—even when these leaders may in the end be more committed to themselves than to the company?

Blame Iacocca. According to James Surowiecki, writing in *Slate*, Iacocca's rise to prominence was a turning point for American business. Before him, the days of tycoons and moguls seemed long past. In the public's mind, *CEO* meant "a buttoned-down organization man, well-treated and well-paid, but essentially bland and characterless." With Iacocca, all of that changed. Business journalists began dubbing executives "the next J. P. Morgan" or "the next Henry Ford." And fixed-mindset executives started vying for those labels.

Surowiecki even traces the recent corporate scandals to this change, for as the trend continued, CEOs became superheroes. But the people who preen their egos and look for the next self-image boost are not the same people who foster long-term corporate health.

Maybe Iacocca is just a charismatic guy who, like rock and roll, is being blamed for the demise of civilization. Is that fair? Let's look at him more closely. And let's look at some other fixed-mindset CEOs: Albert Dunlap of Scott Paper and Sunbeam; Jerry Levin and Steve Case of AOL Time Warner; and Kenneth Lay and Jeffrey Skilling of Enron.

You'll see they all start with the belief that some people are superior; they all have the need to prove and display *their* superiority; they all use their subordinates to feed this need, rather than fostering the development of their workers; and they all end by sacrificing their companies to this need. The fixed mindset helps us understand where gargantuan egos come from, how they operate, and why they become self-defeating.

FIXED-MINDSET LEADERS IN ACTION

Iacocca: I'm a Hero

Warren Bennis, the leadership guru, studied the world's greatest corporate leaders. These great leaders said they didn't set out to be leaders. They'd had no interest in proving themselves. They just did what they loved—with tremendous drive and enthusiasm—and it led where it led.

Iacocca wasn't like that. Yes, he loved the car business, but more than anything he yearned to be a muckamuck at Ford. He craved the approval of Henry Ford II and the royal trappings of office. These were the things he could measure himself by, the things that would prove he was somebody. I use the term *royal* with good reason. Iacocca tells us the Glass House, Ford corporate headquarters, was a palace and Henry Ford was the king. What's more, "If Henry was king, I was the crown prince." "I was His Majesty's special protégé." "All of us . . . lived the good life in the royal court. We were part of something beyond first class—royal class. . . . White coated waiters were on call throughout the day, and we all ate lunch together in the executive dining room . . . Dover sole was flown over from England on a daily basis."

Iacocca achieved great things at Ford, like nurturing and promoting the Ford Mustang, and he dreamed of succeeding Henry Ford as the CEO of the company. But Henry Ford had other ideas and, much to Iacocca's shock and rage, he eventually forced Iacocca out. It's interesting that Iacocca was shocked and that he harbored an enduring rage against Henry Ford. After all, he had seen Henry Ford fire top people, and he, Iacocca, had used the ax quite liberally on others. He knew the corporate game. Yet his fixed mindset clouded his vision: "I had always clung to the idea that I was different, that somehow *I was smarter or luckier* than the rest. I didn't think it would ever happen to me." (Italics added.)

His belief in his inherent superiority had blinded him. Now the other side of the fixed mindset kicked in. He wondered whether Henry Ford had detected a flaw in him. Maybe he wasn't superior after all. And that's why he couldn't let go. Years later, his second wife told him to get over it. "You don't realize what a favor Henry Ford did for you. Getting fired from Ford brought you to greatness. You're richer, more famous and more influential because of Henry Ford. Thank him." Shortly thereafter, he divorced her.

So the king who had defined him as competent and worthy now rejected him as flawed. With ferocious energy, Iacocca applied himself to the monumental task of saving face and, in the process, Chrysler Motors. Chrysler, the once thriving Ford rival, was on the brink of death, but Iacocca as its new CEO acted quickly to hire the right people, bring out new models, and lobby the government for bailout loans. Just a few years after his humiliating exit from Ford, he was able to write a triumphant autobiography and in it declare, "Today, I'm a hero."

Within a short time, however, Chrysler was in trouble again. Iacocca's fixed mindset would not stay put. He needed to prove his greatness—to himself, to Henry Ford, to the world—on a larger and larger scale. He spent his company time on things that would enhance his public image, and he spent the company's money on things that would impress Wall Street and hike up Chrysler's stock prices. But he did this instead of investing in new car designs or manufacturing improvements that would keep the company profitable in the long run.

He also looked to history, to how he would be judged and remembered. But he did not address this concern by building the company. Quite the contrary. According to one of his biographers, he worried that his underlings might get credit for successful new designs, so he balked at approving them. He worried, as Chrysler faltered, that his underlings might be seen as the new saviors, so he tried to get rid of them. He worried that he would be written out of Chrysler history, so he desperately hung on as CEO long after he had lost his effectiveness.

Iacocca had a golden opportunity to make a difference, to leave a great legacy. The American auto industry was facing its biggest challenge ever. Japanese imports were taking over the American market. It was simple: They looked better and they ran better. Iacocca's own people had done a detailed study of Honda, and made excellent suggestions to him.

But rather than taking up the challenge and delivering better cars, Iacocca, mired in his fixed mindset, delivered blame and excuses. He went on the rampage, spewing angry diatribes against the Japanese and demanding that the American government impose tariffs and quotas that would stop them. In an editorial against Iacocca, *The New York Times* scolded, "The solution lies in making better cars in this country, not in angrier excuses about Japan."

Nor was Iacocca growing as a leader of his workforce. In fact, he was shrinking into the insulated, petty, and punitive tyrant he had accused Henry Ford of being. Not only was he firing people who were critical of him, he'd done little to reward the workers who had sacrificed so much to save the company. Even when the money was rolling in, he seemed to have little interest in sharing it with them. Their pay remained low and their working conditions remained poor. Yet even when Chrysler was in trouble again, he maintained a regal lifestyle. Two million dollars were spent renovating his corporate suite at the Waldorf in New York.

Finally, while there was still time to save Chrysler, the board of directors eased Iacocca out. They gave him a grand pension, showered him with stock options, and continued many of his corporate perks. But he was beside himself with rage, especially since his successor seemed to be managing the company quite nicely. So in a bid to regain the throne, he joined a hostile takeover attempt, one that placed the future of Chrysler at risk. It failed. But for many, the suspicion that he put his ego before the welfare of the company was confirmed.

Iacocca lived the fixed mindset. Although he started out loving the car business and having breakthrough ideas, his need to prove his superiority started to dominate, eventually killing his enjoyment and stifling his creativity. As time went on and he became less and less responsive to challenges from competitors, he resorted to the key weapons of the fixed mindset—blame, excuses, and the stifling of critics and rivals.

And as is so often the case with the fixed mindset, because of these very things, Iacocca lost the validation he craved.

When students fail tests or athletes lose games, it tells them that they've dropped the ball. But the power that CEOs wield allows them to create a world that caters night and day to their need for validation. It allows them to surround themselves only with the good news of their perfection and the company's success, no matter what the warning signs may be. This, as you may recall, is CEO disease and a peril of the fixed mindset.

You know, lately I've wondered whether Iacocca has recuperated from CEO disease. He's raising money (and giving a lot of his own) for innovative diabetes research. He's working for the development of environment-friendly vehicles. Maybe, released from the task of trying to prove himself, he's now going for things he deeply values.

Albert Dunlap: I'm a Superstar

Albert Dunlap saved dying companies, although I'm not sure *saved* is the right word. He didn't get them ready to thrive in the future. He got them ready to sell for a profit, for example by firing thousands of workers. And profit he did. He got a hundred million dollars from the turnaround and sale of Scott Paper. One hundred million for little more than a year and a half of work. "Did I earn it? Damn right I did. I'm a superstar in my field, much like Michael Jordan in basketball and Bruce Springsteen in rock 'n' roll."

Iacocca paid lip service to teamwork, the importance of the little guy, and other good things. Albert Dunlap didn't even pay lip service: "If you're in business, you're in business for one thing—to make money."

He proudly reports an incident at an employee meeting at Scott Paper. A woman stood up and asked, "Now that the company is improving, can we restart charitable donations?" To which he replied, "If you want to give on your own, that is your business and I encourage you to do it. But this company is here to make a buck. . . . The answer, in a word, is no."

I'm not here to argue that business isn't about money, but I do want to ask: Why was Dunlap so focused on it?

Let's let him tell us. "Making my way in the world became a matter of self-respect for me, of a kid trying to prove he was worth something. . . . To this day, I feel I have to prove and reprove myself." And if he has to prove himself, he needs a yardstick. Employee satisfaction or community responsibility or charitable contributions are not good yardsticks. They cannot be reduced to one number that represents his self-worth. But shareholder profits can.

In his own words, "The most ridiculous term heard in boardrooms these days is 'stakeholders.' " The term refers to the employees, the community, and the other companies, such as suppliers, that the company deals with. "You can't measure success by the interest of multiple stakeholders. You *can* measure success by how the shareholder fares."

The long haul held no interest for Dunlap. Really learning about a company and figuring out how to make it grow didn't give him the big blast of superhero juice. "Eventually, I have gotten bored every place I have been." In his book, there is a whole chapter called "Impressing the Analysts," but there is no chapter about making a business work. In other words, it's always about Dunlap proving his genius.

Then in 1996, Dunlap took over Sunbeam. In his typical "Chainsaw Al" style, he closed or sold two-thirds of Sunbeam's plants and fired half of the twelve thousand employees. Ironically, the Sunbeam stock rose so high, it ruined his plan to sell the company. It was too expensive to buy! Uh-oh, now he had to run the company. Now he had to keep it profitable, or at least looking profitable. But instead of turning to his staff or learning what to do, he inflated revenues, fired people who questioned him, and covered up the increasingly dire straits his company was in. Less than two years after the self-proclaimed superstardom in his book (and one year after an even more self-congratulatory revision), Dunlap fell apart and was kicked out. As he left, Sunbeam was under investigation by the Securities and Exchange Commission and was expected to be in technical default on a $1.7 billion bank loan.

Dunlap deeply misunderstood Michael Jordan and Bruce Springsteen. Both of these superstars reached the pinnacle and stayed there a long time because they constantly dug down, faced challenges, and kept growing. Al Dunlap thought that he was inherently superior, so he opted out of the kind of learning that would have helped him succeed.

The Smartest Guys in the Room

Yes, it seems as though history led inevitably from Iacocca to the moguls of the 1990s, and none more so than Kenneth Lay and Jeffrey Skilling, the leaders of Enron.

Ken Lay, the company's founder, chairman, and CEO, considered himself a great visionary. According to Bethany McLean and Peter Elkind, authors of *The Smartest Guys in the Room,* Lay looked down his nose at the people who actually made the company run, much the way a king might look at his serfs. He looked down on Rich Kinder, the Enron president, who rolled up his sleeves and tried to make sure the company would reach its earning targets. Kinder was the man who made Lay's royal lifestyle possible. Kinder was also the only person at the top who constantly asked if they were fooling themselves: "Are we smoking our own dope? Are we drinking our own whiskey?"

Naturally, his days were numbered. But in his sensible and astute way, as he departed he arranged to buy the one Enron asset that was inherently valuable, the energy pipelines—the asset that Enron held in disdain. By the middle of 2003, Kinder's company had a market value of seven billion dollars.

Even as Lay was consumed by his view of himself and the regal manner in which he wished to support it, he wanted to be seen as a "good and thoughtful man" with a credo of respect and integrity. Even as Enron merrily sucked the life out of its victims, he wrote to his staff, "Ruthlessness, callousness and arrogance don't belong here. . . . We work with customers and prospects openly, honestly and sincerely." As with Iacocca and the others, the perception—usually Wall Street's perception—was all-important. The reality less so.

Right there with Lay was Jeff Skilling, successor to Rich Kinder as president and chief operating officer, and later the CEO. Skilling was not just smart, he was said to be "the smartest person I ever met" and "incandescently brilliant." He used his brainpower, however, not to learn but to intimidate. When he thought he was smarter than others, which was almost always, he treated them harshly. And anyone who disagreed with him was just not bright enough to "get it." When a co-CEO with superb management skills was brought in to help Skilling during a hard time in his life, Skilling was contemptuous of him: "Ron doesn't get it." When financial analysts or Wall Street traders tried to press Skilling to go beyond his pat explanations, he treated them as though they were stupid. "Well, it's so obvious. How can you not get it?" In most cases, the Wall Street guys, ever concerned about their own intellect, made believe they got it.

As resident genius, Skilling had unlimited faith in his ideas. He had so much regard for his ideas that he believed Enron should be able to proclaim profits as soon as he or his people had the idea that might lead to profits. This is a radical extension of the fixed mindset: *My genius not only defines and validates me. It defines and validates the company. It is what creates value. My genius is profit.* Wow!

And in fact, this is how Enron came to operate. As McLean and Elkind report, Enron recorded "millions of dollars in profits on a business before it had generated a penny in actual revenues." Of course, after the creative act no one cared about follow-through. That was beneath them. So, often as not, the profit never occurred. If genius equaled profit, it didn't matter that Enron people sometimes wasted millions competing against each other. Said Amanda Martin, an Enron executive, "To put one over on one of your own was a sign of creativity and greatness."

Skilling not only thought he was smarter than everyone else but, like Iacocca, also thought he was luckier. According to insiders, he thought he could beat the odds. Why should he feel vulnerable? There was never anything wrong. Skilling still does not admit that there was anything wrong. The world simply didn't get it.

Two Geniuses Collide

Resident geniuses almost brought down AOL and Time Warner, too. Steve Case of AOL and Jerry Levin of Time Warner were *two* CEOs with the fixed mindset who merged their companies. Can you see it coming?

Case and Levin had a lot in common. Both of them cultivated an aura of supreme intelligence. Both tried to intimidate people with their brilliance. And both were known to take more credit than they deserved. As resident geniuses, neither wanted to hear complaints, and both were ready to fire people who weren't "team players," meaning people who wouldn't keep up the façade that they had erected.

When the merger actually took place, AOL was in such debt that the merged company was on the brink of ruin. You would think that the two CEOs might work together, marshaling their resources to save the company they created. Instead, Levin and Case scrambled for personal power.

Levin was the first to fall. But Case was still not trying to make things work. In fact, when the new CEO, Richard Parsons, sent someone down to fix AOL, Case was intensely against it. If someone else fixed AOL, someone else would get the credit. As with Iacocca, better to let the company collapse than let another prince be crowned. When Case was finally counseled to resign, he was furious. Like Iacocca, he denied all responsibility for the company's problems and vowed to get back at those who had turned against him.

Because of the resident geniuses, AOL Time Warner ended the year 2002 with a loss of almost one hundred billion dollars. It was the largest yearly loss in American history.

Invulnerable, Invincible, and Entitled

Iacocca, Dunlap, Lay and Skilling, Case and Levin. They show what can happen when people with the fixed mindset are put in charge of companies. In each case, a brilliant man put his company in jeopardy because measuring himself and his legacy outweighed everything else. They were not evil in the usual sense. They didn't set out to do harm. But at critical decision points, they opted for what would make them feel good and look good over what would serve the longer-term corporate goals. Blame others, cover mistakes, pump up the stock prices, crush rivals and critics, screw the little guy—these were the standard operating procedures.

What is fascinating is that as they led their companies toward ruin, all of these leaders felt invulnerable and invincible. In many cases, they were in highly competitive industries, facing onslaughts from fierce rivals. But they lived in a different reality.

It was a world of personal greatness and entitlement. Kenneth Lay felt a powerful sense of entitlement. Even as he was getting millions a year in compensation from Enron, he took large personal loans from the company, gave jobs and contracts to his relatives, and used the corporate jets as his family fleet. Even during bad years at Chrysler, Iacocca threw lavish Christmas parties for the company elite. At every party, as king, he presented himself with an expensive gift, which the executives were later billed for. Speaking about AOL executives, a former official said, "You're talking about men who thought they had a right to anything."

As these leaders cloaked themselves in the trappings of royalty, surrounded themselves with flatterers who extolled their virtues, and hid from problems, it is no wonder they felt invincible. Their fixed mindset created a magic realm in which the brilliance and perfection of the king were constantly validated. Within that mindset, they were completely fulfilled. Why would they want to step outside that realm to face the uglier reality of warts and failures?

As Morgan McCall, in his book *High Flyers*, points out, "Unfortunately, people often *like* the things that work against their growth. . . . People like to use their strengths . . . to achieve quick, dramatic results, even if . . . they aren't developing the new skills they will need later on. People like to believe they are as good as everyone says . . . and not take their weaknesses as seriously as they might. People don't like to hear bad news or get criticism. . . . There is tremendous risk . . . in leaving what one does well to attempt to master something new." And the fixed mindset makes it seem all that much riskier.

Brutal Bosses

McCall goes on to point out that when leaders feel they are inherently better than others, they may start to believe that the needs or feelings of the lesser people can be ignored. None of our fixed-mindset leaders cared much about the little guy, and many were outright contemptuous of those beneath them on the corporate ladder. Where does this lead? In the guise of "keeping people on their toes," these bosses may mistreat workers.

Iacocca played painful games with his executives to keep them off balance. Jerry Levin of Time Warner was likened by his colleagues to the brutal Roman emperor Caligula. Skilling was known for his harsh ridicule of those less intelligent than he.

Harvey Hornstein, an expert on corporate leadership, writes in his book *Brutal Bosses* that this kind of abuse represents the bosses' desire "to enhance their own feelings of power, competence, and value at the subordinate's expense." Do you remember in our studies how people with the fixed mindset wanted to compare themselves with people who were worse off than they were? The principle is the same, but there is an important difference: These bosses have the power to *make* people worse off. And when they do, they feel better about themselves.

Hornstein describes Paul Kazarian, the former CEO of Sunbeam-Oster. He called himself a "perfectionist," but that was a euphemism for "abuser." He threw things at subordinates when they upset him. One day, the comptroller, after displeasing Mr. Kazarian, saw an orange juice container flying toward him.

Sometimes the victims are people the bosses consider to be less talented. This can feed their sense of superiority. But often the victims are the *most* competent people, because these are the ones who pose the greatest threat to a fixed-mindset boss. An engineer at a major aircraft builder, interviewed by Hornstein, talked about his boss: "His targets were usually those of us who were most competent. I mean, if you're really concerned about our performance, you don't pick on those who are performing best." But if you're really concerned about your competence, you do.

When bosses mete out humiliation, a change comes over the place. Everything starts revolving around pleasing the boss. In *Good to Great,* Collins notes that in many of his comparison companies (the ones that didn't go from good to great, or that went there and declined again), the leader became the main thing people worried about. "The minute a leader allows himself to become the primary reality people worry about, rather than reality being the primary reality, you have a recipe for mediocrity, or worse."

In the 1960s and '70s, the Chase Manhattan Bank was ruled by David Rockefeller, an excessively controlling leader. According to Collins and Porras in *Built to Last,* his managers lived day-to-day in fear of his disapproval. At the end of each day, they breathed a sigh of relief: "Whew! One more day gone and I'm not in trouble." Even long past his heyday, senior managers refused to venture a new idea because "David might not like it." Ray Macdonald of Burroughs, Collins and Porras report, publicly ridiculed managers for mistakes to the point where he inhibited them from innovating. As a result, even though Burroughs was ahead of IBM in the early stages of the computer industry, the company lost out. The same thing happened at Texas Instruments, another leader in the exciting early days of the computer. If they didn't like a presentation, Mark Shepherd and Fred Bucy would yell, bang on tables, insult the speaker, and hurl things. No wonder their people lost their enterprising spirit.

When bosses become controlling and abusive, they put everyone into a fixed mindset. This means that instead of learning, growing, and moving the company forward, everyone starts worrying about being judged. It starts with the bosses' worry about being judged, but it winds up being everybody's fear about being judged. It's hard for courage and innovation to survive a companywide fixed mindset.

GROWTH-MINDSET LEADERS IN ACTION

Andrew Carnegie once said, "I wish to have as my epitaph: 'Here lies a man who was wise enough to bring into his service men who knew more than he.'"

Okay, let's open the windows and let some air in. The fixed mindset feels so stifling. Even when those leaders are globe-trotting and hobnobbing with world figures, their world seems so small and confining—because their minds are always on one thing: *Validate me!*

When you enter the world of the growth-mindset leaders, everything changes. It brightens, it expands, it fills with energy, with possibility. You think, *Gee, that seems like fun!* It has never entered my mind to lead a corporation, but when I learned about what these leaders had done, it sounded like the most exciting thing in the world.

I've chosen three of these leaders to explore as a contrast to the fixed-mindset leaders. I chose Jack Welch of General Electric because he is a larger-than-life figure with an ego he held in check—not your straight-ahead naturally self-effacing growth-minded guy. And I chose Lou Gerstner (the man who came in and saved IBM) and Anne Mulcahy (the woman who brought Xerox back to life) as contrasts to Alfred Dunlap, the other turnaround expert.

Jack Welch, Lou Gerstner, and Anne Mulcahy are also fascinating because they transformed their companies. They did this by rooting out the fixed mindset and putting a culture of growth and teamwork in its place. With Gerstner and IBM, it's like watching Enron morph into a growth-mindset mecca.

As growth-minded leaders, they start with a belief in human potential and development—both their own and other people's. Instead of using the company as a vehicle for their greatness, they use it as an engine of growth—for themselves, the employees, and the company as a whole.

Warren Bennis has said that too many bosses are driven and driving but going nowhere. Not these people. They don't talk royalty. They talk journey. An inclusive, learning-filled, rollicking journey.

Jack: Listening, Crediting, Nurturing

When Jack Welch took over GE in 1980, the company was valued at fourteen billion dollars. Twenty years later, it was valued by Wall Street at $490 billion. It was the most valuable company in the world. *Fortune* magazine called Welch "the most widely admired, studied, and imitated CEO of his time. . . . His total economic impact is impossible to calculate but must be a staggering multiple of his GE performance."

But to me even more impressive was an op-ed piece in *The New York Times* by Steve Bennett, the CEO of Intuit. "I learned about nurturing employees from my time at General Electric from Jack Welch. . . . He'd go directly to the front-line employee to figure out what was going on. Sometime in the early 1990s, I saw him in a factory where they made refrigerators in Louisville. . . . He went right to the workers in the assembly line to hear what they had to say. I do frequent CEO chats with front-line employees. I learned that from Jack."

This vignette says a lot. Jack was obviously a busy guy. An important guy. But he didn't run things like Iacocca—from the luxurious corporate headquarters where his most frequent contacts were the white-gloved waiters. Welch never stopped visiting the factories and hearing from the workers. These were people he respected, learned from, and, in turn, nurtured.

Then there is the emphasis on teamwork, not the royal *I*. Right away—right from the "Dedication" and the "Author's Note" of Welch's autobiography—you know something is different. It's not the "I'm a hero" of Lee Iacocca or the "I'm a superstar" of Alfred Dunlap—although he could easily lay claim to both.

Instead, it's "I hate having to use the first person. Nearly everything I've done in my life has been accomplished with other people. . . . Please remember that every time you see the word *I* in these pages, it refers to all those colleagues and friends and some I might have missed."

Or "[These people] filled my journey with great fun and learning. They often made me look better than I am."

Already we see the *me me me* of the validation-hungry CEO becoming the *we* and *us* of the growth-minded leader.

Interestingly, before Welch could root the fixed mindset out of the company, he had to root it out of himself. And believe me, Welch had a long way to go. He was not always the leader he learned to be. In 1971, Welch was being considered for a promotion when the head of GE human resources wrote a cautioning memo. He noted that despite

Welch's many strengths, the appointment "carries with it more than the usual degree of risk." He went on to say that Welch was arrogant, couldn't take criticism, and depended too much on his talent instead of hard work and his knowledgeable staff. Not good signs.

Fortunately, every time his success went to his head, he got a wake-up call. One day, young "Dr." Welch, decked out in his fancy suit, got into his new convertible. He proceeded to put the top down and was promptly squirted with dark, grungy oil that ruined both his suit and the paint job on his beloved car. "There I was, thinking I was larger than life, and smack came the reminder that brought me back to reality. It was a great lesson."

There is a whole chapter titled "Too Full of Myself" about the time he was on an acquisition roll and felt he could do no wrong. Then he bought Kidder, Peabody, a Wall Street investment banking firm with an Enron-type culture. It was a disaster that lost hundreds of millions of dollars for GE. "The Kidder experience never left me." It taught him that "there's only a razor's edge between self-confidence and hubris. This time hubris won and taught me a lesson I would never forget."

What he learned was this: True self-confidence is "the courage to be open—to welcome change and new ideas regardless of their source." Real self-confidence is not reflected in a title, an expensive suit, a fancy car, or a series of acquisitions. It is reflected in your mindset: your readiness to grow.

Well, humility is a start, but what about the management skills?

From his experiences, Welch learned more and more about the kind of manager he wanted to be: a growth-minded manager—a guide, not a judge. When Welch was a young engineer at GE, he caused a chemical explosion that blew the roof off the building he worked in. Emotionally shaken by what happened, he nervously drove the hundred miles to company headquarters to face the music and explain himself to the boss. But when he got there, the treatment he received was understanding and supportive. He never forgot it. "Charlie's reaction made a huge impression on me. . . . If we're managing good people who are clearly eating themselves up over an error, our job is to help them through it."

He learned how to select people: for their mindset, not their pedigrees. Originally, academic pedigrees impressed him. He hired engineers from MIT, Princeton, and Caltech. But after a while, he realized that wasn't what counted. "Eventually I learned that I was really looking for people who were filled with passion and a desire to get things done. A resume didn't tell me much about that inner hunger."

Then came a chance to become the CEO. Each of the three candidates had to convince the reigning CEO he was best for the job. Welch made the pitch on the basis of his capacity to grow. He didn't claim that he was a genius or that he was the greatest leader who ever lived. He promised to develop. He got the job and made good on his promise.

Immediately, he opened up dialogue and the channels for honest feedback. He quickly set to work asking executives what they liked and disliked about the company and what they thought needed changing. Boy, were they surprised. In fact, they'd been so used to kissing up to the bosses that they couldn't even get their minds around these questions.

Then he spread the word: This company is about growth, not self-importance.

He shut down elitism—quite the opposite of our fixed-mindset leaders. One evening, Welch addressed an elite executive club at GE that was *the* place for movers and shakers to see and be seen. To their shock, he did not tell them how wonderful they were. He told them, "I can't find any value in what you're doing." Instead, he asked them to think of a role that made more sense for them and for the company. A month later, the president of the club came to Welch with a new idea: to turn the club into a force of community volunteers. Twenty years later that program, open to all employees, had forty-two thousand members. They were running mentoring programs in inner-city schools and building parks, playgrounds, and libraries for communities in need. They were now making a contribution to others' growth, not to their own egos.

He got rid of brutal bosses. Iacocca tolerated and even admired brutal bosses who could make the workers produce. It served his bottom line. Welch admitted that he, too, had often looked the other way. But in the organization he now envisioned, he could not do that. In front of five hundred managers, "I explained why four corporate officers were asked to leave during the prior year—even though they delivered good financial performance. . . . [They] were asked to go because they didn't practice our values." The approved way to foster productivity was now through mentoring, not through terror.

And he rewarded teamwork rather than individual genius. For years, GE, like Enron, had rewarded the single originator of an idea, but now Welch wanted to reward the team that brought the ideas to fruition. "As a result, leaders were encouraged to share the credit for ideas with their teams rather than take full credit themselves. It made a huge difference in how we all related to one another."

Jack Welch was not a perfect person, but he was devoted to growth. This devotion kept his ego in check, kept him connected to reality, and kept him in touch with his humanity. In the end, it made his journey prosperous and fulfilling for thousands of people.

Lou: Rooting Out the Fixed Mindset

By the late 1980s, IBM had become Enron, with one exception. The board of directors knew it was in trouble.

It had a culture of smugness and elitism. Within the company, it was the old *We are royalty, but I'm more royal than you are* syndrome. There was no teamwork, only turf wars. There were deals but no follow-up. There was no concern for the customer. Yet this probably wouldn't have bothered anyone if business weren't suffering.

In 1993, they turned to Lou Gerstner and asked him to be the new CEO. He said no. They asked him again. "You owe it to America. We're going to have President Clinton call and tell you to take the job. Please, please, please. We want exactly the kind of strategy and culture change you created at American Express and RJR."

In the end he caved, although he can't remember why. But IBM now had a leader who believed in personal growth and in creating a corporate culture that would foster it. How did he produce it at IBM?

First, as Welch had done, he opened the channels of communication up and down the company. Six days after he arrived, he sent a memo to every IBM worker, telling them: "Over the next few months, I plan to visit as many of our operations and offices as I can. And whenever possible, I plan to meet with many of you to talk about how together we can strengthen the company."

He dedicated his book to them: "This book is dedicated to the thousands of IBMers who never gave up on their company, their colleagues, and themselves. They are the real heroes of the reinvention of IBM."

As Welch had done, he attacked the elitism. Like Enron, the whole culture was about grappling for personal status within the company. Gerstner disbanded the management committee, the ultimate power role for IBM executives, and often went outside the upper echelons for expertise. From a growth mindset, it's not only the select few that have something to offer. "Hierarchy means very little to me. Let's put together in meetings the people who can help solve a problem, regardless of position."

Then came teamwork. Gerstner fired politicians, those who indulged in internal intrigue, and instead rewarded people who helped their colleagues. He stopped IBM sales divisions from putting each other down to clients to win business for themselves. He started basing executives' bonuses more on IBM's overall performance and less on the performance of their individual units. The message: We're not looking to crown a few princes; we need to work as a team.

As at Enron, the deal was the glamorous thing; the rest was pedestrian. Gerstner was appalled by the endless failure to follow through on deals and decisions, and the company's unlimited tolerance of it. He demanded and inspired better execution. Message: Genius is not enough; we need to get the job done.

Finally, Gerstner focused on the customer. IBM customers felt betrayed and angry. IBM was so into itself that it was no longer serving their computer needs. They were upset about pricing. They were frustrated by the bureaucracy at IBM. They were irritated that IBM was not helping them to integrate their systems. At a meeting of 175 chief information officers of the largest U.S. companies, Gerstner announced that IBM would now put the customer first and backed it up by announcing a drastic cut in their mainframe computer prices. Message: We are not hereditary royalty; we serve at the pleasure of our clients.

At the end of his first three arduous months, Gerstner received his report card from Wall Street: "[IBM stock] has done nothing, because he has done nothing."

Ticked off but undaunted, Gerstner continued his anti-royalty campaign and brought IBM back from its "near-death experience." This was the sprint. This is when Dunlap would have taken his money and run. What lay ahead was the even harder task of maintaining his policies until IBM regained industry leadership. That was the marathon. By the time he gave IBM back to the IBMers in March 2002, the stock had increased in value by 800 percent and IBM was "number one in the world in IT services, hardware, enterprise software (excluding PCs), and custom-designed, high performance computer chips." What's more, IBM was once again defining the future direction of the industry.

Anne: Learning, Toughness, and Compassion

Take IBM. Plunge it into debt to the tune of seventeen billion. Destroy its credit rating. Make it the target of SEC investigations. And drop its stock from $63.69 to $4.43 a share. What do you get? Xerox.

That was the Xerox Anne Mulcahy took over in 2000. Not only had the company failed to diversify, it could no longer even sell its copy machines. But three years later, Xerox had had four straight profitable quarters, and in 2004 *Fortune* named Mulcahy "the hottest turnaround act since Lou Gerstner." How did she do it?

She went into an incredible learning mode, *making* herself into the CEO Xerox needed to survive. She and her top people, like Ursula Burns, learned the nitty-gritty of every part of the business. For example, as *Fortune* writer Betsy Morris explains, Mulcahy took Balance Sheet 101. She learned about debt, inventory, taxes, and currency so she could predict how each decision she made would play out on the balance sheet. Every weekend, she took home large binders and pored over them as though her final exam was on Monday. When she took the helm, people at Xerox units couldn't give her simple answers about what they had, what they sold, or who was in charge. She became a CEO who knew those answers or knew where to get them.

She was tough. She told everyone the cold, hard truth they didn't want to know—like how the Xerox business model was not viable or how close the company was to running out of money. She cut the employee rolls by 30 percent. But she was no Chainsaw Al. Instead, she bore the emotional brunt of her decisions, roaming the halls, hanging out with the employees, and saying "I'm sorry." She was tough but compassionate. In fact, she'd wake up in the middle of the night worrying about what would happen to the remaining employees and retirees if the company folded.

She worried constantly about the morale and development of her people, so that even with the cuts, she refused to sacrifice the unique and wonderful parts of the Xerox culture. Xerox was known throughout the industry as the company that gave retirement parties and hosted retiree reunions. As the employees struggled side by side with her, she refused to abolish their raises and, in a morale-boosting gesture, gave them all their birthdays off. She wanted to save the company in body *and* spirit. And not for herself or her ego, but for all her people who were stretching themselves to the limit for the company.

After slaving away for two years, Mulcahy opened *Time* magazine only to see a picture of herself grouped with the notorious heads of Tyco and WorldCom, men responsible for two of the biggest corporate management disasters of our time.

But a year later she knew her hard work was finally paying off when one of her board members, the former CEO of Procter & Gamble, told her, "I never thought I would be proud to have my name associated with this company again. I was wrong."

Mulcahy was winning the sprint. Next came the marathon. Could Xerox win that, too? Maybe it had rested on its laurels too long, resisting change and letting too many chances go by. Or maybe the growth mindset—Mulcahy's mission to transform herself and her company— would help save another American institution.

Jack, Lou, and Anne—all believing in growth, all brimming with passion. And all believing that leadership is about growth and passion, not about brilliance. The fixed-mindset leaders were, in the end, full of bitterness, but the growth-minded leaders were full of gratitude. They looked up with gratitude to their workers who had made their amazing journey possible. They called them the real heroes.

Are CEO *and* Male *Synonymous?*

When you look at the books written by and about CEOs, you would think so. Jim Collins's good-to-great leaders (and his comparison not-so-great leaders) were all men. Perhaps that's because men are the ones who've been at the top for a long while.

A few years ago, you'd have been hard-pressed to think of women at the top of big companies. In fact, many women who've run big companies had to create them, like Mary Kay Ash (the cosmetics tycoon), Martha Stewart, or Oprah Winfrey. Or inherit them, like Katharine Graham, the former head of *The Washington Post*.

Things are beginning to change. Women now hold more key positions in big business. They've been the CEOs of not only Xerox, but also eBay, Hewlett-Packard, Viacom's MTV Networks, Time Warner's Time, Inc., Lucent Technologies, and Rite Aid. Women have been the presidents or chief financial officers of Citigroup, PepsiCo, and Verizon. In fact, *Fortune* magazine called Meg Whitman of eBay "maybe . . . the best CEO in America" of the "world's hottest company."

I wonder whether, in a few years, I'll be able to write this whole chapter with women as the main characters. On the other hand, I hope not. I hope that in a few years, it will be hard to find fixed-mindset leaders— men *or* women—at the top of our most important companies.

A STUDY OF GROUP PROCESSES

Researcher Robert Wood and his colleagues did another great study. This time they created management *groups,* thirty groups with three people each. Half of the groups had three people with a fixed mindset and half had three people with a growth mindset.

Those with the fixed mindset believed that: "People have a certain fixed amount of management ability and they cannot do much to change it." In contrast, those with the growth mindset believed: "People can always substantially change their basic skills for managing other people." So one group thought that you have it or you don't; the other thought your skills could grow with experience.

Every group had worked together for some weeks when they were given, jointly, the task I talked about before: a complex management task in which they ran a simulated organization, a furniture company. If you remember, on this task people had to figure out how to match workers with jobs and how to motivate them for maximum productivity. But this time, instead of working individually, people could discuss their choices and the feedback they got, and work together to improve their decisions.

The fixed- and growth-mindset groups started with the same ability, but as time went on the growth-mindset groups clearly outperformed the fixed-mindset ones. And this difference became ever larger the longer the groups worked. Once again, those with the growth mindset profited from their mistakes and feedback far more than the fixed-mindset people. But what was even more interesting was how the groups functioned.

The members of the growth-mindset groups were much more likely to state their honest opinions and openly express their disagreements as they communicated about their management decisions. Everyone was part of the learning process. For the fixed-mindset groups—with their concern about who was smart or dumb or their anxiety about disapproval for their ideas—that open, productive discussion did not happen. Instead, it was more like groupthink.

GROUPTHINK VERSUS WE THINK

In the early 1970s, Irving Janis popularized the term *groupthink*. It's when everyone in a group starts thinking alike. No one disagrees. No one takes a critical stance. It can lead to catastrophic decisions, and, as the Wood study suggests, it often can come right out of a fixed mindset.

Groupthink can occur when people put unlimited faith in a talented leader, a genius. This is what led to the disastrous Bay of Pigs invasion, America's half-baked secret plan to invade Cuba and topple Castro.

President Kennedy's normally astute advisers suspended their judgment. Why? Because they thought he was golden and everything he did was bound to succeed.

According to Arthur Schlesinger, an insider, the men around Kennedy had unbounded faith in his ability and luck. "Everything had broken right for him since 1956. He had won the nomination and the election against all the odds in the book. Everyone around him thought he had the Midas touch and could not lose."

Schlesinger also said, "Had one senior advisor opposed the adventure, I believe that Kennedy would have canceled it. No one spoke against it." To prevent this from happening to him, Winston Churchill set up a special department. Others might be in awe of his titanic persona, but the job of this department, Jim Collins reports, was to give Churchill all the worst news. Then Churchill could sleep well at night, knowing he had not been groupthinked into a false sense of security.

Groupthink can happen when the group gets carried away with its brilliance and superiority. At Enron, the executives believed that because they were brilliant, all of their ideas were brilliant. Nothing would ever go wrong. An outside consultant kept asking Enron people, "Where do you think you're vulnerable?" Nobody answered him. Nobody even understood the question. "We got to the point," said a top executive, "where we thought we were bullet proof."

Alfred P. Sloan, the former CEO of General Motors, presents a nice contrast. He was leading a group of high-level policy makers who seemed to have reached a consensus. "Gentlemen," he said, "I take it we are all in complete agreement on the decision here. . . . Then I propose we postpone further discussion of this matter until our next meeting to give ourselves time to develop disagreement and perhaps gain some understanding of what the decision is all about."

Herodotus, writing in the fifth century B.C., reported that the ancient Persians used a version of Sloan's techniques to prevent groupthink. Whenever a group reached a decision while sober, they later reconsidered it while intoxicated.

Groupthink can also happen when a fixed-mindset leader punishes dissent. People may not stop thinking critically, but they stop speaking up. Iacocca tried to silence (or get rid of) people who were critical of his ideas and decisions. He said the new, rounder cars looked like flying potatoes, and that was the end of it. No one was allowed to differ, as Chrysler and its square cars lost more and more of the market share.

David Packard, on the other hand, gave an employee a medal for defying him. The co-founder of Hewlett-Packard tells this story. Years ago at a Hewlett-Packard lab, they told a young engineer to give up work on a display monitor he was developing. In response, he went "on vacation," touring California and dropping in on potential customers to show them the monitor and gauge their interest. The customers loved it, he continued working on it, and then he somehow persuaded his manager to put it into production. The company sold more than seventeen thousand of his monitors and reaped a sales revenue of thirty-five million dollars. Later, at a meeting of Hewlett-Packard engineers, Packard gave the young man a medal "for extraordinary contempt and defiance beyond the normal call of engineering duty."

There are so many ways the fixed mindset creates groupthink. Leaders are seen as gods who never err. A group invests itself with special talents and powers. Leaders, to bolster their ego, suppress dissent. Or workers, seeking validation from leaders, fall into line behind them. That's why it's critical to be in a growth mindset when important decisions are made. As Robert Wood showed in his study, a growth mindset—by relieving people of the illusions or the burdens of fixed ability—leads to a full and open discussion of the information and to enhanced decision making.

THE PRAISED GENERATION HITS THE WORKFORCE

Are we going to have a problem finding leaders in the future? You can't pick up a magazine or turn on the radio without hearing about the problem of praise in the workplace. We could have seen it coming.

We've talked about all the well-meaning parents who've tried to boost their children's self-esteem by telling them how smart and talented they are. And we've talked about all the negative effects of this kind of praise. Well, these children of praise have now entered the workforce, and sure enough, many can't function without getting a sticker for their every move. Instead of yearly bonuses, some companies are giving quarterly or even monthly bonuses. Instead of employee of the month, it's the employee of the day. Companies are calling in consultants to teach them how best to lavish rewards on this overpraised generation. We now have a workforce full of people who need constant reassurance and can't take criticism. Not a recipe for success in business, where taking on challenges, showing persistence, and admitting and correcting mistakes are essential.

Why are businesses perpetuating the problem? Why are they continuing the same misguided practices of the overpraising parents, and paying money to consultants to show them how to do it? Maybe we need to step back from this problem and take another perspective.

If the wrong kinds of praise lead kids down the path of entitlement, dependence, and fragility, maybe the right kinds of praise can lead them down the path of hard work and greater hardiness. We have shown in our research that with the right kinds of feedback even adults can be motivated to choose challenging tasks and confront their mistakes.

What would this feedback look or sound like in the workplace? Instead of just giving employees an award for the smartest idea or praise for a brilliant performance, they would get praise for taking initiative, for seeing a difficult task through, for struggling and learning something new, for being undaunted by a setback, or for being open to and acting on criticism. Maybe it could be praise for not needing constant praise!

Through a skewed sense of how to love their children, many parents in the '90s (and, unfortunately, many parents of the '00s) abdicated their responsibility. Although corporations are not usually in the business of picking up where parents left off, they may need to this time. If businesses don't play a role in developing a more mature and growth-minded workforce, where will the leaders of the future come from?

ARE NEGOTIATORS BORN OR MADE?

One of the key things that the successful businessperson must be good at is negotiation. In fact, it's hard to imagine how a business could thrive without skilled negotiators at the helm. Laura Kray and Michael Haselhuhn have shown that mindsets have an important impact on negotiation success. In one study, they taught people either a fixed or a growth mindset about negotiation skills. Half of the participants read an article called "Negotiation Ability, Like Plaster, Is Pretty Stable Over Time." The other half read one called "Negotiation Ability Is Changeable and Can Be Developed." To give you a flavor for the articles, the growth mindset article started by saying, "While it used to be believed that negotiating was a fixed skill that people were either born with or not, experts in the field now believe that negotiating is a dynamic skill that can be cultivated and developed over a lifetime."

The participants were then asked to select the kind of negotiation task they wanted. They could choose one that showed off their negotiation skills, although they would not learn anything new. Or they could choose one in which they might make mistakes and get confused, but they would learn some useful negotiation skills. Almost half (47 percent) of the people who were taught the fixed mindset about negotiation skills chose the task that simply showed off their skills, but only 12 percent of those who were taught the growth mindset cared to pursue this show-offy task. This means that 88 percent of the people who learned a growth mindset wanted to dig into the task that would improve their negotiation skills.

In their next study, Kray and Haselhuhn monitored people as they engaged in negotiations. Again, half of the people were given a fixed mindset about negotiation skills and the other half were given a growth mindset. The people, two at a time, engaged in an employment negotiation. In each pair, one person was the job candidate and the other was the recruiter, and they negotiated on eight issues, including salary, vacation time, and benefits. By the end of the negotiation, those with the growth mindset were the clear winners, doing almost twice as well as those with the fixed mindset. The people who had learned the growth mindset persevered through the rough spots and stalemates to gain more favorable outcomes.

In three final studies, the researchers looked at MBA students enrolled in a course on negotiation. Here they measured the mindsets the

MBA students already had, asking them how much they agreed with fixed mindset statements ("The kind of negotiator someone is is very basic and it can't be changed very much," "Good negotiators are born that way") and growth mindset statements ("All people can change even their most basic negotiation qualities," "In negotiations, experience is a great teacher"). Similar to before, they found that the more of a growth mindset the student had, the better he or she did on the negotiation task.

But does a growth mindset make people good just at getting their own way? Often negotiations require people to understand and try to serve the other person's interests as well. Ideally, at the end of a negotiation, both parties feel their needs have been met. In a study with a more challenging negotiation task, those with a growth mindset were able to get beyond initial failures by constructing a deal that addressed *both* parties' underlying interests. So, not only do those with a growth mindset gain more lucrative outcomes for themselves, but, more important, they also come up with more creative solutions that confer benefits all around.

Finally, a growth mindset promoted greater learning. Those MBA students who endorsed a growth mindset on the first day of the negotiation course earned higher final grades in the course weeks later. This grade was based on performance on written assignments, in class discussions, and during class presentations, and reflected a deeper comprehension of negotiation theory and practice.

CORPORATE TRAINING: ARE MANAGERS BORN OR MADE?

Millions of dollars and thousands of hours are spent each year trying to teach leaders and managers how to coach their employees and give them effective feedback. Yer much of this training is ineffective, and many leaders and mangers remain poor coaches. Is that because this can't be trained? No, that's not the reason. Research sheds light on why corporate training often fails.

Studies by Peter Heslin, Don VandeWalle, and Gary Latham show that many managers do not believe in personal change. These fixed-mindset managers simply look for existing talent—they judge employees as competent or incompetent at the start and that's that. They do relatively little developmental coaching and when employees *do* improve, they may fail to take notice, remaining stuck in their initial impression. What's more (like managers at Enron), they are far less likely to seek or accept critical feedback from their employees. Why bother to coach employees if they can't change and why get feedback from them if you can't change?

Managers with a growth mindset think it's nice to have talent, but that's just the starting point. These managers are more committed to their employees' development, and to their own. They give a great deal more developmental coaching, they notice improvement in employees' performance, and they welcome critiques from their employees.

Most exciting, the growth mindset can be taught to managers. Heslin and his colleagues conducted a brief workshop based on well-established psychological principles. (By the way, with a few changes, it could just as easily be used to promote a growth mindset in teachers or coaches.) The workshop starts off with a video and a scientific article about how the brain changes with learning. As with our "Brainology" workshop (described in chapter 8), it's always compelling for people to understand how dynamic the brain is and how it changes with learning. The article goes on to talk about how change is possible throughout life and how people can develop their abilities at most tasks with coaching and practice. Although managers, of course, want to find the right person for a job, the exactly right person doesn't always come along. However, training and experience can often draw out and develop the qualities required for successful performance.

The workshop then takes managers through a series of exercises in which a) they consider why it's important to understand that people can develop their abilities, b) they think of areas in which they once had low ability but now perform well, c) they write to a struggling protégé about how his or her abilities can be developed, and d) they recall times they have seen people learn to do things they never thought these people could do. In each case, they reflect upon why and how change takes place.

After the workshop, there was a rapid change in how readily the participating managers detected improvement in employee performance, in how willing they were to coach a poor performer, and in the quantity and quality of their coaching suggestions. What's more, these changes persisted over the six-week period in which they were followed up.

What does this mean? First, it means that our best bet is not simply to hire the most talented managers we can find and turn them loose, but to look for managers who also embody a growth mindset: a zest for teaching and learning, an openness to giving and receiving feedback, and an ability to confront and surmount obstacles.

It also means we need to train leaders, managers, and employees to believe in growth, in addition to training them in the specifics of effective communication and mentoring. Indeed, a growth mindset workshop might be a good first step in any major training program.

Finally, it means creating a growth-mindset environment in which people can thrive. This involves:

- Presenting skills as learnable
- Conveying that the organization values learning and perseverance, not just ready-made genius or talent
- Giving feedback in a way that promotes learning and future success
- Presenting managers as resources for learning

Without a belief in human development, many corporate training programs become exercises of limited value. With a belief in development, such programs give meaning to the term "human resources" and become a means of tapping enormous potential.

ARE LEADERS BORN OR MADE?

When Warren Bennis interviewed great leaders, "They all agreed leaders are made, not born, and made more by themselves than by any external means." Bennis concurred: "I believe . . . that everyone, of whatever age and circumstance, is capable of self-transformation." Not that everyone *will* become a leader. Sadly, most managers and even CEOs become bosses, not leaders. They wield power instead of transforming themselves, their workers, and their organization.

Why is this? John Zenger and Joseph Folkman point out that most people, when they first become managers, enter a period of great learning. They get lots of training and coaching, they are open to ideas, and they think long and hard about how to do their jobs. They are looking to develop. But once they've learned the basics, they stop trying to improve. It may seem like too much trouble, or they may not see where improvement will take them. They are content to do their jobs rather than making themselves into leaders.

Or, as Morgan McCall argues, many organizations believe in natural talent and don't look for people with the *potential* to develop. Not only are these organizations missing out on a big pool of possible leaders, but their belief in natural talent might actually squash the very people they think are the naturals, making them into arrogant, defensive nonlearners. The lesson is: Create an organization that prizes the development of ability—and watch the leaders emerge.

Grow Your Mindset

- Are you in a fixed-mindset or growth-mindset workplace? Do you feel people are just judging you or are they helping you develop? Maybe you could try making it a more growth-mindset place, starting with yourself. Are there ways you could be less defensive about your mistakes? Could you profit more from the feedback you get? Are there ways you can create more learning experiences for yourself?

- How do *you* act toward others in your workplace? Are you a fixed-mindset boss, focused on your power more than on your employees' well-being? Do you ever reaffirm your status by demeaning others? Do you ever try to hold back high-performing employees because they threaten you?

  Consider ways to help your employees develop on the job: Apprenticeships? Workshops? Coaching sessions? Think about how you can start seeing and treating your employees as your collaborators, as a team. Make a list of strategies and try them out. Do this even if you already think of yourself as a growth-mindset boss. Well-placed support and growth-promoting feedback never hurt.

- If you run a company, look at it from a mindset perspective. Does it need you to do a Lou Gerstner on it? Think seriously about how to root out elitism and create a culture of self-examination, open communication, and teamwork. Read Gerstner's excellent book *Who Says Elephants Can't Dance?* to see how it's done.

- Is your workplace set up to promote groupthink? If so, the whole decision-making process is in trouble. Create ways to foster alternative views and constructive criticism. Assign people to play the devil's advocate, taking opposing viewpoints so you can see the holes in your position. Get people to wage debates that argue different sides of the issue. Have an anonymous suggestion box that employees must contribute to as part of the decision-making process. Remember, people can be independent thinkers and team players at the same time. Help them fill both roles.

Chapter 6

RELATIONSHIPS: MINDSETS IN LOVE (OR NOT)

What was that about the course of true love never running smooth? Well, the course *to* true love isn't so smooth, either. That path is often strewn with disappointments and heartbreaks. Some people let these experiences scar them and prevent them from forming satisfying relationships in the future. Others are able to heal and move on. What separates them? To find out, we recruited more than a hundred people and asked them to tell us about a terrible rejection.

> When I first got to New York I was incredibly lonely. I didn't know a soul and I totally felt like I didn't belong here. After about a year of misery I met Jack. It's almost an understatement to say that we clicked instantly, we felt like we had known each other forever. It wasn't long before we were living together and doing everything together. I thought I would spend my whole life with him and he said he felt the same way. Two really happy years passed. Then one day I came home and found a note. He said he had to leave, don't try to find him. He didn't even sign it love. I never heard from him again. Sometimes when the phone rings I still think maybe it's him.

We heard a variation of that story over and over again. People with both mindsets told stories like this. Almost everyone, at one time or another, had been in love and had been hurt. What differed—and differed dramatically—was how they dealt with it.

After they told their stories, we asked them follow-up questions: What did this mean to you? How did you handle it? What were you hoping for?

When people had the fixed mindset, they felt judged and labeled by the rejection. Permanently labeled. It was as though a verdict had been handed down and branded on their foreheads: UNLOVABLE! And they lashed out.

Because the fixed mindset gives them no recipe for healing their wound, all they could do was hope to wound the person who inflicted it. Lydia, the woman in the story above, told us that she had lasting, intense feelings of bitterness: "I would get back at him, hurt him any way I could if I got the chance. He deserves it."

In fact, for people with the fixed mindset, their number one goal came through loud and clear. Revenge. As one man put it, "She took my worth with her when she left. Not a day goes by I don't think about how to make her pay." During the study, I asked one of my fixed-mindset friends about her divorce. I'll never forget what she said. "If I had to choose between me being happy and him being miserable, I would definitely want him to be miserable."

It had to be a person with the fixed mindset who coined the phrase "Revenge is sweet"—the idea that with revenge comes your redemption—because people with the growth mindset have little taste for it. The stories they told were every bit as wrenching, but their reactions couldn't have been more different.

For them, it was about understanding, forgiving, and moving on. Although they were often deeply hurt by what happened, they wanted to learn from it: "That relationship and how it ended really taught me the importance of communicating. I used to think love conquers all, but now I know it needs a lot of help." This same man went on to say, "I also learned something about who's right for me. I guess every relationship teaches you more about who's right for you."

There is a French expression: *"Tout comprendre c'est tout pardonner."* To understand all is to forgive all. Of course, this can be carried too far, but it's a good place to start. For people with the growth mindset, the number one goal was forgiveness. As one woman said: "I'm no saint, but I knew for my own peace of mind that I had to forgive and forget. He hurt me but I had a whole life waiting for me and I'll be damned if I was going to live it in the past. One day I just said, 'Good luck to him and good luck to me.'"

Because of their growth mindset, they did not feel permanently branded. Because of it, they tried to learn something useful about themselves and relationships, something they could use toward having a better experience in the future. And they knew how to move on and embrace that future.

My cousin Cathy embodies the growth mindset. Several years ago, after twenty-three years of marriage, her husband left her. Then, to add insult to injury, she was in an accident and hurt her leg. There she sat, home alone one Saturday night, when she said to herself, "I'll be damned if I'm going to sit here and feel sorry for myself!" (Perhaps this phrase should be the mantra of the growth mindset.) Out she went to a dance (leg and all) where she met her future husband.

The Contos family had pulled out all the stops. Nicole Contos, in her exquisite wedding dress, arrived at the church in a Rolls-Royce. The archbishop was inside waiting to perform the ceremony, and hundreds of friends and relatives from all over the world were in attendance. Everything was perfect until the best man went over to Nicole and told her the news. The groom would not be coming. Can you imagine the shock, the pain?

The family, thinking of the hundreds of guests, decided to go through with the reception and dinner. Then, rallying around Nicole, they asked her what she wanted to do. In an act of great courage, she changed into a little black dress, went to the party, and danced solo to "I Will Survive." It was not the dance she had anticipated, but it was one that made her an icon of gutsiness in the national press the next day. Nicole was like the football player who ran the wrong way. Here was an event that could have defined and diminished her. Instead it was one that enlarged her.

It's interesting. Nicole spoke repeatedly about the pain and trauma of being stood up at her wedding, but she never used the word *humiliated*. If she had judged herself, felt flawed and unworthy—humiliated—she would have run and hidden. Instead, her good clean pain made her able to surround herself with the love of her friends and relatives and begin the healing process.

What, by the way, had happened to the groom? As it turned out, he had gone on the honeymoon, flying off to Tahiti on his own. What happened to Nicole? A couple of years later, in the same wedding dress and the same church, she married a great guy. Was she scared? No, she says: "I knew he was going to be there."

When you think about how rejection wounds and inflames people with the fixed mindset, it will come as no surprise that kids with the fixed mindset are the ones who react to taunting and bullying with thoughts of violent retaliation. I'll return to this later.

RELATIONSHIPS ARE DIFFERENT

In his study of gifted people, Benjamin Bloom included concert pianists, sculptors, Olympic swimmers, tennis players, mathematicians, and research neurologists. But not people who were gifted in interpersonal relationships. He planned to. After all, there are so many professions in which interpersonal skills play a key role—teachers, psychologists, administrators, diplomats. But no matter how hard Bloom tried, he couldn't find any agreed-upon way of measuring social ability.

Sometimes we're not even sure it's an ability. When we see people with outstanding interpersonal skills, we don't really think of them as gifted. We think of them as cool people or charming people. When we see a great marriage relationship, we don't say these people are brilliant relationship makers. We say they're fine people. Or they have chemistry. Meaning what?

Meaning that as a society, we don't understand relationship skills. Yet everything is at stake in people's relationships. Maybe that's why Daniel Goleman's *Emotional Intelligence* struck such a responsive chord. It said: There are social-emotional skills and I can tell you what they are.

Mindsets add another dimension. They help us understand even more about why people often don't learn the skills they need or use the skills they have. Why people throw themselves so hopefully into new relationships, only to undermine themselves. Why love often turns into a battlefield where the carnage is staggering. And, most important, they help us understand why some people *are* able to build lasting and satisfying relationships.

MINDSETS FALLING IN LOVE

So far, having a fixed mindset has meant believing your personal traits are fixed. But in relationships, two more things enter the picture—your partner and the relationship itself. Now you can have a fixed mindset about *three* things. You can believe that *your* qualities are fixed, your *partner's* qualities are fixed, and the *relationship's* qualities are fixed—that it's inherently good or bad, meant-to-be or not meant-to-be. Now all of these things are up for judgment.

The growth mindset says all of these things can be developed. All—you, your partner, and the relationship—are capable of growth and change.

In the fixed mindset, the ideal is instant, perfect, and perpetual compatibility. Like it was meant to be. Like riding off into the sunset. Like "they lived happily ever after."

Many people want to feel their relationship is special and not just some chance occurrence. This seems okay. So what's the problem with the fixed mindset? There are two.

1. If You Have to Work at It, It Wasn't *Meant to Be*

One problem is that people with the fixed mindset expect everything good to happen automatically. It's not that the partners will work to help each other solve their problems or gain skills. It's that this will magically occur through their love, sort of the way it happened to Sleeping Beauty, whose coma was cured by her prince's kiss, or to Cinderella, whose miserable life was suddenly transformed by her prince.

Charlene's friends told her about Max, the new musician in town. He had come to play cello with the symphony orchestra. The next night, Charlene and her friends went to see the orchestra's performance, and when they went backstage afterward, Max took Charlene's hand and said, "Next time, let's make it longer." She was taken with his intense, romantic air, and he was taken with her charming manner and exotic looks. As they went out, the intensity grew. They seemed to understand each other deeply. They enjoyed the same things—food, analyzing people, travel. They both thought, *Where have you been all my life?*

Over time, though, Max became moody. Actually, that's how he was. It just didn't show at first. When he was in a bad mood, he wanted to be left alone. Charlene wanted to talk about what was bothering him, but that irritated him. "Just leave me alone," he would insist, more and more forcefully. Charlene, however, would feel shut out.

Plus, his moods didn't always happen at convenient times. Sometimes the couple was scheduled to go out. Sometimes they had planned a special dinner alone. Either he didn't want to do it, or she would endure his sullen silence throughout the evening. If she tried to make light conversation, he would be disappointed in her: "I thought you understood me."

Friends, seeing how much they cared about each other, urged them to work on this problem. But they both felt, with great sorrow, that if the relationship were the right one, they wouldn't have to work so hard. If it were the right relationship, they would just be able to understand and honor each other's needs. So they grew apart and eventually broke up.

In the growth mindset, there may still be that exciting initial combustion, but people in this mindset don't expect magic. They believe that a good, lasting relationship comes from effort and from working through inevitable differences.

But those with the fixed mindset don't buy that. Remember the fixed-mindset idea that if you have ability, you shouldn't have to work hard? This is the same belief applied to relationships: If you're compatible, everything should just come naturally.

Every single relationship expert disagrees with this.

Aaron Beck, noted marriage authority, says that one of the most destructive beliefs for a relationship is "If we need to work at it, there's something seriously wrong with our relationship."

Says John Gottman, a foremost relationship researcher: "Every marriage demands an effort to keep it on the right track; there is a constant tension . . . between the forces that hold you together and those that can tear you apart."

As with personal achievement, this belief—that success should not need effort—robs people of the very thing they need to make their relationship thrive. It's probably why so many relationships go stale—because people believe that being in love means never having to do anything taxing.

MIND READING

Part of the low-effort belief is the idea that couples should be able to read each other's minds: *We are like one. My partner should know what I think, feel, and need and I should know what my partner thinks, feels, and needs.* But this is impossible. Mind reading instead of communicating inevitably backfires.

Elayne Savage, noted family psychologist, describes Tom and Lucy. After three months together, Tom informed Lucy that there was an imbalance in their relationship. Lucy, reading his mind, decided Tom meant that he was less into the relationship than she was. She felt discouraged. Should she break off the relationship before he did? However, after a therapy session, Lucy got up the courage to find out what he meant. Tom, it turned out, had been using a musical term to convey his wish to fine-tune the relationship and move it to the next level.

I almost fell into the same trap. My husband and I had met a few months before, and everything seemed to be going great. Then one evening, as we were sitting together, he said to me, "I need more space." Everything went blank. I couldn't believe what I was hearing. Was I completely mistaken about the relationship? Finally, I summoned my courage. "What do you mean?" I asked. He said, "I need you to move over so I can have more room." I'm glad I asked.

AGREEING ON EVERYTHING

It's strange to believe in mind reading. But it makes sense when you realize that many people with a fixed mindset believe that *a couple should share all of each other's views.*

If you do, then you don't need communication; you can just assume your partner sees things the way you do.

Raymond Knee and his colleagues had couples come in and discuss their views of their relationship. Those with the fixed mindset felt threatened and hostile after talking about even *minor discrepancies* in how they and their partner saw their relationship. Even a minor discrepancy threatened their belief that they shared all of each other's views.

It's impossible for a couple to share all of each other's assumptions and expectations. One may assume the wife will stop working and be supported; the other, that she will be an equal breadwinner. One may assume they will have a house in the suburbs, the other that they will have a bohemian love nest.

Michael and Robin had just finished college and were about to get married. He was the bohemian-love-nest type. He imagined that after they were married, they'd enjoy the young, hip Greenwich Village life together. So when he found the ideal apartment, he thought she'd be delighted. When she saw it, she went berserk. She'd been living in crummy little apartments all her life, and here it was all over again. Married people were supposed to live in nice houses with new cars parked outside. They both felt betrayed, and it didn't get any better from there.

Couples may erroneously believe they agree on each person's rights and duties. Fill in the blank:

"As a husband, I have a right to ____, and my wife has the duty to ____."

"As a wife, I have a right to ____, and my husband has the duty to ____."

Few things can make partners more furious than having their rights violated. And few things can make a partner more furious than having the other feel entitled to something you don't think is coming to them.

John Gottman reports: "I've interviewed newlywed men who told me with pride, 'I'm not going to wash the dishes, no way. That's a woman's job.' Two years later the same guys ask me, 'Why don't my wife and I have sex anymore?'"

Now, a couple may agree on traditional roles. That's up to them. But that's different from assuming it as an entitlement.

When Janet (a financial analyst) and Phil (a real estate agent) met, he had just gotten a new apartment and was thinking he'd like to have a housewarming party, a dinner for a bunch of his friends. When Janet said, "Let's do it," he was thrilled. Her emphasis was on the " 's," the *us*. Because she was the more experienced cook and party giver, however, she did most of the preparation, and she did it gladly. She was delighted to see how happy he was to be having this event. The problem started after the guests arrived. Phil just went to the party. He acted like a guest. Like she was supposed to continue doing all the work. She was enraged.

The mature thing to do would have been to take him aside to have a discussion. Instead, she decided to teach him a lesson. She, too, went to the party. Fortunately, entitlement and retaliation did not become a pattern in their relationship. Communication did. In the future, things were discussed, not assumed.

A no-effort relationship is a doomed relationship, not a great relationship. It takes work to communicate accurately and it takes work to expose and resolve conflicting hopes and beliefs. It doesn't mean there is no "they lived happily ever after," but it's more like "they worked happily ever after."

2. Problems Indicate Character Flaws

The second big difficulty with the fixed mindset is the belief that problems are a sign of deep-seated flaws. But just as there are no great achievements without setbacks, there are no great relationships without conflicts and problems along the way.

When people with a fixed mindset talk about their conflicts, they assign blame. Sometimes they blame themselves, but often they blame their partner. And they assign blame to a *trait*—a character flaw.

But it doesn't end there. When people blame their partner's personality for the problem, they feel anger and disgust toward them.

And it barrels on: Since the problem comes from fixed traits, it can't be solved.

So once people with the fixed mindset see flaws in their partners, they become contemptuous of them and dissatisfied with the whole relationship. (People with the growth mindset, on the other hand, can see their partners' imperfections and still think they have a fine relationship.)

Sometimes people with the fixed mindset blind themselves to problems in the partner or the relationship so they won't have to go that route.

Everybody thought Yvonne was having a flirtation. She was getting mysterious phone calls. She was often late picking up the kids. Her "nights out with the girls" doubled. Her mind was often elsewhere. Her husband, Charlie, said she was just going through a phase. "All women go through times like this," he insisted. "It doesn't mean she's got a guy."

Charlie's best friend urged him to look into it. But Charlie felt that if he confronted the reality—and it was negative—his world would come crashing down. In the fixed mindset, he'd have to confront the idea that either (1) the woman he loved was a bad person, (2) he was a bad person and drove her away, or (3) their relationship was bad and irreparable.

He couldn't handle any of those. It didn't occur to him that there were problems that could be solved, that she was sending him a message she desperately wanted him to hear: *Don't take me for granted. I need more attention.*

A growth mindset doesn't mean he would necessarily confront her, but he would confront *it*—the situation. He'd think about what was wrong. Maybe explore the issue with a counselor. Make an informed decision about what to do next. If there *were* problems to be solved, at least there'd be a chance.

EACH ONE A LOSER

Penelope's friends sat at home complaining that there were no good men. Penelope went out and found them. Each time, she would find a great guy and fall head over heels. "He's the one," she'd tell her friends as she began reading the bridal magazines and practically writing the announcement for the local paper. They'd believe her because he was always a guy with a lot going for him.

But then something would happen. It was over for one of them when he got her a tacky birthday present. Another put ketchup on his food and sometimes wore white shoes. Another had bad electronic habits: His cell phone etiquette was poor and he watched too much TV. And this is only a partial list.

Assuming traits were fixed, Penelope would decide that she couldn't live with these flaws. But most of these were not deep or serious character problems that couldn't be addressed with a little communication.

My husband and I had been together almost a year and, as my birthday approached, I sent a clear message: "I'm not mercenary, but I like a good present." He said, "Isn't it the thought that counts?" I replied, "That's what people say when they don't want to put thought into it.

"Once a year," I continued, "we each have our day. I love you and I plan to put time and effort into choosing a present for you. I would like you to do that for me, too." He's never let me down.

Penelope assumed that somewhere out there was someone who was already perfect. Relationship expert Daniel Wile says that choosing a partner is choosing a set of problems. There are no problem-free candidates. The trick is to acknowledge each other's limitations, and build from there.

THE FLAWS FLY

Brenda and Jack were clients of Daniel Wile, and he tells this tale. Brenda came home from work and told Jack a long, detailed story with no apparent point. Jack was bored to tears but tried to hide it to be polite. Brenda, however, could sense his true feelings, so, hoping to be more amusing, she launched into another endless story, also about a project at work. Jack was ready to burst. They were both mentally hurling traits right and left. According to Wile, they were both thinking: *Brenda is boring, Jack is selfish,* and *our relationship is no good.*

In fact, both meant well. Brenda was afraid to say outright that she did some great work at the office that day. She didn't want to be boastful. So instead she talked about the tiny details of her project. Jack didn't want to be impolite, so instead of asking Brenda questions or expressing his puzzlement, he steeled himself and waited for her story to end.

Jack just needed to say, "You know, honey, when you get into so many details, I lose your point and get frustrated. Why don't you tell me why you're excited about this project? I'd really love to hear that."

It was a problem of communication, not a problem of personality or character. Yet in the fixed mindset, the blame came fast and furious.

By the way, I love these stories. When I was a kid, *Reader's Digest* used to have a feature in each issue called "Can This Marriage Be Saved?" Usually, the answer was yes. I ate up those stories, fascinated by all the ways a marriage could go wrong and even more fascinated by how it could be repaired.

The story of Ted and Karen, told by Aaron Beck, is a story of how two people with the fixed mindset went from all good traits to all bad ones in each other's eyes.

When Ted and Karen met, they were opposites attracting. Karen radiated spontaneity and lightness. Ted, a serious guy with the weight of the world on his shoulders, felt that her carefree presence transformed his life. "Everything she says and does is charming," he effused. In turn, Ted represented the rock-like "father figure" she had never had. He was just the kind of stable, reliable guy who could give her a sense of security.

But a few short years later, Ted saw Karen as an irresponsible airhead. "She never takes anything seriously . . . I can't depend on her." And Karen saw Ted as a judgmental tyrant, dissecting her every move.

In the end, this marriage was saved—only because the couple learned to respond to each other not with angry labels, but with helpful actions. One day, when Karen was swamped with work, Ted came home to a messy house. He was angry and wanted to scold her, but, drawing on what he'd learned from Beck, he instead said to himself, "What is the mature thing to do?" He answered his own question by starting to clean things up. He was offering Karen support rather than judgment.

CAN *THIS* MARRIAGE BE SAVED?

Aaron Beck tells couples in counseling never to think these fixed-mindset thoughts: *My partner is incapable of change. Nothing can improve our relationship.* These ideas, he says, are almost always wrong.

Sometimes it's hard not to think those thoughts—as in the case of Bill and Hillary Clinton. When he was president, Clinton lied to the nation and to his wife about his relationship with Monica Lewinsky. Hillary defended him: "My husband may have his faults, but he has never lied to me."

The truth came out, as it has a way of doing, especially when helped by a special prosecutor. Hillary, betrayed and furious, now had to decide whether Bill was a permanently bad and untrustworthy husband or a man who needed a lot of help.

This is a good time to bring up an important point: The belief that partners have the potential for change should not be confused with the belief that the partner *will* change. The partner has to want to change, commit to change, and take concrete actions toward change.

The Clintons went into counseling, spending one full day a week for a year in the process. Through counseling, Bill came to understand how, as the child of alcoholic parents, he had learned to lead a dual life. On the one hand, he'd learned to shoulder excessive responsibility at an early age—for example, as a boy sternly forbidding his stepfather to strike his mother. On the other hand, he had another part of his life where he took little responsibility, where he made believe everything was okay no matter what was going on. That's how he could appear on TV and earnestly vow that he was not involved with Lewinsky. He was in that no-responsibility and high-denial space.

People were urging Hillary to forgive him. One evening, Stevie Wonder called the White House to ask if he could come over. He had written a song for her on the power of forgiveness, and he played it to her that night.

Yet Hillary could not have forgiven a person she saw as a liar and a cheat. She could only forgive a man she thought was earnestly struggling with his problems and trying to grow.

THE PARTNER AS ENEMY

With the fixed mindset, one moment your partner is the light of your life, the next they're your adversary. Why would people want to transform the loved one into an enemy?

When you fail at other tasks, it's hard to keep blaming someone else. But when something goes wrong in a relationship, it's easy to blame someone else. In fact, in the fixed mindset you have a limited set of choices. One is to blame your own permanent qualities. And one is to blame your partner's. You can see how tempting it is to foist the blame onto the other guy.

As a legacy of my fixed mindset, I still have an irresistible urge to defend myself and assign blame when something in a relationship goes wrong. "It's not my fault!" To deal with this bad habit, my husband and I invented a third party, an imaginary man named Maurice. Whenever I start in on who's to blame, we invoke poor Maurice and pin it on him.

Remember how hard it is for people with the fixed mindset to forgive? Part of it is that they feel branded by a rejection or breakup. But another part is that if they forgive the partner, if they see him or her as a decent person, then they have to shoulder more of the blame themselves: If my partner's a good guy, then I must be a bad guy. I must be the person who was at fault.

The same thing can happen with parents. If you have a troubled relationship with a parent, whose fault is it? If your parents didn't love you enough, were they bad parents or were you unlovable? These are the ugly questions that haunt us within a fixed mindset. Is there a way out?

I had this very dilemma. My mother didn't love me. Most of my life I'd coped with this by blaming her and feeling bitter. But I was no longer satisfied just protecting myself. I longed for a loving relationship with my mother. Yet the last thing I wanted to be was one of those kids who begged for approval from a withholding parent. Then I realized something. I controlled half of the relationship, my half. I could have my half of the relationship. At least I could be the loving daughter I wanted to be. In a sense, it didn't matter what she did. I would still be ahead of where I was.

How did it turn out? I experienced a tremendous sense of growth letting go of my bitterness and stepping forward to have the relationship. The rest is not really relevant since I wasn't seeking validation, but I'll tell you anyway. Something unexpected happened. Three years later, my mother said to me: "If anyone had told me I didn't love my children, I would have been insulted. But now I realize it was true. Whether it was because my parents didn't love us or because I was too involved in myself or because I didn't know what love was, I don't know. But now I know what it is."

From that time until her death twenty-five years later, we became closer and closer. As lively as each of us was, we came even more to life in each other's presence. Once, a few years ago, after she'd had a stroke, the doctors warned me she couldn't speak and might never speak again. I walked into her room, she looked at me and said, "Carol, I love your outfit."

What allowed me to take that first step, to choose growth and risk rejection? In the fixed mindset, I had needed my blame and bitterness. It made me feel more righteous, powerful, and whole than thinking I was at fault. The growth mindset allowed me to give up the blame and move on. The growth mindset gave me a mother.

I remember when we were kids and did something dumb, like drop our ice-cream cone on our foot, we'd turn to our friend and say "Look what you made me do." Blame may make you feel less foolish, but you still have a shoe full of ice cream—and a friend who's on the defensive. In a relationship, the growth mindset lets you rise above blame, understand the problem, and try to fix it—together.

COMPETITION: WHO'S THE GREATEST?

In the fixed mindset, where you've got to keep proving your competence, it's easy to get into a competition with your partner. Who's the smarter, more talented, more likable one?

Susan had a boyfriend who worried that she would be the center of attention and he would be the tagalong. If she were someone, he would be no one. But Martin was far from no one. He was very successful, even revered, in his field. He was handsome and well liked, too. So at first Susan pooh-poohed the whole thing. Then they attended a conference together. They'd arrived separately and, in checking in, Susan had chatted with the friendly hotel staff in the lobby. That evening when the couple walked through the lobby, the whole staff greeted her warmly. Martin grunted. Next, they took a taxi to dinner. Toward the end of the ride, the driver started singing her praises: "You better hold on to her. Yes, sir, she's a good one." Martin winced. The whole weekend continued in this vein, and by the time they got home from the conference their relationship was very strained.

Martin wasn't actively competitive. He didn't try to outdo Susan, he just lamented her seemingly greater popularity. But some partners throw their hats right into the ring.

Cynthia, a scientist, was amazing at almost everything she did—so much so that she left her partners in the dust. That might have been all right if she didn't always venture into their territory. She married an actor, and then started writing plays and acting in them—superbly. She said she was just trying to share his life and his interests, but her part-time hobby outshone his career. He felt he had to escape from the relationship to find himself again. Next, she married a musician who was a great cook, and in no time flat she was tickling the ivories and inventing unbelievable recipes. Once again, the depressed husband eventually fled. Cynthia left her partners no room for their own identity; she needed to equal or surpass them in every skill they arrived with.

There are many good ways to support our partners or show interest in their lives. This is not one of them.

DEVELOPING IN RELATIONSHIPS

When people embark on a relationship, they encounter a partner who is different from them, and they haven't learned how to deal with the differences. In a good relationship, people develop these skills and, as they do, both partners grow and the relationship deepens. But for this to happen, people need to feel they're on the same side.

Laura was lucky. She could be self-centered and defensive. She could yell and pout. But James never took it personally and always felt that she was there for him when he needed her. So when she lashed out, he calmed her down and made her talk things through with him. Over time, she learned to skip the yelling and pouting.

As an atmosphere of trust developed, they became vitally interested in each other's development. James was forming a corporation, and Laura spent hours with him discussing his plans and some of the problems he was encountering. Laura had always dreamed of writing children's books. James got her to spell out her ideas and write a first draft. He urged her to contact someone they knew who was an illustrator. In the context of this relationship, each partner was helping the other to do the things they wanted to do and become the person they wanted to be.

Not long ago, I was talking to a friend about the view some people hold of childrearing—that parents make little difference. In explaining that view, she likened it to a marriage relationship: "It's like partners in a marriage. Each comes to the relationship fully formed, and you don't expect to influence who the partner is."

"Oh no," I replied. "To me the whole point of marriage is to encourage your partner's development and have them encourage yours."

By that I didn't mean a *My Fair Lady* kind of thing where you attempt an extreme makeover on partners, who then feel they aren't good enough as they are. I mean helping partners, within the relationship, to reach their own goals and fulfill their own potential. This is the growth mindset in action.

FRIENDSHIP

Friendships, like partnerships, are places where we have a chance to enhance each other's development, and to validate each other. Both are important. Friends can give each other the wisdom and courage to make growth-enhancing decisions, and friends can reassure each other of their fine qualities. Despite the dangers of praising traits, there are times when we need reassurance about ourselves: "Tell me I'm not a bad person for breaking up with my boyfriend." "Tell me I'm not stupid even though I bombed on the exam."

In fact, these occasions give us a chance to provide support and give a growth message: "You gave that relationship everything you had for three years and he made no effort to improve things. I think you're right to move on." Or "What happened on that exam? Do you understand the material? Did you study enough? Do you think you need a tutor? Let's talk about it."

But as in all relationships, people's need to prove themselves can tilt the balance in the wrong direction. Sheri Levy did a study that was not about friendship, but makes an important and relevant point.

Levy measured adolescent boys' self-esteem and then asked them how much they believed in negative stereotypes about girls. For example, how much did they believe that girls were worse in math or that girls were less rational than boys? She then measured their self-esteem again.

Boys who believed in the fixed mindset showed a boost in self-esteem when they endorsed the stereotypes. Thinking that girls were dumber and more scatterbrained made them feel better about themselves. (Boys with the growth mindset were less likely to agree with the stereotypes, but even when they did, it did not give them an ego boost.)

This mentality can intrude on friendships. *The lower you are, the better I feel* is the idea.

One day I was talking to a dear, wise friend. I was puzzled about why she put up with the behavior of some of her friends. Actually, I was puzzled about why she even had these friends. One often acted irresponsibly; another flirted shamelessly with her husband. Her answer was that everyone has virtues and foibles, and that, really, if you looked only for perfect people, your social circle would be impoverished. There was, however, one thing she would not put up with: People who made her feel bad about herself.

We all know these people. They can be brilliant, charming, and fun, but after being with them, you feel diminished. You may ask: "Am I just doing a number on myself?" But it is often them, trying to build themselves up by establishing their superiority and your inferiority. It could be by actively putting you down, or it could be by the careless way they treat you. Either way, you are a vehicle for (and a casualty of) confirming their worth.

I was at a friend's fiftieth-birthday party and her sister gave a speech, supposedly in her honor. Her sister talked about my friend's insatiable sexual appetite and how lucky it was she found a younger man to marry who could handle it. "All in good fun," she took care of my friend's looks, brains, and mothering skills. After this tribute, I suddenly recalled the saying "With friends like this, you don't need enemies."

It's difficult to realize when friends don't wish you well. One night I had the most vivid dream. Someone, someone I knew well, came into my house and one by one took all my prized possessions. In the dream I could see what was happening, but I couldn't see who it was. At one point, I asked the intruder: "Couldn't you please leave that one, it means a lot to me." But the person just kept taking everything of value. The next morning I realized who it was and what it meant. For the past year a close friend had been calling upon me constantly to help him with his work. I obliged. He was under a great deal of stress, and I was at first happy to use whatever skills I had for his benefit. But it was endless, it was not reciprocal, and on top of that he punished me for it: "Don't think *you* could ever do work this good. You can help me polish my work, but you could never be this creative." He needed to reduce me so he wouldn't feel one down. My dream told me it was time to draw the line.

I'm afraid that in the fixed mindset, I was also a culprit. I don't think I put people down, but when you need validation, you use people for it. One time, when I was a graduate student, I was taking the train to New York and sat next to a very nice businessman. In my opinion, we chatted back and forth pleasantly through the hour-and-a-half journey, but at the end he said to me, "Thank you for telling me about yourself." It really hit me. He was the dream validator—handsome, intelligent, successful. And that's what I had used him for. I had shown no interest in him as a person, only in him as a mirror of my excellence. Luckily for me, what he mirrored back was a far more valuable lesson.

Conventional wisdom says that you know who your friends are in your times of need. And of course this view has merit. Who will stand by you day after day when you're in trouble? However, sometimes an even tougher question is: Who can you turn to when good things happen? When you find a wonderful partner. When you get a great job offer or promotion. When your child does well. Who would be glad to hear it?

Your failures and misfortunes don't threaten other people's self-esteem. Ego-wise, it's easy to be sympathetic to someone in need. It's your assets and your successes that are problems for people who derive their self-esteem from being superior.

SHYNESS

In some ways, shyness is the flip side of what we've been talking about. We've been examining people who use others to buoy themselves up. Shy people worry that others will bring them down. They often worry about being judged or embarrassed in social situations.

People's shyness can hold them back from making friends and developing relationships. When they're with new people, shy people report that they feel anxious, their hearts race, they blush, they avoid eye contact, and they may try to end the interaction as soon as possible. Underneath it all, shy people may be wonderful and interesting, but they often can't show it with someone new. And they know it.

What can mindsets teach us about shyness? Jennifer Beer studied hundreds of people to find out. She measured people's mindsets, she assessed their shyness, and then she brought them together two at a time to get acquainted. The whole thing was filmed, and, later on, trained raters watched the film and evaluated the interactions.

Beer found, first, that people with the fixed mindset were more likely to be shy. This makes sense. The fixed mindset makes you concerned about judgment, and this can make you more self-conscious and anxious. But there were plenty of shy people with both mindsets, and when she looked at them more closely, she found something even more interesting.

Shyness harmed the social interactions of people with the fixed mindset but did not harm the social relations of people with the growth mindset. The observers' ratings showed that, although both fixed- and growth-minded shy people looked very nervous for the first five minutes of the interaction, after that the shy growth-minded people showed greater social skills, were more likable, and created a more enjoyable interaction. In fact, they began to look just like non-shy people.

This happened for good reasons. For one thing, the shy growth-minded people looked on social situations as challenges. Even though they felt anxious, they actively welcomed the chance to meet someone new. The shy fixed people, instead, wanted to avoid meeting someone who might be more socially skilled than they were. They said they were more worried about making mistakes. So the fixed- and growth-mindset people confronted the situation with different attitudes. One embraced the challenge and the other feared the risk.

Armed with these different attitudes, the shy growth-mindset people felt less shy and nervous as the interaction wore on, but the shy fixed-mindset people continued to be nervous and continued to do more socially awkward things, like avoiding eye contact or trying to avoid talking.

You can see how these different patterns would affect making friends. The shy growth-mindset people take control of their shyness. They go out and meet new people, and, after their nerves settle down, their relationships proceed normally. The shyness doesn't tyrannize them.

But for fixed-mindset people, the shyness takes control. It keeps them out of social situations with new people, and when they're in them, they can't let down their guard and let go of their fears.

Scott Wetzler, a therapist and professor of psychiatry, paints a portrait of his client George, a picture of the shy fixed-mindset person. George was incredibly shy, especially with women. He was so eager to look cool, witty, and confident—and so worried that he'd look overeager and inept—that he froze and acted cold. When his attractive co-worker Jean started flirting with him, he became so flustered that he began avoiding her. Then one day she approached him in a nearby coffee shop and cutely suggested he ask her to join him. When he couldn't think of a clever response to impress her, he replied, "It doesn't matter to me if you sit down or not."

George, *what* were you doing? He was trying to protect himself from rejection—by trying not to seem too interested. And he was trying to end this awkward situation. In a strange way, he succeeded. He certainly didn't seem too interested, and the interaction soon ended, as Jean got out of there real fast. He was just like the people in Jennifer Beer's study, controlled by his fear of social judgment and prevented from making contact.

Wetzler slowly helped George get over his exclusive focus on being judged. Jean, he came to see, was not out to judge and humiliate him, but was trying to get to know him. With the focus switched from being judged to developing a relationship, George was eventually able to reciprocate. Despite his anxiety, he approached Jean, apologized for his rude behavior, and asked her to lunch. She accepted. What's more, she was not nearly as critical as he feared.

BULLIES AND VICTIMS: REVENGE REVISITED

We're back to rejection, because it's not just in love relationships that people experience terrible rejections. It happens every day in schools. Starting in grade school, some kids are victimized. They are ridiculed, tormented, and beaten up, not for anything they've done wrong. It could be for their more timid personality, how they look, what their background is, or how smart they are (sometimes they're not smart enough; sometimes they're too smart). It can be a daily occurrence that makes life a nightmare and ushers in years of depression and rage.

To make matters worse, schools often do nothing about it. This is because it's often done out of sight of teachers or because it's done by the school's favorite students, such as the jocks. In this case, it may be the *victims*, not the bullies, who are considered to be the problem kids or the misfits.

As a society, we've paid little attention until recently. Then came the school shootings. At Columbine, the most notorious one, both boys had been mercilessly bullied for years. A fellow bullying victim describes what they endured in their high school.

In the hallways, the jocks would push kids into lockers and call them demeaning names while everyone laughed at the show. At lunch the jocks would knock their victims' food trays onto the floor, trip them, or pelt them with food. While the victims were eating, they would be pushed down onto the table from behind. Then in the locker rooms before gym class, the bullies would beat the kids up because the teachers weren't around.

Who Are the Bullies?

Bullying is about judging. It's about establishing who is more worthy or important. The more powerful kids judge the less powerful kids. They judge them to be less valuable human beings, and they rub their faces in it on a daily basis. And it's clear what the bullies get out of it. Like the boys in Sheri Levy's study, they get a boost in self-esteem. It's not that bullies are low in self-esteem, but judging and demeaning others can give them a self-esteem rush. Bullies also gain social status from their actions. Others may look up to them and judge them to be cool, powerful, or funny. Or may fear them. Either way, they've upped their standing.

There's a big dose of fixed-mindset thinking in the bullies: Some people are superior and some are inferior. And the bullies are the judges. Eric Harris, one of the Columbine shooters, was their perfect target. He had a chest deformity, he was short, he was a computer geek, and he was an outsider, not from Colorado. They judged him mercilessly.

Victims and Revenge

The fixed mindset may also play a role in how the victim reacts to bullying. When people feel deeply judged by a rejection, their impulse is to feel bad about themselves and to lash out in bitterness. They have been cruelly reduced and they wish to reduce in return. In our studies, we have seen perfectly normal people—children and adults—respond to rejection with violent fantasies of revenge.

Highly educated, well-functioning adults, after telling us about a serious rejection or betrayal, say and mean "I wanted him dead" or "I could easily have strangled her."

When we hear about acts of school violence, we usually think it's only bad kids from bad homes who could ever take matters into their own hands. But it's startling how quickly average, everyday kids with a fixed mindset think about violent revenge.

We gave eighth-grade students in one of our favorite schools a scenario about bullying to read. We asked them to imagine it was happening to them.

It is a new school year and things seem to be going pretty well. Suddenly some popular kids start teasing you and calling you names. At first you brush it off—these things happen. But it continues. Every day they follow you, they taunt you, they make fun of what you're wearing, they make fun of what you look like, they tell you you're a loser—in front of everybody. Every day.

We then asked them to write about what they would think and what they would do or want to do.

First, the students with the fixed mindset took the incident more personally. They said, "I would think I was a nobody and that nobody likes me." Or "I would think I was stupid and weird and a misfit."

Then they wanted violent revenge, saying that they'd explode with rage at them, punch their faces in, or run them over. They *strongly* agreed with the statement: "My number one goal would be to get revenge."

They had been judged and they wanted to judge back. That's what Eric Harris and Dylan Klebold, the Columbine shooters, did. They judged back. For a few long, terrible hours, they decided who would live and who would die.

In our study, the students with the growth mindset were not as prone to see the bullying as a reflection of who they were. Instead, they saw it as a psychological problem of the bullies, a way for the bullies to gain status or charge their self-esteem: "I'd think that the reason he is bothering me is probably that he has problems at home or at school with his grades." Or "They need to get a life—not just feel good if they make me feel bad."

Their plan was often designed to educate the bullies: "I would really actually talk to them. I would ask them questions (why are they saying all of these things and why are they doing all of this to me)." Or "Confront the person and discuss the issue; I would feel like trying to help them see they are not funny."

The students with the growth mindset also strongly agreed that: "I would want to forgive them eventually" and "My number one goal would be to help them become better people."

Whether they'd succeed in personally reforming or educating determined bullies is doubtful. However, these are certainly more constructive first steps than running them over.

Brooks Brown, a classmate of Eric Harris and Dylan Klebold, was bullied from third grade on. He suffered tremendously, yet he didn't look for revenge. He rejected the fixed mindset and the right of people to judge others, as in "I am a football player, and therefore I'm better than you." Or "I am a basketball player . . . pathetic geeks like you are not on my level."

More than that, he actively embraced a growth mindset. In his own words, "People do have the potential to change." Even maybe Eric Harris, the more depressed, hostile leader of the shootings. Brown had had a very serious run-in with Eric Harris several years before, but in their senior year of high school, Brown offered a truce. "I told him that I had changed a lot since that year . . . and that I hoped he felt the same way about himself." Brooks went on to say that if he found that Eric hadn't changed, he could always pull back. "However, if he had grown up, then why not give him the chance to prove it."

Brooks hasn't given up. He still wants to change people. He wants to wake up the world to the problem of bullying, and he wants to reach victims and turn them off their violent fantasies. So he's worked for the filmmaker Michael Moore on *Bowling for Columbine* and he's set up an innovative website where bullied kids can communicate with each other and learn that the answer isn't to kill. "It's to use your mind and make things better."

Brooks, like me, does not see the shooters as people who are a world apart from everyone else. His friend Dylan Klebold, he says, was once a regular kid from a fine home with loving, involved parents. In fact, he warns, "We can just sit back and call the shooters 'sick monsters, completely different from us.' . . . Or we can accept that there are more Erics and Dylans out there, who are slowly being driven . . . down the same path."

Even if a victim doesn't have a fixed mindset to begin with, prolonged bullying can instill it. Especially if others stand by and do nothing, or even join in. Victims say that when they're taunted and demeaned and no one comes to their defense, they start to believe they deserve it. They start to judge themselves and to think that they *are* inferior.

Bullies judge. Victims take it in. Sometimes it remains inside and can lead to depression and suicide. Sometimes it explodes into violence.

What Can Be Done?

Individual children can't usually stop the bullies, especially when the bullies attract a group of supporters. But the school can—by changing the school mindset.

School cultures often promote, or at least accept, the fixed mindset. They accept that some kids feel superior to others and feel entitled to pick on them. They also consider some kids to be misfits whom they can do little to help.

But some schools have created a dramatic reduction in bullying by fighting the atmosphere of judgment and creating one of collaboration and self-improvement. Stan Davis, a therapist, school counselor, and consultant, has developed an anti-bullying program that works. Building on the work of Dan Olweus, a researcher in Norway, Davis's program helps bullies change, supports victims, and empowers bystanders to come to a victim's aid. Within a few years, physical bullying in his school was down 93 percent and teasing was down 53 percent.

Darla, a third grader, was overweight, awkward, and a "crybaby." She was such a prime target that half of the class bullied her, hitting her and calling her names on a daily basis—and winning one another's approval for it. Several years later, because of Davis's program, the bullying had stopped. Darla had learned better social skills and even had friends. Then Darla went to middle school and, after a year, came back to report what had happened. Her classmates from elementary school had seen her through. They'd helped her make friends and protected her from her new peers when they wanted to harass her.

· Davis also gets the bullies changing. In fact, some of the kids who rushed to Darla's support in middle school were the same ones who had bullied her earlier. What Davis does is this. First, while enforcing consistent discipline, he doesn't judge the bully as a person. No criticism is directed at traits. Instead, he makes them feel liked and welcome at school every day.

Then he praises every step in the right direction. But again, he does not praise the person; he praises their effort. "I notice that you have been staying out of fights. That tells me you are working on getting along with people." You can see that Davis is leading students directly to the growth mindset. He is helping them see their actions as part of an effort to improve. Even if the change was not intentional on the part of the bullies, they may now try to make it so.

Stan Davis has incorporated our work on praise, criticism, and mindsets into his program, and it has worked. This is a letter I got from him.

Dear Dr. Dweck:

Your research has radically changed the way I work with students. I am already seeing positive results from my own different use of language to give feedback to young people. Next year our whole school is embarking on an initiative to build student motivation based on [growth] feedback.

Yours,
Stan Davis

Haim Ginott, the renowned child psychologist, also shows how teachers can point bullies away from judgment and toward improvement and compassion. Here is a letter from a teacher to an eight-year-old bully in her class. Notice that she doesn't imply he's a bad person, and she shows respect by referring to his leadership, by using big words, and by asking for his advice.

Dear Jay,

Andy's mother has told me that her son has been made very unhappy this year. Name-calling and ostracism have left him sad and lonely. I feel concerned about the situation. Your experience as a leader in your class makes you a likely person for me to turn to for advice. I value your ability to sympathize with those who suffer. Please write me your suggestions about how we can help Andy.

Sincerely,
Your teacher.

In a *New York Times* article on bullying, Eric Harris and Dylan Klebold are referred to as "two misfit teenagers." It's true. They didn't fit in. But you never hear the bullies referred to as misfits. Because they weren't. They fit right in. In fact, they defined and ruled the school culture.

The notion that some people are entitled to brutalize others is not a healthy one. Stan Davis points out that as a society, we rejected the idea that people were entitled to brutalize blacks and harass women. Why do we accept the idea that people are entitled to brutalize our children?

By doing so, we also insult the bullies. We tell them we don't think they're capable of more, and we miss the chance to help them become more.

Grow Your Mindset

- After a rejection, do you feel judged, bitter, and vengeful? Or do you feel hurt, but hopeful of forgiving, learning, and moving on? Think of the worst rejection you ever had. Get in touch with all the feelings, and see if you can view it from a growth mindset. What did you learn from it? Did it teach you something about what you want and don't want in your life? Did it teach you some positive things that were useful in later relationships? Can you forgive that person and wish them well? Can you let go of the bitterness?

- Picture your ideal love relationship. Does it involve perfect compatibility—no disagreements, no compromises, no hard work? Please think again. In every relationship, issues arise. Try to see them from a growth mindset: Problems can be a vehicle for developing greater understanding and intimacy. Allow your partner to air his or her differences, listen carefully, and discuss them in a patient and caring manner. You may be surprised at the closeness this creates.

- Are you a blamer like me? It's not good for a relationship to pin everything on your partner. Create your own Maurice and blame him instead. Better yet, work toward curing yourself of the need to blame. Move beyond thinking about fault and blame all the time. Think of me trying to do that too.

- Are you shy? Then you really need the growth mindset. Even if it doesn't cure your shyness, it will help keep it from messing up your social interactions. Next time you're venturing into a social situation, think about these things: how social skills are things you can improve and how social interactions are for learning and enjoyment, not judgment. Keep practicing this.

Chapter 7

PARENTS, TEACHERS, AND COACHES: WHERE DO MINDSETS COME FROM?

No parent thinks, "I wonder what I can do today to undermine my children, subvert their effort, turn them off learning, and limit their achievement." Of course not. They think, "I would do anything, give anything, to make my children successful." Yet many of the things they do boomerang. Their helpful judgments, their lessons, their motivating techniques often send the wrong message.

In fact, every word and action can send a message. It tells children— or students, or athletes—how to think about themselves. It can be a fixed-mindset message that says: *You have permanent traits and I'm judging them.* Or it can be a growth-mindset message that says: *You are a developing person and I am interested in your development.*

It's remarkable how sensitive children are to these messages, and how concerned they are about them. Haim Ginott, the childrearing sage of the 1950s through '70s, tells this story. Bruce, age five, went with his mother to his new kindergarten. When they arrived, Bruce looked up at the paintings on the wall and said, "Who made those ugly pictures?" His mother rushed to correct him: "It's not nice to call pictures ugly when they are so pretty." But his teacher knew exactly what he meant. "In here," she said, "you don't have to paint pretty pictures. You can paint mean pictures if you feel like it." Bruce gave her a big smile.

She had answered his real question: What happens to a boy who doesn't paint well?

Next, Bruce spotted a broken fire engine. He picked it up and asked in a self-righteous tone, "Who broke this fire engine?" Again his mother rushed in: "What difference does it make to you who broke it? You don't know anyone here." But the teacher understood. "Toys are for playing," she told him. "Sometimes they get broken. It happens." Again, his question was answered: What happens to boys who break toys?

Bruce waved to his mother and went off to start his first day of kindergarten. This was not a place where he would be judged and labeled.

You know, we never outgrow our sensitivity to these messages. Several years ago, my husband and I spent two weeks in Provence, in the south of France. Everyone was wonderful to us—very kind and very generous. But on the last day, we drove to Italy for lunch. When we got there and found a little family restaurant, tears started streaming down my face. I felt so nurtured. I said to David, "You know, in France, when they're nice to you, you feel like you've passed a test. But in Italy, there is no test."

Parents and teachers who send fixed-mindset messages are like France, and parents and teachers who send growth-mindset messages are like Italy.

Let's start with the messages parents send to their children—but, you know, they are also messages that teachers can send to their students or coaches can send to their athletes.

PARENTS (AND TEACHERS):
MESSAGES ABOUT SUCCESS AND FAILURE

Messages About Success

Listen for the messages in the following examples:

"You learned that so quickly! You're so smart!"

"Look at that drawing. Martha, is he the next Picasso or what?"

"You're so brilliant, you got an A without even studying!"

If you're like most parents, you hear these as supportive, esteem-boosting messages. But listen more closely. See if you can hear another message. It's the one that children hear:

If I don't learn something quickly, I'm not smart.

I shouldn't try drawing anything hard or they'll see I'm no Picasso.

I'd better quit studying or they won't think I'm brilliant.

How do I know this? Remember chapter 3, how I was thinking about all the praise parents were lavishing on their kids in the hope of encouraging confidence and achievement? You're so smart. You're so talented. You're such a natural athlete. And I thought, wait a minute. Isn't it the kids with the fixed mindset—the vulnerable kids—who are obsessed with this? Wouldn't harping on intelligence or talent make kids—all kids—even more obsessed with it?

That's why we set out to study this. After seven experiments with hundreds of children, we had some of the clearest findings I've ever seen: Praising children's intelligence harms their motivation and it harms their performance.

How can that be? Don't children love to be praised?

Yes, children love praise. And they especially love to be praised for their intelligence and talent. It really does give them a boost, a special glow—but only for the moment. The minute they hit a snag, their confidence goes out the window and their motivation hits rock bottom. If success means they're smart, then failure means they're dumb. That's the fixed mindset.

Here is the voice of a mother who saw the effects of well-meant praise for intelligence:

I want to share my real-life experience with you. I am the mother of a very intelligent fifth grader. He consistently scores in the 99 percentile on standardized school tests in math, language and science, but he has had some very real "self-worth" problems. My husband, who is also an intelligent person, felt his parents never valued intellect and he has overcompensated with our son in attempting to praise him for "being smart." Over the past years, I have suspected this was causing a problem, because my son, while he easily excels in school, is reluctant to take on more difficult work or projects (just as your studies show) because then he would think he's not smart. He projects an over-inflated view of his abilities and claims he can perform better than others (both intellectually and in physical activities), but will not attempt such activities, because of course, in his failure he would be shattered.

And here is the voice of one of my Columbia students reflecting on his history:

I remember often being praised for my intelligence rather than my efforts, and slowly but surely I developed an aversion to difficult challenges. Most surprisingly, this extended beyond academic and even athletic challenges to emotional challenges. This was my greatest learning disability—this tendency to see performance as a reflection of character and, if I could not accomplish something right away, to avoid that task or treat it with contempt.

I know, it feels almost impossible to resist this kind of praise. We want our loved ones to know that we prize them and appreciate their successes. Even I have fallen into the trap.

One day I came home and my husband, David, had solved a very difficult problem we had been puzzling over for a while. Before I could stop myself, I blurted out: "You're brilliant!" Needless to say, I was appalled at what I had done, and as the look of horror spread over my face, he rushed to reassure me. "I know you meant it in the most 'growth-minded' way. That I searched for strategies, kept at it, tried all kinds of solutions, and finally mastered it."

"Yes," I said, smiling sweetly, "that's *exactly* what I meant."

Parents think they can hand children permanent confidence—like a gift—by praising their brains and talent. It doesn't work, and in fact has the opposite effect. It makes children doubt themselves as soon as anything is hard or anything goes wrong. If parents want to give their children a gift, the best thing they can do is to teach their children to love challenges, be intrigued by mistakes, enjoy effort, and keep on learning. That way, their children don't have to be slaves of praise. They will have a lifelong way to build and repair their own confidence.

SENDING MESSAGES ABOUT PROCESS AND GROWTH

So what's the alternative to praising talent or intelligence? David's reassurance gives us a hint. One of my students tells us more:

> I went home this weekend to find my 12-year-old sister ecstatic about school. I asked what she was so excited about and she said, "I got 102 on my social studies test!" I heard her repeat this phrase about five more times that weekend. At that point I decided to apply what we learned in class to this real-life situation. Rather than praising her intelligence or her grade, I asked questions that made her reflect on the effort she put into studying and on how she has improved from the year before. Last year, her grades dropped lower and lower as the year progressed so I thought it was important for me to intervene and steer her in the right direction at the beginning of this year.

Does this mean we can't praise our children enthusiastically when they do something great? Should we try to restrain our admiration for their successes? Not at all. It just means that we should keep away from a certain *kind* of praise—praise that judges their intelligence or talent. Or praise that implies that we're proud of them for their intelligence or talent rather than for the work they put in.

We can praise them as much as we want for the growth-oriented process—what they accomplished through practice, study, persistence, and good strategies. And we can ask them about their work in a way that admires and appreciates their efforts and choices.

"You really studied for your test and your improvement shows it. You read the material over several times, you outlined it, and you tested yourself on it. It really worked!"

"I like the way you tried all kinds of strategies on that math problem until you finally got it. You thought of a lot of different ways to do it and found the one that worked!"

"I like that you took on that challenging project for your science class. It will take a lot of work—doing the research, designing the apparatus, buying the parts, and building it. Boy, you're going to learn a lot of great things."

"I know school used to be easy for you and you used to feel like the smart kid all the time. But the truth is that you weren't using your brain to the fullest. I'm really excited about how you're stretching yourself now and working to learn hard things."

"That homework was so long and involved. I really admire the way you concentrated and finished it."

"That picture has so many beautiful colors. Tell me about them."

"You put so much thought into this essay. It really makes me understand Shakespeare in a new way."

"The passion you put into that piano piece gives me a real feeling of joy. How do you feel when you play it?"

What about a student who worked hard and *didn't* do well?

"I liked the effort you put in, but let's work together some more and figure out what it is you don't understand."

"We all have different learning curves. It may take more time for you to catch on to this and be comfortable with this material, but if you keep at it like this you will."

"Everyone learns in a different way. Let's keep trying to find the way that works for you."

(This may be especially important for children with learning disabilities. Often for them it is not sheer effort that works but finding the right strategy.)

I was excited to learn recently that Haim Ginott, through his lifelong work with children, came to the same conclusion. "Praise should deal, not with the child's personality attributes, but with his efforts and achievements."

Sometimes people are careful to use growth-oriented praise with their children but then ruin it by the way they talk about others. I have heard parents say in front of their children, "He's just a born loser," "She's a natural genius," or "She's a pea-brain." When children hear their parents level fixed judgments at others, it communicates a fixed mindset. And they have to wonder, *Am I next?*

This caveat applies to teachers, too! In one study, we taught students a math lesson spiced up with some math history, namely, stories about great mathematicians. For half of the students, we talked about the mathematicians as geniuses who easily came up with their math discoveries. This alone propelled students into a fixed mindset. It sent the message: *There are some people who are born smart in math and everything is easy for them. Then there are the rest of you.* For the other half of the students, we talked about the mathematicians as people who became passionate about math and ended up making great discoveries. This brought students into a growth mindset. The message was: *Skills and achievement come through commitment and effort.* It's amazing how kids sniff out these messages from our innocent remarks.

One more thing about praise. When we say to children, "Wow, you did that so quickly!" or "Look, you didn't make any mistakes!" what message are we sending? We are telling them that what we prize are speed and perfection. Speed and perfection are the enemy of difficult learning: "If you think I'm smart when I'm fast and perfect, I'd better not take on anything challenging." So what *should* we say when children complete a task—say, math problems—quickly and perfectly? Should we deny them the praise they have earned? Yes. When this happens, I say, "Whoops. I guess that was too easy. I apologize for wasting your time. Let's do something you can really learn from!"

REASSURING CHILDREN

How do you make a child feel secure before a test or performance? The same principle applies. Reassuring children about their intelligence or talent backfires. They'll only be more afraid to show a deficiency.

Kristina was a really bright high school student who, much to her shame, did terribly on tests. She always studied, she always knew the material, but every time it came to the test, she got so wound up that her mind went blank. Her grades suffered. She disappointed her teachers.

She let her parents down. And it was only going to get worse as she faced the College Board tests that the schools she longed to attend prized so highly.

The night before each test, her parents, seeing how distraught she was, tried to build her confidence. "Look, *you* know how smart you are and *we* know how smart you are. You've got this nailed. Now, stop worrying."

They were as supportive as they knew how to be, but they were raising the stakes even higher. What could they have said instead?

"It must be a terrible thing to feel that everyone is evaluating you and you can't show what you know. We want you to know that we are not evaluating you. We care about your learning, and we know that you've learned your stuff. We're proud that you've stuck to it and kept learning."

Messages About Failure

Praising success should be the least of our problems, right? Failure seems like a much more delicate matter. Children may already feel discouraged and vulnerable. Let's tune in again, this time to the messages parents can send in times of failure.

Nine-year-old Elizabeth was on her way to her first gymnastics meet. Lanky, flexible, and energetic, she was just right for gymnastics, and she loved it. Of course, she was a little nervous about competing, but she was good at gymnastics and felt confident of doing well. She had even thought about the perfect place in her room to hang the ribbon she would win.

In the first event, the floor exercises, Elizabeth went first. Although she did a nice job, the scoring changed after the first few girls and she lost. Elizabeth also did well in the other events, but not well enough to win. By the end of the evening, she had received no ribbons and was devastated.

What would you do if you were Elizabeth's parents?

1. Tell Elizabeth *you* thought she was the best.
2. Tell her she was robbed of a ribbon that was rightfully hers.
3. Reassure her that gymnastics is not that important.

4. Tell her she has the ability and will surely win next time.
5. Tell her she didn't deserve to win.

There is a strong message in our society about how to boost children's self-esteem, and a main part of that message is: *Protect them from failure!* While this may help with the immediate problem of a child's disappointment, it can be harmful in the long run. Why?

Let's look at the five possible reactions from a mindset point of view—and listen to the messages:

The first (*you* thought she was the best) is basically insincere. She was not the best—you know it, and she does, too. This offers her no recipe for how to recover or how to improve.

The second (she was robbed) places blame on others, when in fact the problem was mostly with her performance, not the judges. Do you want her to grow up blaming others for her deficiencies?

The third (reassure her that gymnastics doesn't really matter) teaches her to devalue something if she doesn't do well in it right away. Is this really the message you want to send?

The fourth (she has the ability) may be the most dangerous message of all. Does ability automatically take you where you want to go? If Elizabeth didn't win this meet, why should she win the next one?

The last option (tell her she didn't deserve to win) seems hardhearted under the circumstances. And of course you wouldn't say it quite that way. But that's pretty much what her growth-minded father told her.

Here's what he actually said: "Elizabeth, I know how you feel. It's so disappointing to have your hopes up and to perform your best but not to win. But you know, you haven't really earned it yet. There were many girls there who've been in gymnastics longer than you and who've worked a lot harder than you. If this is something you really want, then it's something you'll really have to work for."

He also let Elizabeth know that if she wanted to do gymnastics purely for fun, that was just fine. But if she wanted to excel in the competitions, more was required.

Elizabeth took this to heart, spending much more time repeating and perfecting her routines, especially the ones she was weakest in. At the next meet, there were eighty girls from all over the region. Elizabeth won five ribbons for the individual events and was the overall champion of the competition, hauling home a giant trophy. By now, her room is so covered with awards, you can hardly see the walls.

In essence, her father not only told her the truth, but also taught her how to learn from her failures and do what it takes to succeed in the future. He sympathized deeply with her disappointment, but he did not give her a phony boost that would only lead to further disappointment.

I've met with many coaches and they ask me: "What happened to the coachable athletes? Where did they go?" Many of the coaches lament that when they give their athletes corrective feedback, the athletes grumble that their confidence is being undermined. Sometimes the athletes phone home and complain to their parents. They seem to want coaches who will simply tell them how talented they are and leave it at that.

The coaches say that in the old days after a little league game or a kiddie soccer game, parents used to review and analyze the game on the way home and give helpful (process) tips. Now on the ride home, they say, parents heap blame on the coaches and referees for the child's poor performance or the team's loss. They don't want to harm the child's confidence by putting the blame on the child.

But as in the example of Elizabeth above, children need honest and constructive feedback. If children are "protected" from it, they won't learn well. They will experience advice, coaching, and feedback as negative and undermining. Withholding constructive criticism does not help children's confidence; it harms their future.

CONSTRUCTIVE CRITICISM: MORE ABOUT FAILURE MESSAGES

We always hear the term *constructive criticism*. But doesn't everyone think the criticism they give their children is constructive? Why would they give it if they didn't think it was helpful? Yet a lot if it is not helpful at all. It's full of judgment about the child. *Constructive* means helping the child to fix something, build a better product, or do a better job.

Billy rushed through his homework, skipping several questions and answering the others in a short, sloppy way. His father hit the roof. "*This* is your homework? Can't you ever get it right? You are either dense or irresponsible. Which is it?" The feedback managed to question his son's intelligence and character at the same time and to imply that the defects were permanent.

How could the dad have expressed his frustration and disappointment without assassinating his son's attributes? Here are some ways.

"Son, it really makes me upset when you don't do a full job. When do you think you can complete this?"

"Son, is there something you didn't understand in the assignment? Would you like me to go over it with you?"

"Son, I feel sad when I see you missing a chance to learn. Can you think of a way to do this that would help you learn more?"

"Son, this looks like a really boring assignment. You have my sympathy. Can you think of a way to make it more interesting?" or "Let's try to think of a way to lessen the pain and still do a good job. Do you have any ideas?"

"Son, remember I told you how tedious things help us learn to concentrate? This one is a real challenge. This will really take all your concentration skills. Let's see if you can concentrate through this whole assignment!"

Sometimes children will judge and label themselves. Ginott tells of Philip, age fourteen, who was working on a project with his father and accidentally spilled nails all over the floor. He guiltily looked at his dad and said:

PHILIP: Gee, I'm so clumsy.
FATHER: That's not what we say when nails spill.
PHILIP: What do you say?
FATHER: You say, the nails spilled—I'll pick them up!
PHILIP: Just like that?
FATHER: Just like that.
PHILIP: Thanks, Dad.

Children Learn the Messages

Kids with the fixed mindset tell us they get constant messages of judgment from their parents. They say they feel as though their traits are being measured all the time.

We asked them: "Suppose your parents offer to help you with your schoolwork. Why would they do this?"

They said: "The real reason is that they wanted to see how smart I was at the schoolwork I was working on."

We asked: "Suppose your parents are happy that you got a good grade. Why would that be?"

They said: "They were happy to see I was a smart kid."

We asked: "Suppose your parents discussed your performance with you when you did poorly on something in school. Why would they do this?"

They said: "They might have been worried I wasn't one of the bright kids," and "They think bad grades might mean I'm not smart."

So every time something happens, these children hear a message of judgment.

Maybe all kids think their parents are judging them. Isn't that what parents do—nag and judge? That's not what students with the growth mindset think. They think their parents are just trying to encourage learning and good study habits. Here's what they say about their parents' motives:

Q: Suppose your parents offer to help you with your school-work. Why would they do this?
A: They wanted to make sure I learned as much as I could from my schoolwork.
Q: Suppose your parents are happy that you got a good grade.
A: They're happy because a good grade means that I really stuck to my work.
Q: Suppose your parents discussed your performance with you when you did poorly on something in school.
A: They wanted to teach me ways to study better in the future.

Even when it was about their conduct or their relationships, the kids with the fixed mindset felt judged, but the kids with the growth mindset felt helped.

> Q: Imagine that your parents became upset when you didn't do what they asked you to do. Why would they be this way?
>
> FIXED-MINDSET CHILD: They were worried I might be a bad kid.
>
> GROWTH-MINDSET CHILD: They wanted to help me learn ways of doing it better next time.

All kids misbehave. Research shows that normal young children misbehave every three minutes. Does it become an occasion for judgment of their character or an occasion for teaching?

> Q: Imagine that your parents were unhappy when you didn't share with other kids. Why would they be this way?
>
> FIXED-MINDSET CHILD: They thought it showed them what kind of person I was.
>
> GROWTH-MINDSET CHILD: They wanted to help me learn better skills for getting along with other kids.

Children learn these lessons early. Children as young as toddlers pick up these messages from their parents, learning that their mistakes are worthy of judgment and punishment. Or learning that their mistakes are an occasion for suggestions and teaching.

Here's a kindergarten boy we will never forget. You will hear him role-playing different messages from his two parents. This is the situation: He wrote some numbers in school, they contained an error, and now he tells us how his parents would react.

> MOTHER: Hello. What are you sad about?
>
> BOY: I gave my teacher some numbers and I skipped the number 8 and now I'm feeling sad.
>
> MOTHER: Well, there's one thing that can cheer you up.

BOY: What?

MOTHER: If you really tell your teacher that you tried your best, she wouldn't be mad at you. [Turning to father] We're not mad, are we?

FATHER: Oh, yes we are! Son, you better go right to your room.

I wish I could tell you he listened to his mother's growth-oriented message. But in our study, he seemed to heed the judgmental message of his dad, downgrading himself for his errors and having no good plan for fixing them. Yet at least he had his mother's effort message that he could, hopefully, put to use in the future.

Parents start interpreting and reacting to their child's behavior at minute one. A new mother tries to nurse her baby. The baby cries and won't nurse. Or takes a few sucks, gives up, and starts screaming. Is the baby stubborn? Is the baby deficient? After all, isn't nursing an inborn reflex? Aren't babies supposed to be "naturals" at nursing? What's wrong with my baby?

A new mother in this situation told me: "At first I got really frustrated. Then I kept your work in mind. I kept saying to my baby, 'We're both learning how to do this. I know you're hungry. I know it's frustrating, but we're learning.' This way of thinking helped me stay cool and guide her through till it worked. It also helped me understand my baby better so I knew how to teach her other things, too."

Don't judge. Teach. It's a learning process.

CHILDREN PASS ON THE MESSAGES

Another way we know that children learn these messages is that we can see how they pass them on. Even young children are ready to pass on the wisdom they've learned. We asked second-grade children: "What advice would you give to a child in your class who was having trouble in math?" Here's the advice from a child with the growth mindset:

Do you quit a lot? Do you think for a minute and then stop? If you do, you should think for a long time—two minutes maybe and if you can't get it you should read the problem again. If you can't get it then, you should raise your hand and ask the teacher.

Isn't that the greatest? The advice from children with the fixed mindset was not nearly as useful. Since there's no recipe for success in the fixed mindset, their advice tended to be short and sweet. "I'm sorry" was the advice of one child as he offered his condolences.

Even *babies* can pass along the messages they've received. Mary Main and Carol George studied abused children, who had been judged and punished by their parents for crying or making a fuss. Abusive parents often don't understand that children's crying is a signal of their needs, or that babies can't stop crying on command. Instead, they judge the child as disobedient, willful, or bad for crying.

Main and George watched the abused children (who were one to three years old) in their day care setting, observing how they reacted when other children were in distress and crying. The abused children often became angry at the distressed children, and some even tried to assault them. They had gotten the message that children who cry are to be judged and punished.

We often think that the legacy of abuse gets passed on to others only when the victims of abuse become parents. But this amazing study shows that children learn lessons early and they act on them.

How did *non*abused children react to their distressed classmate, by the way? They showed sympathy. Many went over to the crying child to see what was wrong and to see if they could help out.

ISN'T DISCIPLINE TEACHING?

Many parents think that when they judge and punish, they *are* teaching, as in "I'll teach you a lesson you'll never forget." What are they teaching? They are teaching their children that if they go against the parents' rules or values, they'll be judged and punished. They're not teaching their children how to think through the issues and come to ethical, mature decisions on their own.

And chances are, they're not teaching their children that the channels of communication are open.

Sixteen-year-old Alyssa came to her mother and said that she and her friends wanted to try alcohol. Could she invite them over for a "cocktail party"? On the face of it, this might seem outrageous. But here's what Alyssa meant. She and her friends had been going to parties where alcohol was available, but they didn't want to try it in a setting where they didn't feel safe and in control. They also didn't want to drive home after drinking. They wanted to try it in a supervised setting, with their parents' permission, where their parents could come and pick them up afterward.

It doesn't matter whether Alyssa's parents said yes or no. They had a full discussion of the issues involved. They had a far more instructive discussion than what would have followed from an outraged, angry, and judgmental dismissal.

It's not that growth-minded parents indulge and coddle their children. Not at all. They set high standards, but they teach the children how to reach them. They say no, but it's a fair, thoughtful, and respectful no. Next time you're in a position to discipline, ask yourself, What is the message I'm sending here: *I will judge and punish you*? Or *I will help you think and learn*?

MINDSETS CAN BE A LIFE-AND-DEATH MATTER

Of course parents want the best for their children, but sometimes parents put their children in danger. As the director of undergraduate studies for my department at Columbia, I saw a lot of students in trouble. Here is the story of a great kid who almost didn't make it.

Sandy showed up in my office at Columbia one week before graduation. She wanted to change her major to psychology. This is basically a wacky request, but I sensed her desperation and listened carefully to her story. When I looked over her record, it was filled with A+'s and F's. What was going on?

Sandy had been groomed by her parents to go to Harvard. Because of their fixed mindset, the only goal of Sandy's education was to prove her worth and competence (and perhaps theirs) by gaining admission to Harvard. Going there would mean that she was truly intelligent. For them, it was not about learning. It was not about pursuing her love of science. It was not even about making a great contribution. It was about the label. But she didn't get in. And she fell into a depression that had plagued her ever since. Sometimes she managed to work effectively (the A+'s), but sometimes she did not (the F's).

I knew that if I didn't help her she wouldn't graduate, and if she didn't graduate she wouldn't be able to face her parents. And if she couldn't face her parents, I didn't know what would happen.

I was legitimately able to help Sandy graduate, but that isn't really the point. It's a real tragedy to take a brilliant and wonderful kid like Sandy and crush her with the weight of these labels.

I hope these stories will teach parents to "want the best" for their children in the right way—by fostering their interests, growth, and learning.

WANTING THE BEST IN THE WORST WAY

Let's look more closely at the message from Sandy's parents: *We don't care about who you are, what you're interested in, and what you can become. We don't care about learning. We will love and respect you only if you go to Harvard.*

Mark's parents felt the same way. Mark was an exceptional math student, and as he finished junior high he was excited about going to Stuyvesant High School, a special high school in New York with a strong math-and-science curriculum. There, he would study math with the best teachers and talk math with the most advanced students in the city. Stuyvesant also had a program that would let him take college math courses at Columbia as soon as he was ready.

But at the last moment, his parents would not let him go. They had heard that it was hard to get into Harvard from Stuyvesant. So they made him go to a different high school.

It didn't matter that he wouldn't be able to pursue his interests or develop his talents as well. Only one thing mattered, and it starts with an *H*.

"WE LOVE YOU—ON OUR TERMS"

It's not just *I'm judging you*. It's *I'm judging you and I'll only love you if you succeed—on my terms*.

We've studied kids ranging from six years old to college age. Those with the fixed mindset feel their parents won't love and respect them unless they fulfill their parents' aspirations for them. The college students say:

"I often feel like my parents won't value me if I'm not as successful as they would like."

Or: "My parents say I can be anything I like, but deep down I feel they won't approve of me unless I pursue a profession they admire."

John McEnroe's father was like that. He was judgmental—everything was black-and-white—and he put on the pressure. "My parents pushed me. . . . My dad was the one mainly. He seemed to live for my growing little junior career. . . . I remember telling my dad that I wasn't enjoying it. I'd say, 'Do you have to come to every match? Do you have to come to this practice? Can't you take one off?' "

McEnroe brought his father the success he craved, but McEnroe didn't enjoy a moment of it. He says he enjoyed the *consequences* of his success—being at the top, the adulation, and the money. However, he says, "Many athletes seem truly to love to play their sport. I don't think I ever felt that way about tennis."

I think he did love it at the very beginning, because he talks about how at first he was fascinated by all the different ways you could hit a ball and create new shots. But we never hear about that kind of fascination again. Mr. McEnroe saw his boy was good at tennis and on went the pressure, the judgment, and the love that depended on his son's success.

Tiger Woods's father presents a contrast. There's no doubt that this guy is ambitious. He also sees his son as a chosen person with a God-given destiny, but he fostered Tiger's love of golf and raised Tiger to focus on growth and learning. "If Tiger had wanted to be a plumber, I wouldn't have minded, as long as he was a hell of a plumber. The goal was for him to be a good person. He's a great person." Tiger says in return, "My parents have been the biggest influence in my life. They taught me to give of myself, my time, talent, and, most of all, my love." This shows that you can have superinvolved parents who still foster *the child's own growth,* rather than replacing it with their own pressure and judgments.

Dorothy DeLay, the famous violin teacher, encountered pressure-cooker parents all the time. Parents who cared more about talent, image, and labels than about the child's long-term learning.

One set of parents brought their eight-year-old boy to play for DeLay. Despite her warnings, they had made him memorize the Beethoven violin concerto. He was note-perfect, but he played like a frightened robot. They had, in fact, ruined his playing to suit their idea of talent, as in, "My eight-year-old can play the Beethoven violin concerto. What can yours do?"

DeLay spent countless hours with a mother who insisted it was time for her son to be signed by a fancy talent agency. But had she followed DeLay's advice? No. For quite a while, DeLay had been warning her that her son didn't have a large enough repertoire. Rather than heeding the expert advice and fostering her son's development, however, the mother refused to believe that anyone could turn down a talent like his for such a slight reason.

In sharp contrast was Yura Lee's mother. Mrs. Lee always sat serenely during Yura's lesson, without the tension and frantic note taking of some of the other parents. She smiled, she swayed to the music, she enjoyed herself. As a result, Yura did not develop the anxieties and insecurities that children with overinvested, judgmental parents do. Says Yura, "I'm always happy when I play."

IDEALS

Isn't it natural for parents to set goals and have ideals for their children? Yes, but some ideals are helpful and others are not. We asked college students to describe their ideal of a successful student. And we asked them to tell us how they thought they measured up to that ideal.

Students with the fixed mindset described ideals that could not be worked toward. You had it or you didn't.

"The ideal successful student is one who comes in with innate talent."

"Genius, physically fit and good at sports. . . . They got there based on natural ability."

Did they think they measured up to their ideal? Mostly not. Instead, they said these ideals disrupted their thinking, made them procrastinate, made them give up, and made them stressed-out. They were demoralized by the ideal they could never hope to be.

Students with the growth mindset described ideals like these:

"A successful student is one whose primary goal is to expand their knowledge and their ways of thinking and investigating the world. They do not see grades as an end in themselves but as means to continue to grow."

Or: "The ideal student values knowledge for its own sake, as well as for its instrumental uses. He or she hopes to make a contribution to society at large."

Were they similar to their ideal? They were working toward it. "As similar as I can be—hey, it takes effort." Or: "I believed for many years that grades/tests were the most important thing but I am trying to move beyond that." Their ideals were inspiring to them.

When parents give their children a fixed-mindset ideal, they are asking them to fit the mold of the brilliant, talented child, or be deemed unworthy. There is no room for error. And there is no room for the children's individuality—their interests, their quirks, their desires and values. I can hardly count the times fixed-mindset parents have wrung their hands and told me how their children were rebelling or dropping out.

Haim Ginott describes Nicholas, age seventeen:

In my father's mind there is a picture of an ideal son. When he compares him to me, he is deeply disappointed. I don't live up to my father's dream. Since early childhood, I sensed his disappointment. He tried to hide it, but it came out in a hundred little ways—in his tone, in his words, in his silence. He tried hard to make me a carbon copy of his dreams. When he failed he gave up on me. But he left a deep scar, a permanent feeling of failure.

When parents help their children construct growth-minded ideals, they are giving them something they can strive for. They are also giving their children growing room, room to grow into full human beings who will make their contribution to society in a way that excites them. I have rarely heard a growth-minded parent say, "I am disappointed in my child." Instead, with a beaming smile, they say, "I am amazed at the incredible person my child has become."

Everything I've said about parents applies to teachers, too. But teachers have additional concerns. They face large classes of students with differing skills, whose past learning they've had no part in. What's the best way to educate these students?

TEACHERS (AND PARENTS):
WHAT MAKES A GREAT TEACHER (OR PARENT)?

Many educators think that lowering their standards will give students success experiences, boost their self-esteem, and raise their achievement. It comes from the same philosophy as the overpraising of students' intelligence. Well, it doesn't work. Lowering standards just leads to poorly educated students who feel entitled to easy work and lavish praise.

For thirty-five years, Sheila Schwartz taught aspiring English teachers. She tried to set high standards, especially since they were going to pass on their knowledge to generations of children. But they became indignant. "One student, whose writing was full of grammatical mistakes and misspellings," she says, "marched into my office with her husband from West Point—in a dress uniform, his chest covered with ribbons—because her feelings had been hurt by my insistence on correct spelling."

Another student was asked to summarize the theme of *To Kill a Mockingbird,* Harper Lee's novel about a southern lawyer fighting prejudice and (unsuccessfully) defending a black man accused of murder. The student insisted the theme was that "all people are basically nice." When Schwartz questioned that conclusion, the student left the class and reported her to the dean. Schwartz was reprimanded for having standards that were too high. Why, Schwartz asks, should the low standards of these future teachers be honored above the needs of the children they will one day teach?

On the other hand, simply raising standards in our schools, without giving students the means of reaching them, is a recipe for disaster. It just pushes the poorly prepared or poorly motivated students into failure and out of school.

Is there a way to set standards high *and* have students reach them?

In chapter 3, we saw in the work of Falko Rheinberg that teachers with the growth mindset brought many low achievers up into the high-achieving range. We saw in the growth-minded teaching of Jaime Escalante that inner-city high school students could learn college calculus, and in the growth-minded teaching of Marva Collins that inner-city grade school children could read Shakespeare. In this chapter, we'll see more. We'll see *how* growth-oriented teaching unleashes children's minds.

I'll focus on three great teachers, two who worked with students who are considered "disadvantaged" and one who worked with students considered supertalented. What do these great teachers have in common?

Great Teachers

The great teachers believe in the growth of the intellect and talent, and they are fascinated with the process of learning.

Marva Collins taught Chicago children who had been judged and discarded. For many, her classroom was their last stop. One boy had been in and out of thirteen schools in four years. One stabbed children with pencils and had been thrown out of a mental health center. One eight-year-old would remove the blade from the pencil sharpener and cut up his classmates' coats, hats, gloves, and scarves. One child referred to killing himself in almost every sentence. One hit another student with a hammer on his first day. These children hadn't learned much in school, but everyone knew it was their own fault. Everyone but Collins.

When *60 Minutes* did a segment on Collins's classroom, Morley Safer tried his best to get a child to say he didn't like the school. "It's so hard here. There's no recess. There's no gym. They work you all day. You have only forty minutes for lunch. Why do you like it? It's just too hard."

But the student replied, "That's why I like it, because it makes your brains bigger."

Chicago Sun-Times writer Zay Smith interviewed one of the children: "We do hard things here. They fill your brain."

As Collins looks back on how she got started, she says, "I have always been fascinated with learning, with the *process* of discovering something new, and it was exciting to share in the discoveries made by my . . . students." On the first day of school, she always promised her students—all students—that they would learn. She forged a contract with them.

"I know most of you can't spell your name. You don't know the alphabet, you don't know how to read, you don't know homonyms or how to syllabicate. I promise you that you will. None of you has ever failed. School may have failed you. Well, goodbye to failure, children. Welcome to success. You will read hard books in here and understand what you read. You will write every day. . . . But you must help me to help you. If you don't give anything, don't expect anything. Success is not coming to you, you must come to it."

Her joy in her students' learning was enormous. As they changed from children who arrived with "toughened faces and glassed-over eyes" to children who were beginning to brim with enthusiasm, she told them, "I don't know what St. Peter has planned for me, but you children are giving me my heaven on earth."

Rafe Esquith teaches Los Angeles second graders from poor areas plagued with crime. Many live with people who have drug, alcohol, and emotional problems. Every day he tells his students that he is no smarter than they are—just more experienced. He constantly makes them see how much they have grown intellectually—how assignments that were once hard have become easier because of their practice and discipline.

Unlike Collins's school or Esquith's school, the Juilliard School of music accepts only the most talented students in the world. You would think the idea would be, *You're all talented, now let's get down to learning.* But if anything, the idea of talent and genius looms even larger there. In fact, many teachers mentally weeded out the students they weren't going to bother with. Except for Dorothy DeLay, the wondrous violin teacher of Itzhak Perlman, Midori, and Sarah Chang.

DeLay's husband always teased her about her "midwestern" belief that anything is possible. "Here is the empty prairie—let's build a city." That's exactly why she loved teaching. For her, teaching was about watching something grow before her very eyes. And the challenge was to figure out how to make it happen. If students didn't play in tune, it was because they hadn't learned how.

Her mentor and fellow teacher at Juilliard, Ivan Galamian, would say, "Oh, he has no ear. Don't waste your time." But she would insist on experimenting with different ways of changing that. (*How* can I do it?) And she usually found a way. As more and more students wanted a part of this mindset and as she "wasted" more and more of her time on these efforts, Galamian tried to get the president of Juilliard to fire her.

It's interesting. Both DeLay and Galamian valued talent, but Galamian believed that talent was inborn and DeLay believed that it was a quality that could be acquired. "I think it's too easy for a teacher to say, 'Oh this child wasn't born with it, so I won't waste my time.' Too many teachers hide their own lack of ability behind that statement."

DeLay gave her all to every one of her students. Itzhak Perlman was her student and so was his wife, Toby, who says that very few teachers get even a fraction of an Itzhak Perlman in a lifetime. "She got the whole thing, but I don't believe she gave him more than she gave me . . . and I believe I am just one of many, many such people." Once DeLay was asked, about another student, why she gave so much time to a pupil who showed so little promise. "I think she has something special. . . . It's in her person. There is some kind of dignity." If DeLay could get her to put it into her playing, that student would be a special violinist.

High Standards and a Nurturing Atmosphere

Great teachers set high standards for all their students, not just the ones who are already achieving. Marva Collins set extremely high standards, right from the start. She introduced words and concepts that were, at first, way above what her students could grasp. Yet she established on Day One an atmosphere of genuine affection and concern as she promised students they would produce: "I'm gonna love you . . . I love you already, and I'm going to love you even when you don't love yourself," she said to the boy who wouldn't try.

Do teachers have to love all of their students? No, but they have to care about every single student.

Teachers with the fixed mindset create an atmosphere of judging. These teachers look at students' beginning performance and decide who's smart and who's dumb. Then they give up on the "dumb" ones. "They're not *my* responsibility."

These teachers don't believe in improvement, so they don't try to create it. Remember the fixed-mindset teachers in chapter 3 who said:

"According to my experience students' achievement mostly remains constant in the course of a year."

"As a teacher I have no influence on students' intellectual ability."

This is how stereotypes work. Stereotypes tell teachers which groups are bright and which groups are not. So teachers with the fixed mindset know which students to give up on before they've even met them.

More on High Standards and a Nurturing Atmosphere

When Benjamin Bloom studied his 120 world-class concert pianists, sculptors, swimmers, tennis players, mathematicians, and research neurologists, he found something fascinating. For most of them, their first teachers were incredibly warm and accepting. Not that they set low standards. Not at all, but they created an atmosphere of trust, not judgment. It was, "I'm going to teach you," not "I'm going to judge your talent."

As you look at what Collins and Esquith demanded of their students—all their students—it's almost shocking. When Collins expanded her school to include young children, she required that every four-year-old who started in September be reading by Christmas. And they all were. The three- and four-year-olds used a vocabulary book titled *Vocabulary for the High School Student*. The seven-year-olds were reading *The Wall Street Journal*. For older children, a discussion of Plato's *Republic* led to discussions of de Tocqueville's *Democracy in America*, Orwell's *Animal Farm*, Machiavelli, and the Chicago city council. Her reading list for the late-grade-school children included *The Complete Plays of Anton Chekhov, Physics Through Experiment,* and *The Canterbury Tales.* Oh, and always Shakespeare. Even the boys who picked their teeth with switchblades, she says, loved Shakespeare and always begged for more.

Yet Collins maintained an extremely nurturing atmosphere. A very strict and disciplined one, but a loving one. Realizing that her students were coming from teachers who made a career of telling them what was wrong with them, she quickly made known her complete commitment to them as her students and as people.

Esquith bemoans the lowering of standards. Recently, he tells us, his school celebrated reading scores that were twenty points below the national average. Why? Because they were a point or two higher than the year before. "Maybe it's important to look for the good and be optimistic," he says, "but delusion is not the answer. Those who celebrate failure will not be around to help today's students celebrate their jobs flipping burgers. . . . Someone has to tell children if they are behind, and lay out a plan of attack to help them catch up."

All of his fifth graders master a reading list that includes *Of Mice and Men, Native Son, Bury My Heart at Wounded Knee, The Joy Luck Club, The Diary of Anne Frank, To Kill a Mockingbird,* and *A Separate Peace.* Every one of his sixth graders passes an algebra final that would reduce most eighth and ninth graders to tears. But again, all is achieved in an atmosphere of affection and deep personal commitment to every student.

"Challenge and nurture" describes DeLay's approach, too. One of her former students expresses it this way: "That is part of Miss DeLay's genius—to put people in the frame of mind where they can do their best. . . . Very few teachers can actually get you to your ultimate potential. Miss DeLay has that gift. She challenges you at the same time that you feel you are being nurtured."

Hard Work and More Hard Work

But are challenge and love enough? Not quite. All great teachers teach students *how* to reach the high standards. Collins and Esquith didn't hand their students a reading list and wish them *bon voyage.* Collins's students read and discussed every line of *Macbeth* in class. Esquith spent hours planning what chapters they would read in class. "I know which child will handle the challenge of the most difficult paragraphs, and carefully plan a passage for the shy youngster . . . who will begin his journey as a good reader. Nothing is left to chance. . . . It takes enormous energy, but to be in a room with young minds who hang on every word of a classic book and beg for more if I stop makes all the planning worthwhile."

What are they teaching the students en route? To love learning. To eventually learn and think for themselves. And to work hard on the fundamentals. Esquith's class often met before school, after school, and on school vacations to master the fundamentals of English and math, especially as the work got harder. His motto: "There are no shortcuts." Collins echoes that idea as she tells her class, "There is no magic here. Mrs. Collins is no miracle worker. I do not walk on water, I do not part the sea. I just love children and work harder than a lot of people, and so will you."

DeLay expected a lot from her students, but she, too, guided them there. Most students are intimidated by the idea of talent, and it keeps them in a fixed mindset. But DeLay demystified talent. One student was sure he couldn't play a piece as fast as Itzhak Perlman. So she didn't let him see the metronome until he had achieved it. "I know so surely that if he had been handling that metronome, as he approached that number he would have said to himself, I can never do this as fast as Itzhak Perlman, and he would have stopped himself."

Another student was intimidated by the beautiful sound made by talented violinists. "We were working on my sound, and there was this one note I played, and Miss DeLay stopped me and said, 'Now *that* is a beautiful sound.'" She then explained how every note has to have a beautiful beginning, middle, and end, leading into the next note. And he thought, "Wow! If I can do it there, I can do it everywhere." Suddenly the beautiful sound of Perlman made sense and was not just an overwhelming concept.

When students don't know how to do something and others do, the gap seems unbridgeable. Some educators try to reassure their students that they're just fine as they are. Growth-minded teachers tell students the truth and then give them the tools to close the gap. As Marva

Collins said to a boy who was clowning around in class, "You are in sixth grade and your reading score is 1.1. I don't hide your scores in a folder. I tell them to you so you know what you have to do. Now your clowning days are over." Then they got down to work.

Students Who Don't Care

What about students who won't work, who don't care to learn? Here is a shortened version of an interaction between Collins and Gary, a student who refused to work, ripped up his homework assignments, and would not participate in class. Collins is trying to get him to go to the blackboard to do some problems:

> COLLINS: Sweetheart, what are you going to do? Use your life or throw it away?
>
> GARY: I'm not gonna do any damn work.
>
> COLLINS: I am not going to give up on you. I am not going to let you give up on yourself. If you sit there leaning against this wall all day, you are going to end up leaning on something or someone all your life. And all that brilliance bottled up inside you will go to waste.

At that, Gary agreed to go to the board, but then refused to address the work there. After a while Collins said:

"If you do not want to participate, go to the telephone and tell your mother, 'Mother, in this school we have to learn, and Mrs. Collins says I can't fool around, so will you please pick me up.' "

Gary started writing. Eventually, Gary became an eager participant and an avid writer. Later that year, the class was discussing Macbeth and how his misguided thinking led him to commit murder. "It's sort of like Socrates says, isn't it, Miss Collins?" Gary piped up. "Macbeth should have known that 'Straight thinking leads to straight living.' " For a class assignment, he wrote, "Somnus, god of sleep, please awaken us. While we sleep, ignorance takes over the world. . . . Take your spell off us. We don't have long before ignorance makes a coup d'état of the world."

When teachers are judging them, students will sabotage the teacher by not trying. But when students understand that school is for them—a way for them to grow their minds—they do not insist on sabotaging themselves.

In my work, I have seen tough guys shed tears when they realize they can become smarter. It's common for students to turn off to school and adopt an air of indifference, but we make a mistake if we think any student stops caring.

Growth-Minded Teachers: Who Are These People?

How can growth-minded teachers be so selfless, devoting untold hours to the worst students? Are they just saints? Is it reasonable to expect that everyone can become a saint? The answer is that they're not entirely selfless. They love to learn. And teaching is a wonderful way to learn. About people and how they tick. About what you teach. About yourself. And about life.

Fixed-minded teachers often think of themselves as finished products. Their role is simply to impart their knowledge. But doesn't that get boring year after year? Standing before yet another crowd of faces and imparting. Now, that's hard.

Seymour Sarason was a professor of mine when I was in graduate school. He was a wonderful educator, and he always told us to question assumptions. "There's an assumption," he said, "that schools are for students' learning. Well, why aren't they just as much for teachers' learning?" I never forgot that. In all of my teaching, I think about what *I* find fascinating and what *I* would love to learn more about. I use my teaching to grow, and that makes me, even after all these years, a fresh and eager teacher.

One of Marva Collins's first mentors taught her the same thing—that, above all, a good teacher is one who continues to learn along with the students. And she let her students know that right up front: "Sometimes I don't like other grown-ups very much because they think they know everything. I don't know everything. I can learn all the time."

It's been said that Dorothy DeLay was an extraordinary teacher because she was not interested in teaching. She was interested in learning.

So, are great teachers born or made? Can anyone be a Collins, Esquith, or DeLay? It starts with the growth mindset—about yourself and about children. Not just lip service to the idea that all children can learn, but a deep desire to reach in and ignite the mind of every child. Michael Lewis, in *The New York Times*, tells of a coach who did this for him. "I had a new taste for . . . extra work . . . and it didn't take long to figure out how much better my life could be if I applied this new zeal acquired on a baseball field to the rest of it. It was as if this baseball coach had reached inside me, found a rusty switch marked Turn On Before Attempting to Use and flipped it."

Coaches are teachers, too, but their students' successes and failures are played out in front of crowds, published in the newspapers, and written into the record books. Their jobs rest on producing winners. Let's look closely at three legendary coaches to see their mindsets in action.

COACHES: WINNING THROUGH MINDSET

Everyone who knows me well laughs when I say someone is complicated. "What do you think of so-and-so?" "Oh, he's complicated." It's usually not a compliment. It means that so-and-so may be capable of great charm, warmth, and generosity, but there's an undercurrent of ego that can erupt at any time. You never really know when you can trust him.

The fixed mindset makes people complicated. It makes them worried about their fixed traits and creates the need to document them, sometimes at your expense. And it makes them judgmental.

The Fixed-Mindset Coach in Action

Bobby Knight, the famous and controversial college basketball coach, is complicated. He could be unbelievably kind. One time he passed up an important and lucrative opportunity to be a sportscaster, because a former player of his had been in a bad accident. Knight rushed to his side and saw him through the ordeal.

He could be extremely gracious. After the basketball team he coached won the Olympic gold medal, he insisted that the team pay homage first and foremost to Coach Henry Iba. Iba had never been given proper respect for his Olympic accomplishments, and in whatever way he could, Knight wanted to make up for it. He had the team carry Coach Iba around the floor on their shoulders.

Knight cared greatly about his players' academic records. He wanted them to get an education, and he had a firm rule against missing classes or tutoring sessions.

But he could also be cruel, and this cruelty came from the fixed mindset. John Feinstein, author of *Season on the Brink,* a book about Knight and his team, tells us: "Knight was incapable of accepting failure. Every defeat was personal; *his* team lost, a team *he* had selected and coached. . . . Failure on any level all but destroyed him, especially failure in coaching because it was coaching that gave him his identity, made him special, set him apart." A loss made him a failure, obliterated his identity. So when he was your coach—when your wins and losses measured him—he was mercilessly judgmental. His demeaning of players who let him down was, hopefully, without parallel.

In Daryl Thomas, Feinstein says, "Knight saw a player of huge potential. Thomas had what coaches call a 'million dollar body.' " He was big and strong, but also fast. He could shoot the ball with his left hand or his right hand. Knight couldn't live with the thought that Thomas and his million-dollar body weren't bringing the team success:

"You know what you are Daryl? You are the worst f____ pussy I've ever seen play basketball at this school. The absolute worst pussy ever. You have more goddam ability than 95 percent of the players we've had here but you are a pussy from the top of your head to the bottom of your feet. An absolute f____ pussy. That's my assessment of you after three years."

To make a similar point, Knight once put a Tampax in a player's locker.

Thomas was a sensitive guy. An assistant coach had given this advice: When he's calling you an asshole, don't listen. But when he starts telling you *why* you're an asshole, listen. That way, you'll get better. Thomas couldn't follow that advice. He heard everything, and, after the tirade, he broke down right there on the basketball court.

The ax of judgment came down on players who had the audacity to lose a game. Often Knight did not let the guilty parties ride back home with the rest of the team. They were no longer worthy of respectful treatment. One time, after his team reached the semifinals of a national tournament (but not *the* national tournament), he was asked by an interviewer what he liked best about the team. "What I like best about this team right now," Knight answered, "is the fact that I only have to watch it play one more time."

Some players could take it better than others. Steve Alford, who went on to have a professional career, had come to Indiana with clear goals in mind and was able to maintain a strong growth focus much of the time. He was able to hear and use Knight's wisdom and, for the most part, ignore the obscene or demeaning parts of the tirades. But even he describes how the team broke down under the yoke of Knight's judgments, and how he himself became so personally unhappy at some points that he lost his zest for the sport.

"The atmosphere was poisonous. . . . When I had been playing well I had always stayed upbeat, no matter how much Coach yelled. . . . But now his negativism, piled on top of my own, was drowning me. . . . Mom and Dad were concerned. They could see the love of the game going out of me."

THE HOLY GRAIL: NO MISTAKES

Says Alford, "Coach's Holy Grail was the mistake-free game." Uh-oh. We know which mindset makes mistakes intolerable. And Knight's explosions were legendary. There was the time he threw the chair across the court. There was the time he yanked his player off the court by his jersey. There was the time he grabbed his player by the neck. He often tried to justify his behavior by saying he was toughening the team up, preparing them to play under pressure. But the truth is, he couldn't control himself. Was the chair a teaching exercise? Was the chokehold educational?

He motivated his players, not through respect for them, but through intimidation—through fear. They feared his judgments and explosions. Did it work?

Sometimes it "worked." He had three championship teams. In the "season on the brink" described by John Feinstein, the team did not have size, experience, or quickness, but they were contenders. They won twenty-one games, thanks to Knight's great basketball knowledge and coaching skills.

But other times, it didn't work. Individual players or the team as a whole broke down. In the season on the brink, they collapsed at the end of the season. The year before, too, the team had collapsed under Knight's pressure. Over the years, some players had escaped by transferring to other schools, by breaking the rules (like cutting classes or skipping tutoring sessions), or by going early to the pros, like Isiah Thomas. On a world tour, the players often sat around fantasizing about where they *should* have gone to school, if they hadn't made the mistake of choosing Indiana.

It's not that Knight had a fixed mindset about his players' ability. He firmly believed in their capacity to develop. But he had a fixed mindset about himself and his coaching ability. The team was his product, and they had to prove his ability every time out. They were not allowed to lose games, make mistakes, or question him in any way, because that would reflect on his competence. Nor did he seem to analyze his motivational strategies when they weren't working. Maybe Daryl Thomas needed another kind of incentive aside from ridicule or humiliation.

What are we to make of this complicated man as a mentor to young players? His biggest star, Isiah Thomas, expresses his profound ambivalence about Knight. "You know there were times when if I had a gun, I think I would have shot him. And there were other times when I wanted to put my arms around him, hug him, and tell him I loved him."

I would not consider myself an unqualified success if my best student had considered shooting me.

The Growth-Mindset Coach in Action

A COACH FOR ALL SEASONS

Coach John Wooden produced one of the greatest championships records in sports. He led the UCLA basketball team to the NCAA Championship in 1964, 1965, 1967, 1968, 1969, 1970, 1971, 1972, 1973, and 1975. There were seasons when his team was undefeated, and they once had an eighty-eight-game winning streak. All this I sort of knew.

What I didn't know was that when Wooden arrived at UCLA, it was a far cry from a basketball dynasty. In fact, he didn't want to work at UCLA at all. He wanted to go to Minnesota. It was arranged that Minnesota would phone him at six o'clock on a certain evening to tell him if he had the job. He told UCLA to call him at seven. No one called at six, six thirty, or even six forty-five, so when UCLA called at seven, he said yes. No sooner had he hung up than the call from Minnesota came. A storm had messed up the phone lines and prevented the six o'clock phone call with the job offer from getting through.

UCLA had grossly inadequate facilities. For his first sixteen years, Wooden held practice in a crowded, dark, and poorly ventilated gym, known as the B.O. Barn because of the atmospheric effect of the sweating bodies. In the same gym, there were often wrestling matches, gymnastics training, trampoline jumping, and cheerleading workouts going on alongside basketball practice.

There was also no place for the games. For the first few years, they had to use the B.O. Barn, and then for fourteen more years, they had to travel around the region borrowing gyms from schools and towns.

Then there were the players. When he put them through their first practice, he was shattered. They were so bad that if he'd had an honorable way to back out of the job, he would have. The press had (perceptively) picked his team to finish last in their division, but Wooden went to work, and this laughable team did not finish last. It won the division title, with twenty-two wins and seven losses for the season. The next year, they went to the NCAA play-offs.

What did he give them? He gave them constant training in the basic skills, he gave them conditioning, and he gave them mindset.

THE HOLY GRAIL: FULL PREPARATION AND FULL EFFORT

Wooden is *not* complicated. He's wise and interesting, but not complicated. He's just a straight-ahead growth-mindset guy who lives by this rule: "You have to apply yourself each day to becoming a little better. By applying yourself to the task of becoming a little better each and every day over a period of time, you will become a *lot* better."

He didn't ask for mistake-free games. He didn't demand that his players never lose. He asked for full preparation and full effort from them. "Did I win? Did I lose? Those are the wrong questions. The correct question is: Did I make my best effort?" If so, he says, "You may be outscored but *you will never lose.*"

He was not a softy. He did not tolerate coasting. If the players were coasting during practice, he turned out the lights and left: "Gentlemen, practice is over." They had lost their opportunity to become better that day.

EQUAL TREATMENT

Like DeLay, Wooden gave equal time and attention to all of his players, regardless of their initial skills. They, in turn, gave all, and blossomed. Here is Wooden talking about two new players when they arrived at UCLA: "I looked at each one to see what he had and then said to myself, 'Oh gracious, if he can make a real contribution, a *playing* contribution, to our team then we must be pretty lousy.' However, what I couldn't see was what these men had inside." Both gave just about everything they could possibly give and both became starters, one as the starting center on a national championship team.

He respected all players equally. You know how some players' numbers are retired after they move on, in homage to their greatness? No player's number was retired while Wooden was coach, although he had some of the greatest players of all time, like Kareem Abdul-Jabbar and

Bill Walton. Later on, when their numbers were retired, he was against it. "Other fellows who played on our team also wore those numbers. Some of those other players gave me close to everything they had. . . . The jersey and the number on it never belong to just one single player, no matter how great or how big a 'star' that particular player is. It goes against the whole concept of what a team is."

Wait a minute. He was in the business of winning games. Don't you have to go with your talented players and give less to the second stringers? Well, he didn't *play* all players equally, but he gave to all players equally. For example, when he recruited another player the same year as Bill Walton, he told him that he would play very little in actual games because of Walton. But he promised him, "By the time you graduate you'll get a pro contract. You'll be that good." By his third year, the player was giving Bill Walton all he could handle in practice. And when he turned pro, he was named rookie of the year in his league.

PREPARING PLAYERS FOR LIFE

Was Wooden a genius, a magician able to turn mediocre players into champions? Actually, he admits that in terms of basketball tactics and strategies, he was quite average. What he was really good at was analyzing and motivating his players. With these skills he was able to help his players fulfill their potential, not just in basketball, but in life—something he found even more rewarding than winning games.

Did Wooden's methods work? Aside from the ten championship titles, we have the testimony of his players, none of whom refer to firearms.

Bill Walton, Hall of Famer: "Of course, the real competition he was preparing us for was life. . . . He taught us the values and characteristics that could make us not only good players, but also good people."

Denny Crum, successful coach: "I can't imagine what my life would have been had Coach Wooden not been my guiding light. As the years pass, I appreciate him more and more and can only pray that I can have half as much influence on the young people I coach as he has had on me."

Kareem Abdul-Jabbar, Hall of Famer: "The wisdom of Coach Wooden had a profound influence on me as an athlete, but an even greater influence on me as a human being. He is responsible, in part, for the person I am today."

Listen to this story.

It was the moment of victory. UCLA had just won its first national championship. But Coach Wooden was worried about Fred Slaughter, a player who had started every game and had had a brilliant year up until this final, championship game. The game had not been going well, and, as it got worse and worse, Wooden felt a change had to made. So he pulled Fred. The replacement player did a great job, and Wooden left him in until the game was virtually won.

The victory was a peak moment. Not only had they just won their first NCAA title by beating Duke, but they had ended the season with thirty wins and zero losses. Yet Wooden's concern for Fred dampened his euphoria. As Wooden left the press conference and went to find Fred, he opened the door to the dressing room. Fred was waiting for him. "Coach . . . I want you to know I understand. You had to leave Doug in there because he played so well, and I didn't. I wanted to play in the worst way, but I do understand, and if anyone says I was upset, it's not true. Disappointed, yes, but upset, no. And I was very happy for Doug."

"There are coaches out there," Wooden says, "who have won championships with the dictator approach, among them Vince Lombardi and Bobby Knight. I had a different philosophy. . . . For me, concern, compassion, and consideration were always priorities of the highest order."

Read the story of Fred Slaughter again and you tell me whether, under the same circumstances, Coach Knight would have rushed to console Daryl Thomas. And would Knight have allowed Thomas to reach down to find his pride, dignity, and generosity in his moment of disappointment?

Which Is the Enemy: Success or Failure?

Pat Summitt is the coach of the Tennessee women's basketball team, the Lady Vols. She has coached them to six national championships. She didn't come into the game with Wooden's philosophical attitude, but was at first more Knight-like in her stance. Every time the team lost, she couldn't let go of it. She continued to live it, beating it to death and torturing herself and the team with it. Then she graduated to a love–hate relationship with losing. Emotionally, it still makes her feel sick. But she loves what it does. It forces everyone, players and coaches, to develop a more complete game. It is success that has become the enemy.

Wooden calls it being "infected" with success. Pat Riley, former coach of the championship Los Angeles Lakers team, calls it the "disease of me"—thinking *you* are the success, and chucking the discipline and the work that got you there. Summitt explains, "Success lulls you. It makes the most ambitious of us complacent and sloppy." As Summitt spoke, Tennessee had won five NCAA Championships, but only *once* when they were favored to win. "On every other occasion, we were upset. We've lost as many as four or five titles that we were predicted to win."

After the 1996 championship, the team was complacent. The older players were the national champions, and the new players expected to be swept to victory merely by being at Tennessee. It was a disaster. They began to lose and lose badly. On December 15, they were crushed by Stanford on their own home court. A few games later, they were crushed again. Now they had five losses and everyone had given up on them. The North Carolina coach, meaning to comfort Summitt, told her, "Well, just hang in there 'til next year." HBO had come to Tennessee to film a documentary, but now the producers were looking for another team. Even her assistants were thinking they wouldn't make it into the March championship play-offs.

So before the next game, Summitt met with the team for five hours. That night, they played Old Dominion, the second-ranked team in the country. For the first time that season, they gave all. But they lost again. It was devastating. They had invested, gone for it, and still lost. Some were sobbing so hard, they couldn't speak, or even breathe. "Get your heads up," Summitt told them. "If you give effort like this all the time, if you fight like this, I'm telling you, I *promise* you, we'll be there in March." Two months later they were the national champions.

Conclusion? Beware of success. It can knock you into a fixed mindset: "I won because I have talent. Therefore I will keep winning." Success can infect a team or it can infect an individual. Alex Rodriguez, one of the best players in baseball, is not infected with success. "You never stay the same," he says, "You either go one way or the other."

OUR LEGACY

As parents, teachers, and coaches, we are entrusted with people's lives. They are our responsibility and our legacy. We now know that the growth mindset has a key role to play in helping *us* fulfill our mission and in helping *them* fulfill their potential.

Grow Your Mindset

- Every word and action from parent to child sends a message. Tomorrow, listen to what you say to your kids and tune in to the messages you're sending. Are they messages that say: *You have permanent traits and I'm judging them*? Or are they messages that say *You're a developing person and I'm interested in your development*?

- How do you use praise? Remember that praising children's intelligence or talent, tempting as it is, sends a fixed-mindset message. It makes their confidence and motivation more fragile. Instead, try to focus on the *processes* they used—their strategies, effort, or choices. Practice working the process praise into your interactions with your children.

- Watch and listen to yourself carefully when your child messes up. Remember that constructive criticism is feedback that helps the child understand how to fix something. It's not feedback that labels or simply excuses the child. At the end of each day, write down the constructive criticism (and the process praise) you've given your kids.

- Parents often set goals their children can work toward. Remember that having innate talent is not a goal. Expanding skills and knowledge is. Pay careful attention to the goals you set for your children.

- If you're a teacher, remember that lowering standards doesn't raise students' self-esteem. But neither does raising standards without giving students ways of reaching them. The growth mindset gives you a way to set high standards *and* have students reach them. Try presenting topics in a growth framework and giving students process feedback. I think you'll like what happens.

- Do you think of your slower students as kids who will never be able to learn well? Do they think of themselves as permanently dumb? Instead, try to figure out what they don't understand and what learning strategies they don't have. Remember that great teachers believe in the growth of talent and intellect, and are fascinated by the process of learning.

- Are you a fixed-mindset coach? Do you think first and foremost about your record and your reputation? Are you intolerant of mistakes? Do you try to motivate your players though judgment? That may be what's holding up your athletes.

  Try on the growth mindset. Instead of asking for mistake-free games, ask for full commitment and full effort. Instead of judging the players, give them the respect and the coaching they need to develop.

- As parents, teachers, and coaches, our mission is developing people's potential. Let's use all the lessons of the growth mindset—and whatever else we can—to do this.

Chapter 8

CHANGING MINDSETS

The growth mindset is based on the belief in change, and the most gratifying part of my work is watching people change. Nothing is better than seeing people find their way to things they value. This chapter is about kids and adults who found their way to using their abilities. And about how all of us can do that.

THE NATURE OF CHANGE

I was in the middle of first grade when my family moved. Suddenly I was in a new school. Everything was unfamiliar—the teacher, the students, and the work. The work was what terrified me. The new class was way ahead of my old one, or at least it seemed that way to me. They were writing letters I hadn't learned to write yet. And there was a way to do everything that everyone seemed to know except me. So when the teacher said, "Class, put your name on your paper in the right place," I had no idea what she meant.

So I cried. Each day things came up that I didn't know how to do. Each time, I felt lost and overwhelmed. Why didn't I just say to the teacher, "Mrs. Kahn, I haven't learned this yet. Could you show me how?"

Another time when I was little, my parents gave me money to go to the movies with an adult and a group of kids. As I rounded the corner to the meeting place, I looked down the block and saw them all leaving. But instead of running after them and yelling, "Wait for me!" I stood frozen, clutching the coins in my hand and watching them recede into the distance.

Why didn't I try to stop them or catch up with them? Why did I accept defeat before I had tried some simple tactics? I know that in my dreams I had often performed magical or superhuman feats in the face of danger. I even have a picture of myself in my self-made Superman cape. Why, in real life, couldn't I do an ordinary thing like ask for help or call out for people to wait?

In my work, I see lots of young children like this—bright, seemingly resourceful children who are paralyzed by setbacks. In some of our studies, they just have to take the simplest action to make things better. But they don't. These are the young children with the fixed mindset. When things go wrong, they feel powerless and incapable.

Even now, when something goes wrong or when something promising seems to be slipping away, I still have a passing feeling of powerlessness. Does that mean I haven't changed?

No, it means that change isn't like surgery. Even when you change, the old beliefs aren't just removed like a worn-out hip or knee and replaced with better ones. Instead, the new beliefs take their place alongside the old ones, and as they become stronger, they give you a different way to think, feel, and act.

Beliefs Are the Key to Happiness (and to Misery)

In the 1960s, psychiatrist Aaron Beck was working with his clients when he suddenly realized it was their *beliefs* that were causing their problems. Just before they felt a wave of anxiety or depression, something quickly flashed through their minds. It could be: "Dr. Beck thinks I'm incompetent." Or "This therapy will never work. I'll never feel better." These kinds of beliefs caused their negative feelings not only in the therapy session, but in their lives, too.

They weren't beliefs people were usually conscious of. Yet Beck found he could teach people to pay attention and hear them. And then he discovered he could teach them how to work with and change these beliefs. This is how cognitive therapy was born, one of the most effective therapies ever developed.

Whether they're aware of it or not, all people keep a running account of what's happening to them, what it means, and what they should do. In other words, our minds are constantly monitoring and interpreting. That's just how we stay on track. But sometimes the interpretation process goes awry. Some people put more extreme interpretations on things that happen—and then react with exaggerated feelings of anxiety, depression, or anger. Or superiority.

Mindsets Go Further

Mindsets frame the running account that's taking place in people's heads. They guide the whole interpretation process. The fixed mindset creates an internal monologue that is focused on judging: "This means I'm a loser." "This means I'm a better person than they are." "This means I'm a bad husband." "This means my partner is selfish."

In several studies, we probed the way people with a fixed mindset dealt with information they were receiving. We found that they put a very strong evaluation on each and every piece of information. Something good led to a very strong positive label and something bad led to a very strong negative label.

People with a growth mindset are also constantly monitoring what's going on, but their internal monologue is not about judging themselves and others in this way. Certainly they're sensitive to positive and negative information, but they're attuned to its implications for learning and constructive action: What can I learn from this? How can I improve? How can I help my partner do this better?

Now, cognitive therapy basically teaches people to rein in their extreme judgments and make them more reasonable. For example, suppose Alana does poorly on a test and draws the conclusion, "I'm stupid." Cognitive therapy would teach her to look more closely at the facts by asking: What is the evidence for and against your conclusion? Alana may, after prodding, come up with a long list of ways in which she has been competent in the past, and may then confess, "I guess I'm not as incompetent as I thought."

She may also be encouraged to think of reasons she did poorly on the test other than stupidity, and these may further temper her negative judgment. Alana is then taught how to do this for herself, so that when she judges herself negatively in the future, she can refute the judgment and feel better.

In this way, cognitive therapy helps people make more realistic and optimistic judgments. *But it does not take them out of the fixed mindset and its world of judgment.* It does not confront the basic assumption—the idea that traits are fixed—that is causing them to constantly measure themselves. In other words, it does not escort them out of the framework of judgment and into the framework of growth.

This chapter is about changing the internal monologue from a judging one to a growth-oriented one.

THE MINDSET LECTURES

Just learning about the growth mindset can cause a big shift in the way people think about themselves and their lives.

So each year in my undergraduate course, I teach about these mindsets—not only because they are part of the topic of the course but also because I know what pressure these students are under. Every year, students describe to me how these ideas have changed them in all areas of their lives.

Here is Maggie, the aspiring writer:

I recognized that when it comes to artistic or creative endeavors I had internalized a fixed mindset. I believed that people were inherently artistic or creative and that you could not improve through effort. This directly affected my life because I have always wanted to be a writer, but have been afraid to pursue any writing classes or to share my creative writing with others. This is directly related to my mindset because any negative criticism would mean that I am not a writer inherently. I was too scared to expose myself to the possibility that I might not be a "natural."

Now after listening to your lectures, I have decided to register for a creative writing class next term. And I feel that I have really come to understand what was preventing me from pursuing an interest that has long been my secret dream. I really feel this information has empowered me!

Maggie's internal monologue used to say: *Don't do it. Don't take a writing class. Don't share your writing with others. It's not worth the risk. Your dream could be destroyed. Protect it.*

Now it says: *Go for it. Make it happen. Develop your skills. Pursue your dream.*

And here's Jason, the athlete:

As a student athlete at Columbia I had exclusively the fixed mindset. Winning was everything and learning did not enter the picture. However, after listening to your lectures, I realized that this is not a good mindset. I've been working on learning while I compete, under the realization that if I can continually improve, even in matches, I will become a much better athlete.

Jason's internal monologue used to be: *Win. Win. You* have *to win. Prove yourself. Everything depends on it.*

Now it's: *Observe. Learn. Improve. Become a better athlete.*

And finally, here's Tony, the recovering genius:

In high school I was able to get top grades with minimal studying and sleeping. I came to believe that it would always be so because I was naturally gifted with a superior understanding and memory. However, after about a year of sleep deprivation my understanding and memory began to not be so superior anymore. When my natural talents, which I had come to depend on almost entirely for my self-esteem (as opposed to my ability to focus, my determination or my ability to work hard), came into question, I went through a personal crisis that lasted until a few weeks ago when you discussed the different mindsets in class. Understanding that a lot of my problems were the result of my preoccupation with proving myself to be "smart" and avoiding failures has really helped me get out of the self-destructive pattern I was living in.

Tony's internal monologue went from: *I'm naturally gifted. I don't need to study. I don't need to sleep. I'm superior.*

To: *Uh-oh, I'm losing it. I can't understand things, I can't remember things. What am I now?*

To: *Don't worry so much about being smart. Don't worry so much about avoiding failures. That becomes self-destructive. Let's start to study and sleep and get on with life.*

Of course, these people will have setbacks and disappointments, and sticking to the growth mindset may not always be easy. But just knowing it gave them another way to be. Instead of being held captive by some intimidating fantasy about the Great Writer, the Great Athlete, or the Great Genius, the growth mindset gave them courage to embrace their own goals and dreams. And more important, it gave them a way to work toward making them real.

A MINDSET WORKSHOP

Adolescence, as we've seen, is a time when hordes of kids turn off to school. You can almost hear the stampede as they try to get as far from learning as possible. This is a time when students are facing some of the biggest challenges of their young lives, and a time when they are heavily evaluating themselves, often with a fixed mindset. It is precisely the kids with the fixed mindset who panic and run for cover, showing plummeting motivation and grades.

Over the past few years, we've developed a workshop for these students. It teaches them the growth mindset and how to apply it to their schoolwork. Here is part of what they're told:

Many people think of the brain as a mystery. They don't know much about intelligence and how it works. When they do think about what intelligence is, many people believe that a person is born either smart, average, or dumb—and stays that way for life. But new research shows that the brain is more like a muscle—it changes and gets stronger when you use it. And scientists have been able to show just how the brain grows and gets stronger when you learn.

We then describe how the brain forms new connections and "grows" when people practice and learn new things.

When you learn new things, these tiny connections in the brain actually multiply and get stronger. The more that you challenge your mind to learn, the more your brain cells grow. Then, things that you once found very hard or even impossible—like speaking a foreign language or doing algebra—seem to become easy. The result is a stronger, smarter brain.

We go on to point out that nobody laughs at babies and says how dumb they are because they can't talk. They just haven't learned yet. We show students pictures of how the density of brain connections changes during the first years of life as babies pay attention, study their world, and learn how to do things.

Over a series of sessions, through activities and discussions, students are taught study skills and shown how to apply the lessons of the growth mindset to their studying and their schoolwork.

Students love learning about the brain, and the discussions are very lively. But even more rewarding are the comments students make about themselves. Let's revisit Jimmy, the hard-core turned-off student from chapter 3. In our very first workshop, we were amazed to hear him say with tears in his eyes: "You mean I don't have to be dumb?"

You may think these students are turned off, but I saw that they never stop caring. Nobody gets used to feeling dumb. Our workshop told

Jimmy, "You're in charge of your mind. You can help it grow by using it in the right way." And as the workshop progressed, here is what Jimmy's teacher said about him:

> Jimmy, who never puts in any extra effort and often doesn't turn in homework on time, actually stayed up late working for hours to finish an assignment early so I could review it and give him a chance to revise it. He earned a B+ on the assignment (he had been getting C's and lower).

Incidentally, teachers weren't just trying to be nice to us by telling us what we wanted to hear. The teachers didn't *know* who was in our growth-mindset workshop. This was because we had another workshop too. This workshop met just as many times, and taught them even more study skills. And students got just as much personal attention from supportive tutors. But they didn't learn the growth mindset and how to apply it.

Teachers didn't know which of their students went to which of the workshops, but they still singled out Jimmy and *many* of the students in the growth-mindset workshop to tell us that they'd seen real changes in their motivation to learn and improve.

> Lately I have noticed that some students have a greater appreciation for improvement. . . . R. was performing below standards. . . . He has learned to appreciate the improvement from his grades of 52, 46, and 49 to his grades of 67 and 71. . . . He valued his growth in learning Mathematics.

> M. was far below grade level. During the past several weeks, she has voluntarily asked for extra help from me during her lunch period in order to improve her test-taking performance. Her grades drastically improved from failing to an 84 on the most recent exam.

> Positive changes in motivation and behavior are noticeable in K. and J. They have begun to work hard on a consistent basis.

Several students have voluntarily participated in peer tutoring sessions during their lunch periods or after school. Students such as N. and S. were passing when they requested the extra help and were motivated by the prospect of sheer improvement.

We were eager to see whether the workshop affected students' grades, so, with their permission, we looked at students' final marks at the end of the semester. We looked especially at their math grades, since these reflected real learning of challenging new concepts.

Before the workshops, students' math grades had been suffering badly. But afterward, lo and behold, students who'd been in the growth-mindset workshop showed a jump in their grades. They were now clearly doing better than the students who'd been in the other workshop.

The growth-mindset workshop—just eight sessions long—had a real impact. This one adjustment of students' beliefs seemed to unleash their brain power and inspire them to work and achieve. Of course, they were in a school where the teachers were responsive to their outpouring of motivation, and were willing to put in the extra work to help them learn. Even so, these findings show the power of changing mindsets.

The students in the other workshop did not improve. Despite their eight sessions of training in study skills and other good things, they showed no gains. Because they were not taught to think differently about their minds, they were not motivated to put the skills into practice.

The mindset workshop put students in charge of their brains. Freed from the vise of the fixed mindset, Jimmy and others like him could now use their minds more freely and fully.

BRAINOLOGY

The problem with the workshop was that it required a big staff to deliver it. This wouldn't be feasible on a large scale. Plus, the teachers weren't directly involved. They could be a big factor in helping to sustain the students' gains. So we decided to put our workshop on inter-active computer modules and have teachers guide their classes through the modules.

With the advice of educational experts, media experts, and brain experts, we developed the "Brainology"™ program. It presents ani-mated figures, Chris and Dahlia—seventh graders who are cool but are having problems with their schoolwork. Dahlia is having trouble with Spanish, and Chris with math. They visit the lab of Dr. Cerebrus, a slightly mad brain scientist, who teaches them all about the brain and the care and feeding of it. He teaches them what to do for maximum performance from the brain (like sleeping enough, eating the right things, and using good study strategies) and he teaches them how the brain grows as they learn. The program, all along, shows students how Chris and Dahlia apply these lessons to their schoolwork. The interac-tive portions allow students to do brain experiments, see videos of real students with their problems and study strategies, recommend study plans for Chris and Dahlia, and keep a journal of their own problems and study plans.

Here are some of the seventh graders writing about how this pro-gram changed them:

> After Brainology, I now have a new look at things. Now, my atti-tude towards the subjects I have trouble in [is] I try harder to study and master the skills. . . . I have been using my time more wisely, studying everyday and reviewing the notes that I took on that day. I am really glad that I joined this program because it in-creased my intelligence about the brain.

> I did change my mind about how the brain works and i do things differently. i will try harder because i know that the more you try the more your brain works.

> ALL i can say is that Brainology changed my grades. Bon Voy-age!

The Brainology program kind of made me change the way i work and study and practice for school work now that i know how my brain works and what happens when i learn.

Thank you for making us study more and helping us build up our brain! I actually picture my neurons growing bigger as they make more connections.

Teachers told us how formerly turned-off students were now talking the Brainology talk. For example, they were taught that when they studied well and learned something, they transferred it from temporary storage (working memory) to more permanent storage (long-term memory). Now they were saying to each other: "I'll have to put that into my long-term memory." "Sorry, that stuff is not in my long-term memory." "I guess I was only using my working memory."

Teachers said that students were also offering to practice, study, take notes, or pay attention more to make sure that neural connections would be made. As one student said:

"Yes the [B]rainology program helped a lot. . . . Every time I thought about not doing work I remembered that my neurons could grow if I did do the work."

The teachers also changed. Not only did they say great things about how their students benefited, they also said great things about the insights they themselves had gained. In particular, they said Brainology was essential for understanding:

"That *all* students can learn, even the ones who struggle with math and with self-control."

"That I have to be more patient because learning takes a great deal of time and practice."

"How the brain works. . . . Each learner learns differently. Brainology assisted me in teaching for various learning styles."

Our workshop went to children in twenty schools. Some children admitted to being skeptical at first: "i used to think it was just free time and a good cartoon but i started listening to it and i started doing what they told me to do." In the end, just about every child reported meaningful benefits.

MORE ABOUT CHANGE

Is change easy or hard? So far it sounds easy. Simply learning about the growth mindset seems to mobilize people for meeting challenges and persevering.

The other day one of my former grad students told me a story. But first some background. In my field, when you submit a research paper for publication, that paper often represents years of work. Some months later you receive your reviews: ten or so pages of criticism—single-spaced. If the editor still thinks the paper has potential, you will be invited to revise it and resubmit it *provided you can address every criticism.*

My student reminded me of the time she had sent her thesis research to the top journal in our field. When the reviews came back, she was devastated. She had been judged—the work was flawed and, by extension, so was she. Time passed, but she couldn't bring herself to go near the reviews again or work on the paper.

Then I told her to change her mindset. "Look," I said, "it's not about you. That's their job. Their job is to find every possible flaw. Your job is to learn from the critique and make your paper even better." Within hours she was revising her paper, which was warmly accepted. She tells me: "I never felt judged again. Never. Every time I get that critique, I tell myself, 'Oh, that's their job,' and I get to work immediately on *my* job."

But change is also hard.

When people hold on to a fixed mindset, it's often for a reason. At some point in their lives it served a good purpose for them. It told them who they were or who they wanted to be (a smart, talented child) and it told them how to be that (perform well). In this way, it provided a formula for self-esteem and a path to love and respect from others.

The idea that they are worthy and will be loved is crucial for children, and—if a child is unsure about being valued or loved—the fixed mindset appears to offer a simple, straightforward route to this.

Psychologists Karen Horney and Carl Rogers, working in the mid-

1900s, both proposed theories of children's emotional development. They believed that when young children feel insecure about being accepted by their parents, they experience great anxiety. They feel lost and alone in a complicated world. Since they're only a few years old, they can't simply reject their parents and say, "I think I'll go it alone." They have to find a way to feel safe and to win their parents over.

Both Horney and Rogers proposed that children do this by creating or imagining other "selves," ones that their parents might like better. These new selves are what they think the parents are looking for and what may win them the parents' acceptance.

Often, these steps are good adjustments to the family situation at the time, bringing the child some security and hope.

The problem is that this new self—this all-competent, strong, good self that they now try to be—is likely to be a fixed-mindset self. Over time, the fixed traits may come to be the person's sense of who they are, and validating these traits may come to be the main source of their self-esteem.

Mindset change asks people to give this up. As you can imagine, it's not easy to just let go of something that has felt like your "self" for many years and that has given you your route to self-esteem. And it's especially not easy to replace it with a mindset that tells you to embrace all the things that have felt threatening: challenge, struggle, criticism, setbacks.

When I was exchanging my fixed mindset for a growth one, I was acutely aware of how unsettled I felt. For example, I've told you how as a fixed mindsetter, I kept track each day of all my successes. At the end of a good day, I could look at the results (the high numbers on my intelligence "counter," my personality "counter," and so on) and feel good about myself. But as I adopted a growth mindset and stopped keeping track, some nights I would still check my mental counters and find them at zero. It made me insecure not to be able to tote up my victories.

Even worse, since I was taking more risks, I might look back over the day and see all the mistakes and setbacks. And feel miserable.

What's more, it's not as though the fixed mindset wants to leave gracefully. If the fixed mindset has been controlling your internal monologue, it can say some pretty strong things to you when it sees those counters at zero: "You're *nothing*." It can make you want to rush right out and rack up some high numbers. The fixed mindset once offered you refuge from that very feeling, and it offers it to you again.

Don't take it.

Then there's the concern that you won't be yourself anymore. It may feel as though the fixed mindset gave you your ambition, your edge, your individuality. Maybe you fear you'll become a bland cog in the wheel just like everyone else. Ordinary.

But opening yourself up to growth makes you *more* yourself, not less. The growth-oriented scientists, artists, athletes, and CEOs we've looked at were far from humanoids going through the motions. They were people in the full flower of their individuality and potency.

TAKING THE FIRST STEP

The rest of the book is pretty much about you. It's a mindset exercise in which I ask you to venture with me into a series of dilemmas. In each case, you'll first see the fixed-mindset reactions, and then work through to a growth-mindset solution.

The First Dilemma. Imagine you've applied to graduate school. You applied to just one place because it was the school you had your heart set on. And you were confident you'd be accepted since many people considered your work in your field to be original and exciting. But you were rejected.

The Fixed-Mindset Reaction. At first you tell yourself that it was extremely competitive, so it doesn't really reflect on you. They probably had more first-rate applicants than they could accept. Then the voice in your head starts in. It tells you that you're fooling yourself, rationalizing. It tells you that the admissions committee found your work mediocre. After a while, you tell yourself it's probably true. The work is probably ordinary, pedestrian, and they'd seen that. They were experts. The verdict is in and you're not worthy.

With some effort you talk yourself back into your first, reasonable, and more flattering conclusion, and you feel better. In the fixed mindset (and in most cognitive therapies), that's the end of it. You've regained your self-esteem, so the job is finished. But in the growth mindset, that's just the first step. All you've done is talk to yourself. Now comes the learning and self-improvement part.

The Growth-Mindset Step. Think about your goal and think about what you could do to stay on track toward achieving it. What steps could you take to help yourself succeed? What information could you gather?

Well, maybe you could apply to more schools next time. Or maybe, in the meantime, you could gather more information about what makes a good application: What are they looking for? What experiences do they value? You could seek out those experiences before the next application.

Since this is a true story, I know what step the rejected applicant took. She was given some strong growth-mindset advice and, a few days later, she called the school. When she located the relevant person and told him the situation, she said, "I don't want to dispute your decision. I just want to know, if I decide to apply again in the future, how I can improve my application. I would be very grateful if you could give me some feedback along those lines."

Nobody scoffs at an honest plea for helpful feedback. Several days later, he called her back and offered her admission. It had indeed been a close call and, after reconsidering her application, the department decided they could take one more person that year. Plus, they liked her initiative.

She had reached out for information that would allow her to learn from experience and improve in the future. It turned out in this case that she didn't have to improve her application. She got to plunge right into learning in her new graduate program.

Plans That You'll Carry Out and Ones That You Won't

The key part of our applicant's reaction was her call to the school to get more information. It wasn't easy. Every day people plan to do difficult things, but they don't do them. They think, "I'll do it tomorrow," and they swear to themselves that they'll follow through the next day. Research by Peter Gollwitzer and his colleagues shows that vowing, even intense vowing, is often useless. The next day comes and the next day goes.

What works is making a vivid, concrete plan: "Tomorrow during my break, I'll get a cup of tea, close the door to my office, and call the graduate school." Or, in another case: "On Wednesday morning, right after I get up and brush my teeth, I'll sit at my desk and start writing my report." Or: "Tonight, right after the dinner dishes are done, I'll sit down with my wife in the living room and have that discussion. I'll say to her, 'Dear, I'd like to talk about something that I think will make us happier.'"

Think of something you need to do, something you want to learn, or a problem you have to confront. What is it? Now make a concrete plan. *When* will you follow through on your plan? *Where* will you do it? *How* will you do it? Think about it in vivid detail.

These concrete plans—plans you can visualize—about *when, where,* and *how* you are going to do something lead to really high levels of follow-through, which, of course, ups the chances of success.

So the idea is not only to make a growth-mindset plan, but also to visualize, in a concrete way, how you're going to carry it out.

Feeling Bad, But Doing Good

Let's go back a few paragraphs to when you were rejected by the graduate school. Suppose your attempt to make yourself feel better had failed. *You could still have taken the growth-mindset step.* You can feel miserable and still reach out for information that will help you improve.

Sometimes after I have a setback, I go through the process of talking to myself about what it means and how I plan to deal with it. Everything seems fine—until I sleep on it. In my sleep, I have dream after dream of loss, failure, or rejection, depending on what happened. Once when I'd experienced a loss, I went to sleep and had the following dreams: My hair fell out, my teeth fell out, I had a baby and it died, and so on. Another time when I felt rejected, my dreams generated countless rejection experiences—real and imagined. In each instance, the incident triggered a theme, and my too-active imagination gathered up all the variations on the theme to place before me. When I woke up, I felt as though I'd been through the wars.

It would be nice if this didn't happen, *but it's irrelevant.* It might be easier to mobilize for action if I felt better, but it doesn't matter. The plan is the plan. Remember the depressed students with the growth mindset? The worse they felt, the more they did the constructive thing. The less they felt like it, the more they made themselves do it.

The critical thing is to make a concrete, growth-oriented plan, and to stick to it.

The Number One Draft Choice

The last dilemma seemed hard, but, basically, it was solved by a phone call. Now imagine you're a promising quarterback. In fact, you're the winner of the Heisman trophy, college football's highest award. You're the top draft pick of the Philadelphia Eagles, the team you've always dreamed of playing for. So what's the dilemma?

The Second Dilemma. The pressure is overwhelming. You yearn for playing time in the games, but every time they put you in a game to try you out, you turn anxious and lose your focus. You were always cool under pressure, but this is the pros. Now all you see are giant guys coming toward you—twelve hundred pounds of giant guys who want to take you apart. Giant guys who move faster than you ever thought possible. You feel cornered . . . helpless.

The Fixed-Mindset Reaction. You torture yourself with the idea that a quarterback is a leader and you're no leader. How could you ever inspire the confidence of your teammates when you can't get your act together to throw a good pass or scramble for a few yards? To make things worse, the sportscasters keep asking, *What happened to the boy wonder?*

To minimize the humiliation you begin to keep to yourself and, to avoid the sportscasters, you disappear into the locker room right after the game.

Whoa. Is this a recipe for success? What steps could you take to make things better? Think about the resources at your disposal and how you could use them. But first, get your mindset turned around.

The Growth-Mindset Step. In the growth mindset, you tell yourself that the switch to the professionals is a huge step, one that takes a lot of adjustment and a lot of learning. There are many things you couldn't possibly know yet and that you'd better start finding out about.

You try to spend more time with the veteran quarterbacks, asking them questions and watching tapes with them. Instead of hiding your insecurities, you talk about how different it is from college. They, in turn, tell you that's exactly how they felt. In fact, they share their humiliating stories with you.

You ask them what they did to overcome the initial difficulties and they teach you their mental and physical techniques. As you begin to feel more integrated into the team, you realize you're part of an organization that wants to help you grow, not judge and belittle you. Rather than worrying that they overpaid for your talent, you begin to give them their money's worth of incredibly hard work and team spirit.

PEOPLE WHO DON'T WANT TO CHANGE

Entitlement: The World Owes You

Many people with the fixed mindset think the *world* needs to change, not them. They feel entitled to something better—a better job, house, or spouse. The world should recognize their special qualities and treat them accordingly. Let's move to the next dilemma and imagine yourself in this situation.

The Next Dilemma. "Here I am," you think, "in this low-level job. It's demeaning. With my talent I shouldn't have to work like this. I should be up there with the big boys, enjoying the good life." Your boss thinks you have a bad attitude. When she needs someone to take on more responsibilities, she doesn't turn to you. When it's time to give out promotions, she doesn't include you.

The Fixed-Mindset Reaction. "She's threatened by me," you say bitterly. Your fixed mindset is telling you that, because of who you are, you should automatically be thrust into the upper levels of the business. In your mind, people should see your talents and reward you. When they don't, it's not fair. Why should *you* change? You just want your due.

But putting yourself in a growth mindset, what are some new ways you could think and some steps you could take? For example, what are some new ways you could think about effort? About learning? And how could you act on this new thinking in your work?

Well, you could consider working harder and being more helpful to people at work. You could use your time to learn more about the business you're in instead of bellyaching about your low status. Let's see how this might look.

The Growth-Mindset Step. But first, let's be clear. For a long time, it's frightening to think of giving up the idea of being superior. An ordinary, run-of-the-mill human being isn't what you want to be. How could you feel good about yourself if you're no more valuable than the people you look down on?

You begin to consider the idea that some people stand out because of their commitment and effort. Little by little you try putting more effort into things and seeing if you get more of the rewards you wanted. You do.

Although you can slowly accept the idea that effort might be *necessary,* you still can't accept that it's no guarantee. It's enough of an indignity to have to work at things, but to work and *still* not have them turn out the way you want—now, that's really not fair. That means you could work hard and somebody else could still get the promotion. Outrageous.

It's a long time before you begin to *enjoy* putting in effort and a long time before you begin to think in terms of learning. Instead of seeing your time at the bottom of the corporate ladder as an insult, you slowly see that you can learn a lot at the bottom that could help you greatly on your rise to the top. Learning the nuts and bolts of the company could later give you a big advantage. All of our top growth-mindset CEOs knew their companies from top to bottom, inside out, and upside down.

Instead of seeing your discussions with your colleagues as time spent getting what you want, you begin to grasp the idea of building relationships or even helping your colleagues develop in ways they value. This can become a new source of satisfaction. You might say you were following in the footsteps of Bill Murray and his Groundhog Day experience.

As you become a more growth-minded person, you're amazed at how people start to help you, support you. They no longer seem like adversaries out to deny you what you deserve. They're more and more often collaborators toward a common goal. It's interesting, you started out wanting to change other people's behavior—and you did.

In the end, many people with the fixed mindset understand that their cloak of specialness was really a suit of armor they built to feel safe, strong, and worthy. While it may have protected them early on, later it constricted their growth, sent them into self-defeating battles, and cut them off from satisfying, mutual relationships.

Denial: My Life Is Perfect

People in a fixed mindset often run away from their problems. If their life is flawed, then *they're* flawed. It's easier to make believe everything's all right. Try this dilemma.

The Dilemma. You seem to have everything. You have a fulfilling career, a loving marriage, wonderful children, and devoted friends. But one of those things isn't true. Unbeknownst to you, your marriage is ending. It's not that there haven't been signs, but you chose to misinterpret them. You were fulfilling your idea of the "man's role" or the "woman's role," and couldn't hear your partner's desire for more communication and more sharing of your lives. By the time you wake up and take notice, it's too late. Your spouse has disengaged emotionally from the relationship.

The Fixed-Mindset Reaction. You've always felt sorry for divorced people, abandoned people. And now you're one of them. You lose all sense of worth. Your partner, who knew you intimately, doesn't want you anymore.

For months, you don't feel like going on, convinced that even your children would be better off without you. It takes you a while to get to the point where you feel at all useful or competent. Or hopeful. Now comes the hard part because, even though you now feel a little better about yourself, you're still in the fixed mindset. You're embarking on a lifetime of judging. With everything good that happens, your internal voice says, *Maybe I'm okay after all.* But with everything bad that happens, the voice says, *My spouse was right.* Every new person you meet is judged too—as a potential betrayer.

How could you rethink your marriage, yourself, and your life from a growth-mindset perspective? Why were you afraid to listen to your spouse? What could you have done? What should you do now?

The Growth-Mindset Step. First, it's not that the marriage, which you used to think of as inherently good, suddenly turned out to have been all bad or always bad. It was an evolving thing that had stopped developing for lack of nourishment. You need to think about how both you and your spouse contributed to this, and especially about why you weren't able to hear the request for greater closeness and sharing.

As you probe, you realize that, in your fixed mindset, you saw your partner's request as a criticism of you that you didn't want to hear. You also realize that at some level, you were afraid you weren't capable of the intimacy your partner was requesting. So instead of exploring these issues with your spouse, you turned a deaf ear, hoping they would go away.

When a relationship goes sour, these are the issues we all need to explore in depth, not to judge ourselves for what went wrong, but to overcome our fears and learn the communication skills we'll need to build and maintain better relationships in the future. Ultimately, a growth mindset allows people to carry forth not judgments and bitterness, but new understanding and new skills.

Is someone in your life trying to tell you something you're refusing to hear? Step into the growth mindset and listen again.

CHANGING YOUR CHILD'S MINDSET

Many of our children, our most precious resource, are stuck in a fixed mindset. You can give them a personal Brainology workshop. Let's look at some ways to do this.

The Precocious Fixed Mindsetter

Most kids who adopt a fixed mindset don't become truly passionate believers until later in childhood. But some kids take to it much earlier.

The Dilemma. Imagine your young son comes home from school one day and says to you, "Some kids are smart and some kids are dumb. They have a worse brain." You're appalled. "Who told you that?" you ask him, gearing up to complain to the school. "I figured it out myself," he says proudly. He saw that some children could read and write their letters and add a lot of numbers, and others couldn't. He drew his conclusion. And he held fast to it.

Your son is precocious in all aspects of the fixed mindset, and soon the mindset is in full flower. He develops a distaste for effort—he wants his smart brain to churn things out quickly for him. And it often does.

When he takes to chess very quickly, your spouse, thinking to inspire him, rents the movie *Searching for Bobby Fischer,* a film about a young chess champion. What your son learns from the film is that you could lose and not be a champion anymore. So he retires. "I'm a chess champion," he announces to one and all. A champion who won't play.

Because he now understands what losing means, he takes further steps to avoid it. He starts cheating at Candy Land, Chutes and Ladders, and other games.

He talks often about all the things he can do and other children can't. When you and your spouse tell him that other children aren't dumb, they just haven't practiced as much as he has, he refuses to believe it. He watches things carefully at school and then comes home and reports, "Even when the teacher shows us something new, I can do it better than them. I don't have to practice."

This boy is invested in his brain—not in making it grow but in singing its praises. You've already told him that it's about practice and learning, not smart and dumb, but he doesn't buy it. What else can you do? What are other ways you can get the message across?

The Growth-Mindset Step. You decide that, rather than trying to talk him out of the fixed mindset, you have to live the growth mindset. At the dinner table each evening, you and your partner structure the discussion around the growth mindset, asking each child (and each other): "What did you learn today?" "What mistake did you make that taught you something?" "What did you try hard at today?" You go around the table with each question, excitedly discussing your own and one another's effort, strategies, setbacks, and learning.

You talk about skills you have today that you didn't have yesterday because of the practice you put in. You dramatize mistakes you made that held the key to the solution, telling it like a mystery story. You describe with relish things you're struggling with and making progress on. Soon the children can't wait each night to tell their stories. "Oh my goodness," you say with wonder, "you certainly did get smarter today!"

When your fixed-mindset son tells stories about doing things better than other children, everyone says, "Yeah, but what did you learn?" When he talks about how easy everything is for him in school, you all say, "Oh, that's too bad. You're not learning. Can you find something harder to do so you could learn more?" When he boasts about being a champ, you say, "Champs are the people who work the hardest. You can *become* a champ. Tomorrow tell me something you've done to become a champ." Poor kid, it's a conspiracy. In the long run, he doesn't stand a chance.

When he does his homework and calls it easy or boring, you teach him to find ways to make it more fun and challenging. If he has to write words, like *boy*, you ask him, "How many words can you think of that rhyme with *boy*? Write them on separate paper and later we can try to make a sentence that has all the words." When he finishes his home-work, you play that game: "The boy threw the toy into the soy sauce." "The girl with the cirl [curl] ate a pirl [pearl]." Eventually, he starts com-ing up with his own ways to make his homework more challenging.

And it's not just school or sports. You encourage the children to talk about ways they learned to make friends, or ways they're learning to un-derstand and help others. You want to communicate that feats of intel-lect or physical prowess are not all you care about.

For a long time, your son remains attracted to the fixed mindset. He loves the idea that he's inherently special—case closed. He doesn't love the idea that he has to work every day for some little gain in skill or knowledge. Stardom shouldn't be so taxing. Yet as the value system in the family shifts toward the growth mindset, he wants to be a player. So at first he talks the talk (squawking), then he walks the walk (balking). Finally, going all the way, he becomes the mindset watchdog. When anyone in the family slips into fixed-mindset thinking, he delights in catching them. "Be careful what you wish for," you joke to your spouse.

The fixed mindset is so very tempting. It seems to promise children a lifetime of worth, success, and admiration just for sitting there and being who they are. That's why it can take a lot of work to make the growth mindset flourish where the fixed mindset has taken root.

Effort Gone Awry

Sometimes the problem with a child isn't too *little* effort. It's too *much*. And for the wrong cause. We've all heard about schoolchildren who stay up past midnight every night studying. Or children who are sent to tu-tors so they can outstrip their classmates. These children are working hard, but they're typically not in a growth mindset. They're not focused on love of learning. They're usually trying to prove themselves to their parents.

And in some cases, the parents may like what comes out of this high effort: the grades, the awards, the admission to top schools. Let's see how you would handle this one.

The Dilemma. You're proud of your daughter. She's at the top of her class and bringing home straight A's. She's a flute player studying with the best teacher in the country. And you're confident she'll get into the top private high school in the city. But every morning before school, she gets an upset stomach, and some days she throws up. You keep feeding her a blander and blander diet to soothe her sensitive stomach, but it doesn't help. It never occurs to you that she's a nervous wreck.

When your daughter is diagnosed with an ulcer, it should be a wake-up call, but you and your spouse remain asleep. You continue to see it as a gastrointestinal issue. The doctor, however, insists that you consult a family counselor. He tells you it's a mandatory part of your daughter's treatment and hands you a card with the counselor's name and number.

The Fixed-Mindset Reactions. The counselor tells you to ease up on your daughter: Let her know it's okay not to work so hard. Make sure she gets more sleep. So you, dutifully following the instructions, make sure she gets to sleep by ten o'clock each night. But this only makes things worse. She now has less time to accomplish all the things that are expected of her.

Despite what the counselor has said, it doesn't occur to you that she could possibly want your daughter to fall behind other students. Or be less accomplished at the flute. Or risk not getting into the top high school. How could that be good for her?

The counselor realizes she has a big job. Her first goal is to get you more fully in touch with the seriousness of the problem. The second goal is to get you to understand your role in the problem. You and your spouse need to see that it's *your* need for perfection that has led to the problem. Your daughter wouldn't have run herself ragged if she hadn't been afraid of losing your approval. The third goal is to work out a concrete plan that you can all follow.

Can you think of some concrete things that can be done to help your daughter enter a growth mindset so she can ease up and get some pleasure from her life?

The Growth-Mindset Step. The plan the counselor suggests would allow your daughter to start enjoying the things she does. The flute lessons are put on hold. Your daughter is told she can practice as much or as little as she wants for the pure joy of the music and nothing else.

She is to study her school materials to learn from them, not to cram everything possible into her head. The counselor refers her to a tutor who teaches her how to study for understanding. The tutor also discusses the material with her in a way that makes it interesting and enjoyable. Studying now has a new meaning. It isn't about getting the highest grade to prove her intelligence and worth to her parents. It's about learning things and thinking about them in interesting ways.

Your daughter's teachers are brought into the loop to support her in her reorientation toward growth. They're asked to talk to her about (and praise her for) her learning process rather than how she did on tests. ("I can see that you really understand how to use metaphors in your writing." "I can see that you were really into your project on the Incas. When I read it, I felt as though I were in ancient Peru.") You are taught to talk to her this way too.

Finally, the counselor strongly urges that your daughter attend a high school that is less pressured than the one you have your eye on. There are other fine schools that focus more on learning and less on grades and test scores. You take your daughter around and spend time in each of the schools. Then she discusses with you and the counselor which ones she was most excited about and felt most at ease in.

Slowly, you learn to separate your needs and desires from hers. You may have needed a daughter who was number one in everything, but your daughter needed something else: acceptance from her parents and freedom to grow. As you let go, your daughter becomes much more genuinely involved in the things she does. She does them for interest and learning, and she does them very well indeed.

Is your child trying to tell you something you don't want to hear? You know the ad that asks, "Do you know where your child is now?" If you can't hear what your child is trying to tell you—in words or actions—then you don't know where your child is. Enter the growth mindset and listen harder.

MINDSET AND WILLPOWER

Sometimes we don't want to change ourselves very much. We just want to be able to drop some pounds and keep them off. Or stop smoking. Or control our anger.

Some people think about this in a fixed-mindset way. If you're strong and have willpower, you can do it. But if you're weak and don't have willpower, you can't. People who think this way may firmly resolve to do something, but they'll take no special measures to make sure they succeed. These are the people who end up saying, "Quitting is easy. I've done it a hundred times."

It's just like the chemistry students we talked about before. The ones with the fixed-mindset thought: "If I have ability, I'll do well; if I don't, I won't." As a result, they didn't use sophisticated strategies to help themselves. They just studied in an earnest but superficial way and hoped for the best.

When people with a fixed mindset fail their test—in chemistry, dieting, smoking, or anger—they beat themselves up. They're incompetent, weak, or bad people. Where do you go from there?

My friend Nathan's twenty-fifth high school reunion was coming up, and when he thought about how his ex-girlfriend would be there, he decided to lose the paunch. He'd been handsome and fit in high school and he didn't want to show up as a fat middle-aged man.

Nathan had always made fun of women and their diets. What's the big fuss? You just need some self-control. To lose the weight, he decided he would just eat part of what was on his plate. But each time he got into a meal, the food on the plate disappeared. "I blew it!" he'd say, feeling like a failure and ordering dessert—either to seal the failure or to lift his mood.

I'd say, "Nathan, this isn't working. You need a better system. Why not put some of the meal aside at the beginning or have the restaurant wrap it up to take home? Why not fill your plate with extra vegetables, so it'll look like more food? There are lots of things you can do." To this he would say, "No, I have to be strong."

Nathan ended up going on one of those liquid crash diets, losing weight for the reunion, and putting back more than he lost afterward. I wasn't sure how this was being strong, and how using some simple strategies was being weak.

Next time you try to diet, think of Nathan and remember that willpower is not just a thing you have or don't have. Willpower needs help. I'll come back to this point.

Anger

Controlling anger is something else that's a problem for many people. Something triggers their temper and off they go, losing control of their mouths or worse. Here, too, people may vow that next time they'll be different. Anger control is a big issue between partners and between parents and children, not only because partners and children do things that make us angry, but also because we may think we have a greater right to let loose when they do. Try this one.

The Dilemma. Imagine you're a nice, caring person—as you probably are—usually. You love your spouse and feel lucky to have them as your partner. But when they violate one of your rules, like letting the garbage overflow before taking it out, you feel personally betrayed and start criticizing. It begins with "I've told you a thousand times," then moves on to "You never do anything right." When they still don't seem properly ashamed, you flare, insulting their intelligence ("Maybe you aren't smart enough to remember garbage") and their character ("If you weren't so irresponsible, you wouldn't . . ." "If you cared about anyone but yourself, you'd . . ."). Seething with rage, you then bring in everything you can think of to support your case: "My father never trusted you, either," or "Your boss was right when he said you were limited." Your spouse has to leave the premises to get out of range of your mounting fury.

The Fixed-Mindset Reaction. You feel righteous about your anger for a while, but then you realize you've gone too far. You suddenly recall all the ways that your spouse is a supportive partner and feel intensely guilty.

Then you talk yourself back into the idea that you, too, are a good person, who's just slipped up—lost it—temporarily. "I've really learned my lesson," you think, "I'll never do this again."

But believing you can simply keep that good person in the forefront in the future, you don't think of strategies you could use next time to prevent a flare-up. That's why the next time is a carbon copy of the time before.

The Growth Mindset and Self-Control

Some people think about losing weight or controlling their anger in a growth-mindset way. They realize that to succeed, they'll need to learn and practice strategies that work for them.

It's like the growth-mindset chemistry students. They used better study techniques, carefully planned their study time, and kept up their motivation. In other words, they used every strategy possible to make sure they succeeded.

Just like them, people in a growth mindset don't merely make New Year's resolutions and wait to see if they stick to them. They understand that to diet, they need to plan. They may need to keep desserts out of the house. Or think in advance about what to order in restaurants. Or schedule a once-a-week splurge. Or consider exercising more.

They think actively about maintenance. What habits must they develop to continue the gains they've achieved?

Then there are the setbacks. They know that setbacks will happen. So instead of beating themselves up, they ask: "What can I learn from this? What will I do next time when I'm in this situation?" It's a learning process—not a battle between the bad you and the good you.

In that last episode, what could you have done with your anger? First, think about *why* you got so worked up. You may have felt devalued and disrespected when your spouse shirked the tasks or broke your rules—as though they were saying to you, "You're not important. Your needs are trivial. I can't be bothered."

Your first reaction was to angrily remind them of their duty. But on the heels of that was your retaliation, sort of "Okay big shot, if you think you're so important, try this on for size."

Your spouse, rather than reassuring you of your importance, simply braced for the onslaught. Meanwhile, you took the silence as evidence that they felt superior, and it fueled your escalation.

What can be done? Several things. First, spouses can't read your mind, so when an anger-provoking situation arises, you have to matter-of-factly tell them how it makes you feel. "I'm not sure why, but when you do that, it makes me feel unimportant. Like you can't be bothered to do things that matter to me."

They, in turn, can reassure you that they care about how you feel and will try to be more watchful. ("Are you kidding?" you say. "My spouse would never do that." Well, you can request it directly, as I've sometimes done: "Please tell me that you care how I feel and you'll try to be more watchful.")

When you feel yourself losing it, you can learn to leave the room and write down your ugliest thoughts, followed by what is probably *really* happening ("She doesn't understand this is important to me," "He doesn't know what to do when I start to blow"). When you feel calm enough, you can return to the situation.

You can also learn to loosen up on some of your rules, now that each one is not a test of your partner's respect for you. With time, you might even gain a sense of humor about them. For example, if your spouse leaves some socks in the living room or puts the wrong things in the recycling bins, you might point at the offending items and ask sternly, "What is the meaning of this?" You might even have a good laugh.

When people drop the good–bad, strong–weak thinking that grows out of the fixed mindset, they're better able to learn useful strategies that help with self-control. Every lapse doesn't spell doom. It's like anything else in the growth mindset. It's a reminder that you're an unfinished human being and a clue to how to do it better next time.

MAINTAINING CHANGE

Whether people change their mindset in order to further their career, heal from a loss, help their children thrive, lose weight, or control their anger, change needs to be maintained. It's amazing—once a problem improves, people often *stop doing what caused it to improve.* Once you feel better, you stop taking your medicine.

But change doesn't work that way. When you've lost weight, the issue doesn't go away. Or when your child starts to love learning, the problem isn't solved forever. Or when you and your partner start communicating better, that's not the end of it. These changes have to be supported or they can go away faster than they appeared.

Maybe that's why Alcoholics Anonymous tells people they will always be alcoholics—so they won't become complacent and stop doing what they need to do to stay sober. It's a way of saying, "You'll always be vulnerable."

This is why mindset change is not about picking up a few tricks. In fact, if someone stays inside a fixed mindset and uses the growth strategies, it can backfire.

Wes, a dad with a fixed mindset, was at his wit's end. He'd come home exhausted from work every evening and his son, Mickey, would refuse to cooperate. Wes wanted quiet, but Mickey was noisy. Wes would warn him, but Mickey would continue what he was doing. Wes found him stubborn, unruly, and not respectful of Wes's rights as a father. The whole scene would disintegrate into a shouting match and Mickey would end up being punished.

Finally, feeling he had nothing to lose, Wes tried some of the growth-oriented strategies. He showed respect for Mickey's efforts and praised his strategies when he was empathic or helpful. The turnaround in Mickey's behavior was dramatic.

But as soon as the turnaround took place, Wes stopped using the strategies. He had what he wanted and he expected it to just continue. When it didn't, he became even angrier and more punitive than before. Mickey had shown he *could* behave and now refused to.

The same thing often happens with fixed-mindset couples who start communicating better. Marlene and Scott were what my husband and I call the Bickersons. All they did was bicker: "Why don't you ever pick up after yourself?" "I might if you weren't such a nag." "I wouldn't have to nag if you did what you were supposed to do." "Who made *you* the judge of what *I'm* supposed to do?"

With counseling, Marlene and Scott stopped jumping on the negatives. More and more, they started rewarding the thoughtful things their partner did and the efforts their partner made. The love and tenderness they thought were dead returned. But once it returned, they reverted. In the fixed mindset, things shouldn't need such effort. Good people should just act good and good relationships should just unfold in a good way.

When the bickering resumed, it was fiercer than ever because it reflected all of their disappointed hopes.

Mindset change is not about picking up a few pointers here and there. It's about seeing things in a new way. When people—couples, coaches and athletes, managers and workers, parents and children, teachers and students—change to a growth mindset, they change from a *judge-and-be-judged* framework to a *learn-and-help-learn* framework. Their commitment is to growth, and growth takes plenty of time, effort, and mutual support.

Learn and Help Learn

Every day presents you with ways to grow and to help the people you care about grow. How can you remember to look for these chances?

First, make a copy of this graphic summary of the two mindsets, which was created by the wonderful Nigel Holmes, and tape it to your mirror. Each morning, use it to remind yourself of the differences between the fixed and growth mindsets. Then, as you contemplate the day in front of you, try to ask yourself these questions. If you have room on your mirror, copy them over and tape them there, too.

> *What are the opportunities for learning and growth today? For myself? For the people around me?*

As you think of opportunities, form a plan, and ask:

> *When, where, and how will I embark on my plan?*

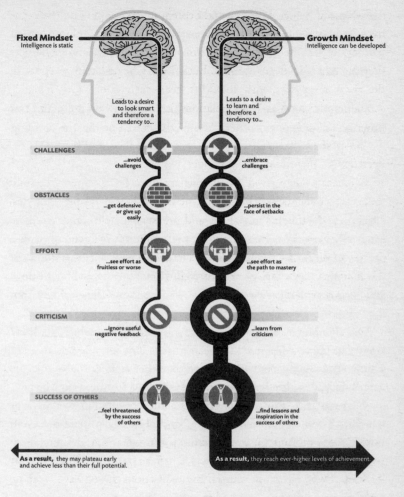

Fixed Mindset
Intelligence is static

Growth Mindset
Intelligence can be developed

Leads to a desire
to look smart
and therefore a
tendency to...

Leads to a desire
to learn and
therefore a
tendency to...

CHALLENGES

...avoid
challenges

...embrace
challenges

OBSTACLES

...get defensive
or give up
easily

...persist in the
face of setbacks

EFFORT

...see effort as
fruitless or worse

...see effort as
the path to mastery

CRITICISM

...ignore useful
negative feedback

...learn from
criticism

SUCCESS OF OTHERS

...feel threatened
by the success
of others

...find lessons and
inspiration in the
success of others

As a result, they may plateau early
and achieve less than their full potential.

As a result, they reach ever-higher levels of achievement.

DIAGRAM BY NIGEL HOLMES

When, where, and *how* make the plan concrete. *How* asks you to think of all the ways to bring your plan to life and make it work.

As you encounter the inevitable obstacles and setbacks, form a new plan and ask yourself the question again:

When, where, and how will I act on my new plan?

Regardless of how bad you may feel, do it!

And when you succeed, don't forget to ask yourself:

What do I have to do to maintain and continue the growth?

Remember, as Alex Rodriguez, the great baseball player, said: "You either go one way or the other." You might as well be the one deciding the direction.

THE ROAD AHEAD

Change can be tough, but I've never heard anyone say it wasn't worth it. Maybe they're just rationalizing, the way people who've gone through a painful initiation say it was worth it. But people who've changed can tell you how their lives have been enhanced. They can tell you about things they have now that they wouldn't have had, and ways they feel now that they wouldn't have felt.

Did changing to a growth mindset solve all my problems? No. But I know that I have a different life because of it—a richer one. And that I'm a more alive, courageous, and open person because of it.

It's for you to decide whether change is right for you now. Maybe it is, maybe it isn't. But either way, keep the growth mindset in your thoughts. Then, when you bump up against obstacles, you can turn to it. It will always be there for you, showing you a path into the future.

NOTES

CHAPTER 1. THE MINDSETS

3 **When I was a young researcher:** This research was conducted with Dick Reppucci and with Carol Diener.

4 **Through the ages, these alleged physical differences:** See Steven J. Gould's *The Mismeasure of Man* (New York: Norton, 1981) for a history of how people have tried to explain human differences in terms of innate physical characteristics.

4 **It may surprise you to know:** Alfred Binet (Suzanne Heisler, trans.), *Modern Ideas About Children* (Menlo Park, CA: Suzanne Heisler, 1975) (original work, 1911). See also: Robert S. Siegler, "The Other Alfred Binet," *Developmental Psychology* 28 (1992), 179–190; René Zazzo, "Alfred Binet," *Prospects: The Quarterly Review of Comparative Education* 23 (1993), 101–112.

5 **"A few modern philosophers":** Binet, *Modern Ideas,* 105–107.

5 **In fact, as Gilbert Gottlieb:** Gilbert Gottlieb, "Normally Occurring Environmental and Behavioral Influences on Gene Activity: From Central Dogma to Probabilistic Epigenesis," *Psychological Review* 105 (1995), 792–802.

5 **Robert Sternberg:** Robert Sternberg, "Intelligence, Competence, and Expertise." In Andrew Elliot and Carol S. Dweck (eds.), *The Handbook of Competence and Motivation* (New York: Guilford Press, 2005).

7 **A View from the Two Mindsets:** This research was conducted with Wenjie Zhao and Claudia Mueller.

11 **In fact, studies show:** See the fine work of David Dunning.

11 **Recently, we set out to see:** This research was conducted with Joyce Ehrlinger.

11 **Howard Gardner:** Howard Gardner, *Extraordinary Minds* (New York: Basic Books, 1997).

12 **In a poll of 143 creativity researchers:** Robert J. Sternberg (ed.), *Handbook of Creativity* (New York: Cambridge University Press, 1999).

12 **Which mindset do you have?:** These measures were developed with Sheri Levy, Valanne MacGyvers, C. Y. Chiu, and Ying-yi Hong.

CHAPTER 2. INSIDE THE MINDSETS

16 **Benjamin Barber, an eminent sociologist:** Carole Hyatt and Linda Gottlieb, *When Smart People Fail* (New York: Penguin Books, 1987/1993), 232.

16 **We offered four-year-olds a choice:** This research was done with Charlene Hebert, and was followed up by work with Pat Smiley, Gail Heyman, and Kathy Cain.

17 **One seventh-grade girl summed it up:** Thanks to Nancy Kim for this quote.

17 **It's another to pass up an opportunity:** This work was done with Ying-yi Hong, C. Y. Chiu, Derek Lin, and Wendy Wan.

18 **Brain Waves:** This research is being conducted with Jennifer Mangels and Catherine Good and is supported by a grant from the Department of Education.

18 **It's not just on intellectual tasks:** This research was carried out with Stephanie Morris and Melissa Kamins.

20 **Lee Iacocca had a bad case:** Doron Levin, *Behind the Wheel at Chrysler: The Iacocca Legacy* (New York: Harcourt Brace, 1995).

20 **Darwin Smith, looking back:** Reported in Jim Collins, *Good to Great: Why Some Companies Make the Leap . . . and Others Don't* (New York: HarperCollins, 2001), 20.

20 **Albert Dunlap, a self-professed fixed mindsetter:** Albert Dunlap with Bob Andelman, *Mean Business: How I Save Bad Companies and Make Good Companies Great* (New York: Fireside/Simon & Schuster, 1996); John A. Byrne, "How Al Dunlap Self-Destructed," *Business Week,* July 6, 1998.

20 **Lou Gerstner, an avowed growth mindsetter:** Lou Gerstner, *Who Says Elephants Can't Dance? Inside IBM's Historic Turnaround* (New York: HarperCollins, 2002).

21 **"All my life I've been playing":** Mia Hamm with Aaron Heifetz, *Go for the Goal: A Champion's Guide to Winning in Soccer and in Life* (New York: HarperCollins, 1999), 3.

21 *Patricia Miranda was a chubby, unathletic:* Judy Battista, "A Tiny Female Pioneer for Olympic Wrestling," *The New York Times,* May 16, 2004.

22 *In 1995, Christopher Reeve, the actor:* Christopher Reeve, *Nothing Is Impossible: Reflections on a New Life* (New York, Random House, 2002).

22 *I watched it happen:* This work was done with Heidi Grant.

23 *We saw the same thing in younger students:* This work was with Claudia Mueller.

23 *Marina Semyonova, a great Russian dancer:* Margaret Henry, "Passion and Will, Undimmed by 80 Years of Ballet," *The New York Times,* January 10, 1999.

24 *When Do You Feel Smart:* This work was carried out with Elaine Elliott and later with Valanne MacGyvers.

25 *"We were stars":* Stephen Glass, *The Fabulist* (New York: Simon & Schuster, 2003). This is a moment-by-moment account, which Glass has published as a novel.

26 *To find out, we showed:* This work was done with Jeremy Stone.

27 *So common is the belief:* Reported in Steve Young, *Great Failures of the Extremely Successful* (Los Angeles: Tallfellow Press, 2002).

27 *"Morton," Kennedy told him:* Ibid., 47.

28 *People with the growth mindset know:* This survey was conducted with Catherine Good and Aneeta Rattan.

29 *Is there another way:* Charles C. Manz, *The Power of Failure* (San Francisco: Berrett-Koehler, 2002), 38.

29 *Jack Welch, the celebrated CEO:* Jack Welch with John A. Byrne, *Jack: Straight from the Gut* (New York: Warner Books, 2001).

31 *John McEnroe had a fixed mindset:* John McEnroe with James Kaplan, *You Cannot Be Serious* (New York: Berkley, 2002).

31 *McEnroe used sawdust:* Ibid., 159.

31 *He goes on to tell us:* Ibid., 160.

31 *"Everything was about you":* Ibid., 158.

32 *"I was shocked":* From Janet Lowe, *Michael Jordan Speaks: Lessons from the World's Greatest Champion* (New York: John Wiley, 1999), 95.

32 *Tom Wolfe, in* The Right Stuff*:* Tom Wolfe, *The Right Stuff* (New York: Bantam, 1980), 31. Also cited in Morgan W. McCall, *High Flyers: Developing the Next Generation of Leaders* (Boston: Harvard Business School Press, 1998), 5.

32 *"There is no such thing":* Chuck Yeager and Leo Janos, *Yeager* (New York: Bantam, 1985), 406. Also cited in McCall, *High Flyers,* 17.

33 *As a* New York Times *article:* Amy Waldman, "Why Nobody Likes a Loser," *The New York Times,* August 21, 1999.

33 *"I would have been a different":* Clifton Brown, "Out of a Bunker, and Out of a Funk, Els Takes the Open," *The New York Times,* July 22, 2002.

33 *Each April when the skinny envelopes:* Amy Dickinson, "Skinny Envelopes," *Time,* April 3, 2000. (Thanks to Nellie Sabin for calling my attention to this article.)

33 *Jim Marshall, former defensive player:* Young, *Great Failures of the Extremely Successful,* 7–11.

34 *Bernard Loiseau was one of the top:* Elaine Ganley, "Top Chef's Death Shocks France, Sparks Condemnation of Powerful Food Critics," *Associated Press,* February 25, 2003.

35 *In one study, seventh graders:* This work was done with Lisa Sorich Blackwell and Kali Trzesniewski.

36 *College students, after doing poorly:* This work was with David Nussbaum.

36 *Jim Collins tells:* Collins, *Good to Great,* 80.

36 *It was never his fault:* McEnroe, *You Cannot Be Serious.*

37 *John Wooden, the legendary:* John Wooden with Steve Jamison, *Wooden: A Lifetime of Observations and Reflections On and Off the Court* (Lincolnwood, IL: Contemporary Books, 1997), 55.

37 *When Enron, the energy giant:* Bethany McLean and Peter Elkind, *The Smartest Guys in the Room: The Amazing Rise and Scandalous Fall of Enron* (New York: Penguin Group, 2003), 414.

37 *Jack Welch, the growth-minded CEO:* Welch, *Jack,* 224.

37 *As a psychologist and an educator:* The work described was carried out with Allison Baer and Heidi Grant.

41 *Malcolm Gladwell:* Presented in an invited address at the annual meeting of the American Psychological Association, Chicago, August 2002.

41 *A report from researchers:* "Report of the Steering Committee for the Women's Initiative at Duke University," August 2003.

41 *Americans aren't the only people:* Jack Smith, "In the Weight Rooms of Paris, There Is a Chic New Fragrance: Sweat," *The New York Times,* June 21, 2004.

41 *Seabiscuit:* Laura Hillenbrand, *Seabiscuit: An American Legend* (New York: Random House, 2001).

41 *Equally moving is the parallel story:* Laura Hillenbrand, "A Sudden Illness," *The New Yorker,* July 7, 2003.

42 *Nadja Salerno-Sonnenberg made her violin debut:* Nadja Salerno-Sonnenberg, *Nadja, On My Way* (New York: Crown, 1989); Barbara L. Sand, *Teaching Genius: Dorothy DeLay and the Making of a Musician* (Portland, OR: Amadeus Press, 2000).

42 *"I was used to success":* Salerno-Sonnenberg, *Nadja*, 49.

42 *"Everything I was going through":* Ibid., 50.

42 *Then, one day:* Ibid., 50.

44 *There were few American women:* Hyatt and Gottlieb, *When Smart People Fail*, 25–27.

44 *"I don't really understand":* Ibid., 27.

44 *"I often thought":* Ibid., 25.

44 *Billie Jean King says:* Billie Jean King with Kim Chapin, *Billie Jean* (New York: Harper & Row, 1974).

48 *A lawyer spent seven years:* Hyatt and Gottlieb, *When Smart People Fail*, 224.

50 *Can everything about people be changed?:* Martin Seligman has written a very interesting book on this subject: *What You Can Change . . . And What You Can't* (New York: Fawcett, 1993).

51 *Joseph Martocchio conducted a study:* Joseph J. Martocchio, "Effects of Conceptions of Ability on Anxiety, Self-Efficacy, and Learning in Training," *Journal of Applied Psychology* 79 (1994), 819–825.

51 *The same thing happened with Berkeley students:* Richard Robins and Jennifer Pals, "Implicit Self-Theories in the Academic Domain: Implications for Goal Orientation, Attributions, Affect, and Self-Esteem Change," *Self and Identity* 1 (2002), 313–336.

51 *Michelle Wie is a teenage golfer:* Clifton Brown, "An Education with Hard Courses," *The New York Times*, January 13, 2004.

52 *"I think I learned that I can":* Clifton Brown, "Wie Shows Power but Her Putter Let Her Down," *The New York Times*, January 16, 2004.

CHAPTER 3. THE TRUTH ABOUT ABILITY AND ACCOMPLISHMENT

55 *Edison was not a loner:* Paul Israel, *Edison: A Life of Invention* (New York: John Wiley & Sons, 1998).

56 *Yet Darwin's masterwork:* Howard E. Gruber, *Darwin on Man: A Psychological Study of Scientific Creativity*, 2nd ed. (Chicago: University of Chicago Press, 1981); Charles Darwin, *Autobiographies* (Michael Neve and Sharon Messenger, eds.) (New York: Penguin Books, 1903/2002).

56 *Mozart labored:* Robert W. Weisberg, "Creativity and Knowledge." In Robert J. Sternberg (ed.), *Handbook of Creativity* (New York: Cambridge University Press, 1999).

57 *Back on earth, we measured:* This work was done in collaboration with Lisa Sorich Blackwell and Kali Trzesniewski. Thanks also to Nancy Kim for collecting quotes from the students.

58 *George Danzig was a graduate student:* Told by George Danzig in Cynthia Kersey, *Unstoppable* (Naperville, IL: Sourcebooks, 1998).

58 *John Holt, the great educator:* John Holt, *How Children Fail* (New York: Addison Wesley, 1964/1982), 14.

60 *The College Transition:* This work was done with Heidi Grant.

62 *In her book* Gifted Children: Ellen Winner, *Gifted Children: Myths and Realities* (New York: Basic Books, 1996).

62 *Michael's mother reports:* Ibid., 21.

64 *Garfield High School:* Jay Matthews, *Escalante: The Best Teacher in America* (New York: Henry Holt, 1998).

64 *Marva Collins:* Marva Collins and Civia Tamarkin, *Marva Collins' Way: Returning to Excellence in Education* (Los Angeles: Jeremy Tarcher, 1982/1990).

65 *He saw four-year-olds:* Ibid., 160.

65 *As the three- and four-years-olds:* Marva Collins, *"Ordinary" Children, Extraordinary Teachers* (Charlottesville, VA: Hampton Roads Publishing, 1992), 4.

65 *Benjamin Bloom:* Benjamin S. Bloom, *Developing Talent in Young People* (New York: Ballantine Books, 1985).

65 *Bloom concludes:* Ibid., 4.

66 *Falko Rheinberg, a researcher in Germany:* Falko Rheinberg, *Leistungsbewertung und Lernmotivation* [Achievement Evaluation and Motivation to Learn] (Göttingen: Hogrefe, 1980), 87, 116. Also reported at the conference of the American Educational Research Association, Seattle, April 2001.

67 *"Come on, peach":* Collins and Tamarkin, *Marva Collins' Way,* 19.

68 *On the opposite page are the before-and-after:* Betty Edwards, *The New Drawing on the Right Side of the Brain* (New York: Tarcher/ Putnam, 1979/1999), 18–20.

70 *Jackson Pollock:* Elizabeth Frank, *Pollock* (New York: Abbeville Press, 1983); Evelyn Toynton, "A Little Here, A Little There," *The New York Times Book Review,* January 31, 1999.

70 *Twyla Tharp:* *The Creative Habit* (New York: Simon & Schuster, 2003).

70 *"There are no 'natural' geniuses":* Ibid., 7.

71 *The Danger of Praise:* This work was conducted with Claudia Mueller and with Melissa Kamins.

71 *Adam Guettel has been called:* Jesse Green, "A Complicated Gift," *The New York Times Magazine,* July, 6, 2003.

75 *Research by Claude Steele and Joshua Aronson:* Claude M. Steele and

Joshua Aronson, "Stereotype Threat and the Intellectual Test Performance of African-Americans," *Journal of Personality and Social Psychology* 68 (1995), 797–811.

76 *We asked African American students:* This research was done with Bonita London.

77 *To find out how this happens:* This work was done with Catherine Good and Aneeta Rattan, and is being supported by a grant from the National Science Foundation.

78 *Many females have a problem not only with:* This has been studied by Tomi-Ann Roberts and Susan Nolen-Hoeksema.

79 *When we observed in grade school:* This research was conducted with William Davidson, Sharon Nelson, and Bradley Enna.

79 *Frances Conley:* Frances K. Conley, *Walking Out on the Boys* (New York: Farrar, Straus & Giroux, 1999).

79 *"Is a honey," she wondered:* Ibid., 65.

79 *Julie Lynch, a budding techie:* Michael J. Ybarra, "Why Won't Women Write Code?" *Sky,* December 1999.

80 *The Polgar family:* Carlin Flora, "The Grandmaster Experiment," *Psychology Today,* August 2005.

CHAPTER 4. SPORTS: THE MINDSET OF A CHAMPION

82 *As Michael Lewis tells us:* Michael Lewis, *Moneyball: The Art of Winning an Unfair Game* (New York: Norton, 2003).

82 *"It wasn't merely":* Ibid., 9.

82 *As one scout said:* Ibid., 48.

83 *"He had no concept of failure":* Ibid., 46.

83 *Beane continues, "I started to get":* Ibid., 47.

84 *Muhammad Ali failed these measurements:* Felix Dennis and Don Atyeo, *Muhammad Ali: The Glory Years* (New York: Hyperion, 2003).

84 *He pulled back his torso:* Ibid., 14.

84 *Not only did he study Liston's:* Ibid., 92.

85 *Ali said, "Liston had to believe":* Ibid., 96.

85 *Float like a butterfly:* Ibid., 74.

85 *"He was a paradox":* Ibid., 14.

85 *Michael Jordan:* Janet Lowe, *Michael Jordan Speaks: Lessons from the World's Greatest Champion* (New York: John Wiley, 1999).

86 *His mother says:* Ibid., 7.

86 *Former Bulls assistant coach John Bach:* Ibid., 29.

86 *For Jordan, success stems:* Ibid., 35.

86   *The Babe was not a natural, either:*   Robert W. Creamer, *Babe: The Legend Comes to Life* (New York: Penguin Books, 1974/1983).

87   *Robert Creamer, his biographer:*   Creamer, *Babe*, 301.

87   *"He could experiment at the plate":*   Ibid., 109.

87   *Yet we cling fast:*   Stephen J. Gould, *Triumph and Tragedy in Mudville: A Lifelong Passion for Baseball* (New York: Norton, 2003).

87   *What about Wilma Rudolph:*   Tom Biracree, *Wilma Rudolph* (New York: Chelsea House, 1988).

88   *After her incredible career, she said:*   Ibid., 107.

88   *What about Jackie Joyner-Kersee:*   Jackie Joyner-Kersee with Sonja Steptoe, *A Kind of Grace* (New York: Warner Books, 1997).

88   *"There is something about seeing myself improve":*   Ibid., 60.

88   *Did you know:*   Clifton Brown, "On Golf: It's Not How for Tiger, It's Just by How Much," *The New York Times*, July 25, 2000.

89   *Wills was an eager baseball player:*   Cynthia Kersey, *Unstoppable* (Naperville, IL: Sourcebooks, 1998).

89   *He proudly announced to his friends:*   Ibid., 152.

89   *At the seven-and-a-half:*   Ibid., 153.

90   *This really hit me:*   Buster Olney, "Speedy Feet, but an Even Quicker Thinker," *The New York Times*, February 1, 2002.

91   *Bruce Jenner, 1976 Olympic gold medalist:*   Mike McGovern and Susan Shelly, *The Quotable Athlete* (New York: McGraw-Hill, 2000), 113.

92   *They hadn't won a World Series:*   Gould, *Triumph and Tragedy in Mudville*.

92   *As* New York Times *writer:*   Jack Curry, "After Melee, Spin Control Takes Over," *The New York Times*, October 13, 2003.

92   *Even the Boston writers were aghast:*   Dan Shaughnessy, "It Is Time for Martinez to Grow Up," *The New York Times*, October 13, 2003. (During this series, the *Globe* sportswriters' columns appeared in the *Times* and vice versa.)

94   *Let's take it from the top:*   William Rhoden, "Momentous Victory, Most Notably Achieved," *The New York Times*, July 10, 2000.

94   *"Just keep pumping your arms":*   Kersee, *A Kind of Grace*, 280.

95   *"The strength for that sixth jump":*   Ibid., 298.

95   *But, as Billie Jean King tells us:*   King, *Billie Jean*, 236.

96   *When the match:*   Ibid., 78.

96   *Jackie Joyner-Kersee had her* Eureka!*:*   Joyner-Kersee, *A Kind of Grace*, 63.

96   *Often called the best woman soccer player:*   Mia Hamm with Aaron

Heifetz, *Go for the Goal: A Champion's Guide to Winning in Soccer and in Life* (New York: HarperCollins, 1999), 31.

96 *"It is," said Hamm:* Ibid., 36.

96 *By the way, did Hamm think:* Ibid., 3.

96 *Jack Nicklaus, the famed golfer:* Tom Callahan, *In Search of Tiger: A Journey Through Gold with Tiger Woods* (New York: Crown, 2003), 24.

96 *John Wooden:* John Wooden with Jack Tobin, *They Call Me Coach* (Waco, TX: Word Books, 1972), 63–65.

97 *"I believe ability":* John Wooden with Steve Jamison, *Wooden* (Lincolnwood, IL: Contemporary Books, 1997), 99.

97 *Stuart Biddle and his colleagues:* "Goal Orientation and Conceptions of the Nature of Sport Ability in Children: A Social Cognitive Approach," *British Journal of Social Psychology* 35 (1996), 399–414; "Motivation for Physical Activity in Young People: Entity and Incremental Beliefs About Athletic Ability," *Journal of Sports Sciences* 21 (2003), 973–989. See also Yngvar Ommundsen, "Implicit Theories of Ability and Self-Regulation Strategies in Physical Education Classes," *Educational Psychology* 23 (2003), 141–157; "Self-Handicapping Strategies in Physical Education Classes: The Influence of Implicit Theories of the Nature of Ability and Achievement Goal Orientations," *Psychology of Sport and Exercise* 2 (2001), 139–156.

98 *Finding #1:* This finding is from the research by Biddle and his colleagues.

98 *"For me the joy of athletics":* Joyner-Kersee, *A Kind of Grace*, 60.

98 *In fact, he says:* Wooden, *Wooden*, 53.

99 *After the '98 Masters tournament:* Dave Anderson, "No Regrets for Woods," *The New York Times*, April 4, 1998.

99 *Or after a British Open:* Callahan, *In Search of Tiger*, 219.

99 *Tiger is a hugely ambitious man:* Ibid., 220.

99 *Mia Hamm tells us:* Hamm, *Go for the Goal*, 201.

99 *"They saw that we truly love":* Ibid., 243.

99 *"There was a time":* John McEnroe with James Kaplan, *You Cannot Be Serious* (New York: Berkley, 2002), 10.

99 *"Some people don't want to rehearse":* Ibid., 155.

99 *Finding #2:* Ommundsen, "Implicit Theories of Ability," 141–157.

99 *"You can't leave":* Lowe, *Michael Jordan Speaks*, 99.

100 *Michael Jordan embraced his failures:* Ibid., 107.

100 *Here's how Kareem Abdul-Jabbar:* Wooden, *Wooden*, 100.

100 *For example, he hoped desperately:* McEnroe, *You Cannot Be Serious*, 112.

100 *"God, if I lose to Patrick":*   Ibid., 259.

100 *Here's how failure motivated him:*   Ibid., 119.

100 *In 1981, McEnroe bought:*   Ibid., 274.

100 *Here's how failure motivated Sergio Garcia:*   Callahan, *In Search of Tiger,* 164, 169.

101 *Finding #3:*   Ommundsen, "Implicit Theories of Ability and Self-Regulation Strategies," *Educational Psychology,* 2003, *23,* 141–157; "Self-Handicapping Strategies," *Psychology of Sport and Exercise,* 2001 2, 139–156.

101 *How come Michael Jordan's skill:*   Lowe, *Michael Jordan Speaks,* 177.

101 *Butch Harmon, the renowned coach:*   Callahan, *In Search of Tiger,* 75.

101 *With this in mind, Tiger's dad:*   Ibid., 237.

101 *"I know my game":*   Ibid., 219.

102 *"I love working on shots":*   Ibid., 300.

102 *"He's twelve":*   Ibid., 23.

102 *Mark O'Meara, Woods's golf partner:*   Ibid., 25.

102 *For example, when he didn't:*   McEnroe, *You Cannot Be Serious,* 166.

102 *In fact, rather than combating:*   Ibid., 29.

102 *He wished someone else:*   Ibid., 207.

102 *"The system let me get away":*   Ibid., 190.

103 *"In our society":*   Lowe, *Michael Jordan Speaks,* 37.

103 *Coach John Wooden claims:*   Wooden, *Wooden,* 113.

103 *"I believe, for example":*   Ibid., 78.

104 *When asked before a game:*   Charlie Nobles, "Johnson Is Gone, So Bucs, Move On," *The New York Times,* November 20, 2003; Dave Anderson, "Regarding Johnson, Jets Should Just Say No," *The New York Times,* November 21, 2003.

104 *"I am a team player, but":*   Anderson, "Regarding Johnson."

104 *When Nyad hatched her plan:*   Kersey, *Unstoppable,* 212.

105 *Iciss Tillis is a college:*   Viv Bernstein, "The Picture Doesn't Tell the Story," *The New York Times,* January 24, 2004.

106 *It's six-foot-three Candace Parker:*   Ira Berkow, "Stardom Awaits a Prodigy and Assist Goes to Her Father," *The New York Times,* January 20, 2004.

CHAPTER 5. BUSINESS: MINDSET AND LEADERSHIP

108 *According to Malcolm Gladwell:*   Malcolm Gladwell, "The Talent Myth," *The New Yorker,* July 22, 2002.

109 *Remember the study where we interviewed:*   That study was performed with Ying-yi Hong, C. Y. Chiu, Derek Lin, and Wendy Wan.

109 *And remember how we put students:* This research was conducted with Claudia Mueller.

109 *Jim Collins set out to discover:* Jim Collins, *Good to Great: Why Some Companies Make the Leap . . . and Others Don't* (New York: Harper-Collins, 2001).

110 *"They used to call me the prosecutor":* Ibid., 75.

111 *Robert Wood and Albert Bandura:* Robert Wood and Albert Bandura, "Impact of Conceptions of Ability on Self-Regulatory Mechanisms and Complex Decision Making," *Journal of Personality and Social Psychology* 56 (1989), 407–415.

112 *As Collins puts it:* Collins, *Good to Great,* 26.

113 *Says Collins: The good-to-great Kroger:* Ibid., 65–69.

113 *According to James Surowiecki:* James Surowiecki, "Blame Iacocca: How the Former Chrysler CEO Caused the Corporate Scandals," *Slate,* July 24, 2002.

114 *Warren Bennis, the leadership guru:* Warren Bennis, *On Becoming a Leader* (Cambridge, MA: Perseus Publishing, 1989/2003), xxix.

114 *Iacocca wasn't like that:* Lee Iacocca with William Novak, *Iacocca: An Autobiography* (New York: Bantam Books, 1984).

114 *What's more, "If Henry was king":* Ibid., 101.

114 *"I was His Majesty's special protégé":* Ibid., 83.

114 *"All of us . . . lived the good life":* Ibid., 101.

115 *"I had always clung to the idea":* Ibid., 144.

115 *He wondered whether Henry Ford:* Doron P. Levin, *Behind the Wheel at Chrysler: The Iacocca Legacy* (New York: Harcourt Brace, 1995), 31.

115 *"You don't realize what a favor":* Ibid., 231.

115 *Just a few years after:* Iacocca, *Iacocca,* xvii.

115 *Within a short time, however:* Levin, *Behind the Wheel at Chrysler.*

116 *In an editorial:* Ibid., 312.

116 *So in a bid:* "Iacocca, Spurned in Return Attempts, Lashes Out," *USA Today,* March 19, 2002.

117 *Albert Dunlap saved dying companies:* Albert J. Dunlap with Bob Andelman, *Mean Business: How I Save Bad Companies and Make Good Companies Great* (New York: Fireside/Simon & Schuster, 1996).

117 *"Did I earn it?":* Ibid., 21.

117 *"If you're in business":* Ibid., 199.

117 *A woman stood up and asked:* Ibid., 62.

118 *"Making my way in the world":* Ibid., 107–108.

118 *"The most ridiculous term":* Ibid., 196.

118 *"Eventually, I have gotten bored":* Ibid., 26.

118 **Then in 1996:** John A. Byrne, "How Al Dunlap Self-Destructed," *Business Week,* July 6, 1998.

119 **Ken Lay, the company's founder:** Bethany McLean and Peter Elkind, *The Smartest Guys in the Room: The Amazing Rise and Scandalous Fall of Enron* (New York: Penguin Group, 2003).

119 **Kinder was also the only person:** Ibid., 92.

119 **Even as Lay:** Ibid., 89.

120 **"Ron doesn't get it":** Ibid., 69.

120 **"Well, it's so obvious":** Ibid., 233.

120 **As McLean and Elkind report:** Ibid., 40.

120 **Said Amanda Martin, an Enron executive:** Ibid., 121.

121 **Resident geniuses almost brought down:** Alec Klein, *Stealing Time: Steve Case, Jerry Levin, and the Collapse of AOL Time Warner* (New York: Simon & Schuster, 2003).

122 **Speaking about AOL executives:** Ibid., 171.

122 **As Morgan McCall:** Morgan W. McCall, *High Flyers: Developing the Next Generation of Leaders* (Boston: Harvard Business School Press, 1998), xiii. McCall also analyzes the effects on corporate culture of believing in natural talent instead of the potential to develop. "The message of *High Flyers,*" he says, "is that leadership ability can be learned, that creating a context that supports the development of talent can become a source of competitive advantage, and that the development of leaders is itself a leadership responsibility," xii.

123 **Harvey Hornstein, an expert:** Harvey A. Hornstein, *Brutal Bosses and Their Prey* (New York: Riverhead Books, 1996), 49.

123 **Hornstein describes Paul Kazarian:** Ibid., 10.

123 **An engineer at a major aircraft:** Ibid., 54.

124 **In Good to Great, *Collins notes:*** Jim Collins, *Good to Great,* 72.

124 **According to Collins and Porras:** James C. Collins and Jerry I. Porras, *Built to Last: Successful Habits of Visionary Companies* (New York: HarperCollins, 1994/2002), 165.

124 **Ray Macdonald of Burroughs:** Ibid., 166.

124 **The same thing happened at Texas:** Ibid.

124 **Andrew Carnegie once said:** John C. Maxwell, *Developing the Leaders Around You* (Nashville, TN: Thomas Nelson, 1995), 15.

125 **Warren Bennis has said:** Bennis, *On Becoming a Leader,* 19.

125 **When Jack Welch took over:** "Overvalued: Why Jack Welch Isn't God," *The New Republic,* June 11, 2001. Even this article, which explains why Welch should *not* be regarded as a god-like figure, details his remarkable accomplishments.

125 **Fortune** *magazine called Welch:* Ibid.

126 *But to me even more impressive:* Steve Bennett, "The Boss: Put It in Writing Please," *The New York Times,* May 9, 2004.

126 *Instead, it's "I hate having to":* Jack Welch with John A. Byrne, *Jack: Straight from the Gut* (New York: Warner Books, 2001), ix.

126 *Or "[These people] filled my journey":* Ibid., 439.

126 *In 1971, Welch was being considered:* Ibid., 42.

127 *One day, young "Dr." Welch:* Ibid., 36.

127 *"The Kidder experience never left me":* Ibid., 228–229.

127 *What he learned was this:* Ibid., 384.

127 *When Welch was a young engineer:* Ibid., 27.

128 *"Eventually I learned":* Ibid., 54.

128 *One evening, Welch addressed:* Ibid., 97–98.

128 *In front of five hundred managers:* Ibid., 189.

129 *"As a result, leaders were encouraged":* Ibid., 186.

129 *"You owe it to America":* Louis V. Gerstner, *Who Says Elephants Can't Dance? Inside IBM's Historic Turnaround* (New York: HarperCollins, 2002), p. 16.

129 *Six days after he arrived:* Ibid., 78.

130 *He dedicated his book to them:* Ibid., v.

130 *"Hierarchy means very little to me":* Ibid., 24.

131 *"[IBM stock] has done nothing":* Ibid., 57.

131 *That was the Xerox Anne Mulcahy:* Betsy Morris, "The Accidental CEO," *Fortune,* June 23, 2003.

131 **Fortune** *named Mulcahy "the hottest turnaround":* "Most Powerful Women in Business 2004," *Fortune,* October 18, 2004.

131 *For example, as* **Fortune** *writer Betsy:* Morris, "The Accidental CEO."

131 *She was tough:* Ibid.

132 *After slaving away:* Ibid.

132 *But a year later she knew:* Ibid.

133 *Women now hold more key positions:* "Most Powerful Women in Business 2004."

133 *In fact,* **Fortune** *magazine called Meg:* Eryn Brown, "How Can a Dot-Com Be This Hot?" *Fortune,* January 21, 2002; Patricia Sellers, "eBay's Secret," *Fortune,* October 18, 2004.

133 *Researcher Robert Wood and his colleagues:* Robert E. Wood, Katherine Williams Phillips, and Carmen Tabernero, "Implicit Theories of Ability, Processing Dynamics and Performance in Decision-Making Groups," Australian Graduate School of Management, Sydney, Australia.

134 In the early 1970s, Irving Janis: Irving Janis, *Groupthink*, 2nd ed. (Boston: Houghton Mifflin, 1972/1982).

135 "Everything had broken right for him": Ibid., 35.

135 Schlesinger also said, "Had one senior": Ibid., 38.

135 To prevent this from happening: Collins, *Good to Great*, 71.

135 An outside consultant kept asking Enron: McLean and Elkind, *The Smartest Guys in the Room*, 241.

135 "We got to the point": Ibid., 230.

135 Alfred P. Sloan, the former CEO: Janis, *Groupthink*, 71. From Peter F. Drucker, *The Effective Executive* (New York: Harper & Row, 1966).

135 Herodotus, writing: Janis, *Groupthink*, 71.

136 He said the new, rounder cars: Levin, *Behind the Wheel*, 102–103.

136 David Packard, on the other hand: David Packard, *The HP Way: How Bill Hewlett and I Built Our Company* (New York: HarperCollins, 1995).

136 You can't pick up a magazine: Jean M. Twenge, *Generation Me: Why Today's Young Americans Are More Confident, Assertive, Entitled—and More Miserable Than Ever Before* (New York: Free Press, 2007).

138 Laura Kray and Michael Haselhuhn have shown: Laura Kray and Michael Haselhuhn, "Implicit Theories of Negotiating Ability and Performance: Longitudinal and Experimental Evidence." *Journal of Personality and Social Psychology* 93 (2007), 49–64.

139 Studies by Peter Heslin: Peter Heslin, Gary Latham, and Don VandeWalle. "The Effect of Implicit Person Theory on Performance Appraisals." *Journal of Applied Psychology* 90 (2005), 842–56; Peter Heslin, Don VandeWalle, and Gary Latham. "Keen to Help? Managers' IPT and Their Subsequent Employee Coaching." *Personnel Psychology* 59 (2006), 871–902.

141 When Warren Bennis interviewed: Bennis, *On Becoming a Leader*, xxix.

141 Bennis concurred: "I believe": Ibid., xxxii.

142 John Zenger and Joseph Folkman: John H. Zenger and Joseph Folkman, *The Extraordinary Leader: Turning Good Managers into Great Leaders* (New York: McGraw-Hill, 2002).

142 Or, as Morgan McCall argues: McCall, *High Flyers*.

CHAPTER 6. RELATIONSHIPS: MINDSETS IN LOVE (OR NOT)

144 What separates them?: This work was carried out with Israela Silberman.

146 The Contos family: Shown on *Weddings Gone Wild*, ABC, June 14, 2004.

147 **In his study of gifted people:** Benjamin S. Bloom, *Developing Talent in Young People* (New York: Ballantine Books, 1985).

147 **Maybe that's why Daniel Goleman's:** Daniel Goleman, *Emotional Intelligence: Why It Can Matter More than IQ* (New York: Bantam, 1995).

150 **Aaron Beck, noted marriage authority:** Aaron T. Beck, *Love Is Never Enough* (New York: Harper & Row, 1988), 202.

150 **Says John Gottman:** John Gottman with Nan Silver, *Why Marriages Succeed or Fail* (New York: Fireside/Simon & Schuster, 1994), 69.

150 **Elayne Savage, noted family psychologist:** Elayne Savage, *Don't Take It Personally: The Art of Dealing with Rejection* (Oakland, CA: New Harbinger, 1997).

151 **Raymond Knee and his colleagues:** C. Raymond Knee, "Implicit Theories of Relationships: Assessment and Prediction of Romantic Relationship Initiation, Coping, and Longevity," *Journal of Personality and Social Psychology* 74 (1998), 360–370.

152 **John Gottman reports:** Gottman, *Why Marriages Succeed or Fail,* 155.

152 **And they assign blame to a trait:** This has been studied by Raymond Knee, and I have found this in my work with Lara Kammrath. (See also the work of Frank Fincham.)

153 **So once people with the fixed mindset:** The idea that a fixed mindset can undermine relationships is also found in the work of Roy Eidelson and Norman Epstein, and of Susan Hendrick and Clyde Hendrick. The idea of criticism—attacking the partner's personality or character—leading to contempt is explored in the work of John Gottman.

154 **Brenda and Jack were clients:** Daniel B. Wile, *After the Honeymoon: How Conflict Can Improve Your Relationship* (New York: John Wiley & Sons, 1988).

155 **The story of Ted and Karen:** Beck, *Love Is Never Enough.*

155 **"Everything she says and does":** Ibid., 36.

155 **"She never takes anything seriously":** Ibid., 36.

155 **"What is the mature thing":** Ibid., 246.

156 **Aaron Beck tells couples:** Ibid., 199.

156 **Hillary defended him:** Hillary Rodham Clinton, *Living History* (New York: Simon & Schuster, 2003), 465.

156 **Through counseling, Bill came to understand:** Bill Clinton, *My Life* (New York: Knopf, 2004); Bill Clinton on *The Charlie Rose Show,* June 23, 2004.

156 **One evening, Stevie Wonder:** H. R. Clinton, *Living History.*

163 **Jennifer Beer studied hundreds of people:** Jennifer S. Beer, "Implicit Self-Theories of Shyness," *Journal of Personality & Social Psychology* 83

(2002), 1009–1024. See also the excellent work of Phil Zimbardo on shyness.

164 *Scott Wetzler, a therapist and professor:* Scott Wetzler, *Is It You or Is It Me? Why Couples Play the Blame Game* (New York: HarperCollins, 1998).

164 *"It doesn't matter to me":* Ibid., 134.

165 *At Columbine, the most notorious:* Brooks Brown and Rob Merritt, *No Easy Answers: The Truth Behind Death at Columbine* (New York: Lantern Books, 2002).

168 *Brooks Brown, a classmate:* Ibid.

168 *He rejected the fixed mindset:* Ibid., 47.

168 *In his own words:* Ibid., 107.

168 *"It's to use your mind":* Ibid., 263.

168 *"We can just sit back":* Ibid., 21.

169 *Stan Davis, a therapist:* Stan Davis, *Schools Where Everyone Belongs: Practical Strategies for Reducing Bullying* (Wayne, ME: Stop Bullying Now, 2003). See also Dan Olweus, *Bullying at School* (Malden, MA: Blackwell, 1993).

170 *"I notice that you have been":* Ibid., 34.

170 *Haim Ginott, the renowned child psychologist:* Haim G. Ginott, *Teacher and Child* (New York: Macmillan, 1972), 167.

171 *In a* **New York Times** *article:* Jane Gross, "Hot Topic at Summer Camps: Ending the Rule of the Bullies," *The New York Times*, June 28, 2004.

CHAPTER 7. PARENTS, TEACHERS, AND COACHES:
WHERE DO MINDSETS COME FROM?

173 *Haim Ginott, the childrearing sage:* Haim G. Ginott, *Between Parent & Child* (New York: Avon Books, 1956), 22–24.

175 *Remember chapter 3:* This work was with Claudia Mueller and Melissa Kamins.

183 *Ginott tells of Philip:* Haim G. Ginott, *Between Parent & Teenager* (New York: Macmillan, 1969), 88.

184 *Children Learn the Messages:* This research was done with Chauncy Lennon and Eva Pomerantz.

185 *Here's a kindergarten boy:* This is from work with Gail Heyman and Kathy Cain: Gail D. Heyman, Carol S. Dweck, and Kathleen Cain, "Young Children's Vulnerability to Self-Blame and Helplessness," *Child Development* 63 (1992), 401–415.

186 We asked second-grade children: This research was with Gail Heyman: Gail D. Heyman and Carol S. Dweck, "Children's Thinking About Traits: Implications for Judgments of the Self and Others," *Child Development* 64 (1998), 391–403.

187 Mary Main and Carol George: Mary Main and Carol George, "Responses of Abused and Disadvantaged Toddlers to Distress in the Day Care Setting," *Developmental Psychology* 21 (1985), 407–412.

190 "My parents pushed me": John McEnroe with James Kaplan, *You Cannot Be Serious* (New York: Berkley, 2002), 31.

190 However, he says, "Many athletes": Ibid., 30.

190 "If Tiger had wanted to be": Tom Callahan, *In Search of Tiger: A Journey Through Gold with Tiger Woods* (New York: Crown, 2003), 213.

190 Tiger says in return: Tiger Woods, *How I Play Golf* (New York: Warner Books, 2001), 302.

191 Dorothy DeLay, the famous violin teacher: Barbara L. Sand, *Teaching Genius: Dorothy DeLay and the Making of a Musician* (Portland, OR: Amadeus Press, 2000).

191 One set of parents: Ibid., 79.

191 DeLay spent countless hours: Ibid., 144.

191 Says Yura, "I'm always happy": Ibid., 153.

191 We asked college students to describe: This work was with Bonita London.

192 Haim Ginott describes Nicholas: Ginott, *Between Parent & Teenager*, 132.

193 For thirty-five years, Sheila Schwartz taught: Sheila Schwartz, "Teaching's Unlettered Future," *The New York Times*, August 6, 1998.

194 Marva Collins taught Chicago children: Marva Collins and Civia Tamarkin, *Marva Collins' Way: Returning to Excellence in Education* (Los Angeles: Jeremy Tarcher, 1982/1990); Marva Collins, *"Ordinary" Children, Extraordinary Teachers* (Charlottesville, VA: Hampton Roads Publishing, 1992).

194 When 60 Minutes *did a segment:* Collins, *"Ordinary" Children*, 43–44.

195 Chicago Sun-Times writer Zay Smith: Collins and Tamarkin, *Marva Collins' Way*, 160.

195 As Collins looks back: Ibid., 47.

195 "I know most of you can't": Ibid., 21–22.

195 As they changed from children: Ibid., 68.

195 Rafe Esquith teaches Los Angeles: Rafe Esquith, *There Are No Shortcuts* (New York: Pantheon, 2003).

196 DeLay's husband always teased her: Sand, *Teaching Genius*, 23.

196 Her mentor and fellow teacher: Ibid., 54.

196 *"I think it's too easy":* Ibid., 70.

196 *Itzhak Perlman was her student:* Ibid., 201.

196 *"I think she has something special":* Ibid., 85.

196 *Yet she established on Day One:* Collins and Tamarkin, *Marva Collins' Way,* 19.

197 *When Benjamin Bloom studied his 120:* Benjamin S. Bloom, *Developing Talent in Young People* (New York: Ballantine Books, 1985).

197 *When Collins expanded her school:* Collins, *"Ordinary" Children.*

198 *Esquith bemoans the lowering of standards:* Esquith, *There Are No Shortcuts,* 53.

198 *"That is part of Miss DeLay's":* Sand, *Teaching Genius,* 219.

199 *"I know which child will handle":* Esquith, *There Are No Shortcuts,* 40.

199 *Collins echoes that idea:* Collins and Tamarkin, *Marva Collins' Way,* 21.

199 *One student was sure he couldn't:* Sand, *Teaching Genius,* 64.

199 *Another student was intimidated:* Ibid., 114.

199–200 *As Marva Collins said to a boy:* Collins and Tamarkin, *Marva Collins' Way,* 208.

200 *Here is a shortened version:* Ibid., 85–88.

200 *"It's sort of like Socrates says":* Ibid., 159.

200 *For a class assignment, he wrote:* Ibid., 165.

201 *And she let her students know:* Ibid., 87.

202 *Michael Lewis, in* The New York Times: Michael Lewis, "Coach Fitz's Management Theory," *The New York Times Magazine,* March 28, 2004.

202 *Bobby Knight, the famous and controversial:* Bob Knight with Bob Hammel, *Knight: My Story* (New York: St. Martin's Press, 2002); Steve Alford with John Garrity, *Playing for Knight* (New York: Fireside/ Simon & Schuster, 1989); John Feinstein, *A Season on the Brink: A Year with Bobby Knight and the Indiana Hoosiers* (New York: Fireside/Simon & Schuster, 1987).

203 *John Feinstein, author of* Season: Feinstein, *Season on the Brink,* 3.

203 *In Daryl Thomas, Feinstein says:* Ibid., 3–4.

203 *"You know what you are Daryl?":* Ibid., 7.

204 *An assistant coach had given this advice:* Ibid., 4.

204 *"What I like best about this team":* Ibid., 25.

204 *Steve Alford, who went on:* Alford, *Playing for Knight,* 101.

204 *"The atmosphere was poisonous":* Ibid., 169.

204 *Says Alford, "Coach's Holy Grail":* Ibid., 63.

205 *In the "season on the brink":* Feinstein, *Season on the Brink,* xi.

205 *"You know there were times":* Ibid., 8–9.

206 **Coach John Wooden produced:** John Wooden with Jack Tobin, *They Call Me Coach* (Waco, TX: Word Books, 1972); John Wooden with Steve Jamison, *Wooden: A Lifetime of Observations and Reflections On and Off the Court* (Lincolnwood, IL: Contemporary Books, 1997).

207 *"You have to apply yourself":* Wooden, *Wooden,* 11.

207 *"Did I win? Did I lose?":* Ibid., 56.

207 *If so, he says:* Ibid., 55.

207 *If the players were coasting:* Ibid., 119.

207 *"I looked at each one":* Ibid., 95.

208 *"Other fellows who played":* Ibid., 67.

208 *But he promised him:* Ibid., 141–142.

208 *Bill Walton, Hall of Famer:* Ibid., ix.

208 *Denny Crum, successful coach:* Ibid., xii.

209 *Kareem Abdul-Jabbar, Hall of Famer:* Ibid., xiii.

209 *It was the moment of victory:* Wooden, *They Call Me Coach,* 9–10.

209 *"There are coaches out there":* Wooden, *Wooden,* 117.

209 *Pat Summitt is the coach:* Pat Summitt with Sally Jenkins, *Reach for the Summit* (New York: Broadway Books, 1998).

210 *Wooden calls it being "infected":* Wooden, *Wooden.*

210 *Pat Riley, former coach:* Pat Riley, *The Winner Within* (New York: Putnam, 1993).

210 *Summitt explains, "Success lulls you":* Summitt, *Reach for the Summit,* 237.

210 *The North Carolina coach:* Ibid., 5.

210 *"Get your heads up":* Ibid., 6.

211 *"You never stay the same":* Tyler Kepner, "The Complete Package: Why A-Rod Is the Best in Business, Even While Learning a New Position," *The New York Times,* April 4, 2004.

CHAPTER 8. CHANGING MINDSETS

214 *In the 1960s, psychiatrist Aaron Beck:* Aaron T. Beck, "Thinking and Depression: Idiosyncratic Content and Cognitive Distortions," *Archives of General Psychology* 9 (1963), 325–333; *Prisoners of Hate: The Cognitive Basis of Anger, Hostility, and Violence* (New York: HarperCollins, 1999). (At about the same time, therapist Albert Ellis was discovering a similar thing: that beliefs are the key to how people feel.)

215 *In several studies, we probed:* This work was done with Ying-yi Hong, C. Y. Chiu, and Russell Sacks.

216 *It does not confront the basic:* However, see Jeffrey E. Young and Janet Klosko, *Reinventing Your Life* (New York: Plume/Penguin, 1994). Although Young and Klosko are working in a cognitive therapy tradition, a core assumption of their approach and one that they teach their clients is that people can change in very basic ways.

218 *A Mindset Workshop:* This workshop was developed with Lisa Sorich Blackwell with grants from the William T. Grant Foundation and the Spencer Foundation: L. S. Blackwell, C. S. Dweck, and K. Trzesniewski, *Implicit Theories of Intelligence Predict Achievement Across an Adolescent Transition: A Longitudinal Study and an Intervention,* 2003. I would also like to acknowledge other psychologists who have developed their own student workshops based on the growth mindset: Jeff Howard, founder of the Efficacy Institute, and Joshua Aronson, Catherine Good, and Michael Inzlicht of New York University and Columbia University.

219 *"Many people think of the brain":* This was written for the workshop by Lisa Sorich Blackwell.

221 *Brainology:* The Brainology computer-based program was also developed with Lisa Sorich Blackwell, with a grant from the William T. Grant Foundation.

224 *Psychologists Karen Horney and Carl Rogers:* Karen Horney, *Neurosis and Human Growth: The Struggle Toward Self-Realization* (New York: Norton, 1950); *Our Inner Conflicts: A Constructive Theory of Neurosis* (New York: Norton, 1945). Carl R. Rogers, *Client-Centered Therapy* (New York: Houghton Mifflin, 1951); *On Becoming a Person* (New York: Houghton Mifflin, 1961).

228 *Research by Peter Gollwitzer:* Peter M. Gollwitzer, "Implementation Intentions: Strong Effects of Simple Plans," *American Psychologist* 54 (1999), 493–503.

239 *Mindset and Willpower:* I am researching this issue with Abigail Scholer, Eran Magen, and James Gross.

RECOMMENDED BOOKS

Beck, Aaron T. *Love Is Never Enough.* New York: Harper & Row, 1988.

———. *Prisoners of Hate.* New York: HarperCollins, 1999.

Beck, Judith S. *Cognitive Therapy.* New York: Guilford Press, 1995.

Bennis, Warren. *On Becoming a Leader.* Cambridge, MA: Perseus Publishing, 1989/2003.

Binet, Alfred (Suzanne Heisler, trans.). *Modern Ideas About Children.* Menlo Park, CA: Suzanne Heisler, 1975 (original work, 1909).

Bloom, Benjamin S. *Developing Talent in Young People.* New York: Ballantine Books, 1985.

Collins, Jim. *Good to Great: Why Some Companies Make the Leap . . . and Others Don't.* New York: HarperCollins, 2001.

Collins, Marva, and Civia Tamarkin. *Marva Collins' Way: Returning to Excellence in Education.* Los Angeles: Jeremy Tarcher, 1982/1990.

Csikszentmihalyi, Mihaly. *Flow: The Psychology of Optimal Experience.* New York: Harper & Row, 1990.

Davis, Stan. *Schools Where Everyone Belongs: Practical Strategies for Reducing Bullying.* Wayne, ME: Stop Bullying Now, 2003.

Edwards, Betty. *The New Drawing on the Right Side of the Brain.* New York: Tarcher/Putnam, 1979/1999.

Ellis, Albert. *Reason and Emotion in Psychotherapy.* Secaucus, NJ: Citadel, 1962.

Ginott, Haim G. *Between Parent & Child.* New York: Avon Books, 1956.

———. *Between Parent & Teenager.* New York: Macmillan, 1969.

———. *Teacher and Child.* New York: Macmillan, 1972.

Goleman, Daniel. *Emotional Intelligence: Why It Can Matter More than IQ.* New York: Bantam, 1995.

Gottman, John, with Nan Silver. *Why Marriages Succeed or Fail.* New York: Fireside/Simon & Schuster, 1994.

Gould, Stephen J. *The Mismeasure of Man.* New York: Norton, 1981.

Holt, John. *How Children Fail.* New York: Addison Wesley, 1964/1982.

Hyatt, Carole, and Linda Gottlieb. *When Smart People Fail.* New York: Penguin Books, 1987/1993.

Janis, Irving. *Groupthink,* 2nd ed. Boston: Houghton Mifflin, 1972/1982.

Lewis, Michael. *Moneyball: The Art of Winning an Unfair Game.* New York: Norton, 2003.

Lewis, Michael. *Coach: Lessons on the Game of Life.* New York: Norton, 2005.

McCall, Morgan W. *High Flyers: Developing the Next Generation of Leaders.* Boston: Harvard Business School Press, 1998.

McLean, Bethany, and Peter Elkind. *The Smartest Guys in the Room: The Amazing Rise and Scandalous Fall of Enron.* New York: Penguin Group, 2003.

Olweus, Dan. *Bullying at School.* Malden, MA: Blackwell, 1993.

Reeve, Christopher. *Nothing Is Impossible: Reflections on a New Life.* New York: Random House, 2002.

Sand, Barbara L. *Teaching Genius: Dorothy DeLay and the Making of a Musician.* Portland, OR: Amadeus Press, 2000.

Seligman, Martin E. P. *Learned Optimism: How to Change Your Mind and Your Life.* New York: Knopf, 1991.

Tharp, Twyla. *The Creative Habit.* New York: Simon & Schuster, 2003.

Wetzler, Scott. *Is It You or Is It Me? Why Couples Play the Blame Game.* New York: HarperCollins, 1998.

Wooden, John, with Steve Jamison. *Wooden: A Lifetime of Observations and Reflections On and Off the Court.* Lincolnwood, IL: Contemporary Books, 1997.

INDEX

CAROL S. DWECK, PH.D., is widely regarded as one of the world's leading researchers in the fields of personality, social psychology, and developmental psychology. She has been the William B. Ransford Professor of Psychology at Columbia University and is now the Lewis and Virginia Eaton Professor of Psychology at Stanford University and a member of the American Academy of Arts and Sciences. Her scholarly book *Self-Theories: Their Role in Motivation, Personality, and Development* was named Book of the Year by the World Education Fellowship. Her work has been featured in such publications as *The New Yorker, Time, The New York Times, The Washington Post,* and *The Boston Globe,* and she has appeared on *Today* and *20/20*. She lives with her husband in Palo Alto, California.